OFFICIALS AND STAFF

INDIANAPOLIS MOTOR SPEEDWAY CORPORATION

Mari H. George
Chairman

Anton H. "Tony" George
President & Chief Executive Officer

M. Josephine George
Nancy L. George

Katherine M. George-Conforti
Jack R. Snyder

EXECUTIVE STAFF

Jeffrey G. Belskus
Executive Vice President &
Chief Operating Officer

W. Curtis Brighton
Vice President &
General Counsel

Laura George
Staff Advisor

Mel Harder
Vice President, Operations

Fred J. Nation
Vice President, Corporate
Communications & Public Relations

Bob Reif
Senior Vice President of Sales &
Marketing and Chief Marketing Officer

Peggy Swalls
Vice President, Administration

Kenneth T. Ungar
Chief of Staff

SPEEDWAY STAFF

Karen Ahrens
Payroll Processing Manager

Mike Archer
Fitness Director

Don Bailey
Vehicle Coordinator

Kelly Bailey
Manager of Brickyard Crossing Inn

Ellen Bireley
Manager of Museum Services

Dr. Henry Bock
Director of Medical Services

Martha Briggs
Manager of Accounting

Jeff Chapman
Director of Marketing & Branding

Randy Clark
Manager of Food & Beverage

Sean Clayton
Manager of Market Research

Donald Davidson
Historian

Derek Decker
Manager of Hospitality Sales

Dawn Dyer
Manager of Creative Services

Chuck Ferguson
Director of Information Systems &
Telecommunications

Brenda Ferryman
Manager of Mail Services

Kevin Forbes
Director of Engineering & Construction

Lee Gardner
Director of Automotive Partnerships

Lynn Greggs
Director of Accounting & Administration

MaryAnn Hawkins
Director of Catering & Conference Services,
Brickyard Crossing Inn

Pat Hayes
Manager of Contract Administration

Michael Hughes
Manager of Internet Development

Marty Hunt
Manager of Track Racing Operations

Paul Kelly
Communications Manager

John Kesler
Manager of Sales

Jon Koskey
Technology Manager

Patricia Kuhn
Director of Human Resources

John Lewis
Manager of Facilities

Lisa Lewis
Human Resources Manager

Kent Liffick
Director of Sponsorship Development

Mai Lindstrom
Director of Public Relations

Bruce Lynch
Director of Retail Sales & Operations

Buddy McAtee
Director of Sales

Matt McCartin
Manager of Promotions

Richard McComb
Director of Finance

Robert McInteer
Director of Safety

Ron McQueeney
Director of Photography

Mark Miller
Applications Manager

Nancy Miller
Manager of Public Relations

David Moroknek
Director of Licensing & Consumer Products

Gloria Novotney
Director of Credentials

Dan Petty
Manager of Retail Merchandise

Nicole Polsky
Manager of Licensing

Bruce Ralston
Manager of Telecommunications

Cheryl Rumer
Medical Manager

Rollie Schroeder
Golf Professional, Brickyard Crossing

Jeff Stuart
Golf Course Superintendent

LuAnn Tanzilli
Director of Sales, Brickyard Crossing Inn

Dennis Vervynckt
Manager of Guest Services,
Brickyard Crossing Inn

Greg Woodsmall
Director of Flight Operations & Chief Pilot

INDY RACING LEAGUE STAFF

Brian Barnhart
Director of Racing Operations

Mark Bridges
Technical Manager

Phil Casey
Technical Director

Ron Green
Manager of Media Relations

Andy Hall
Director of Events

Tiffany Hemmer
Manager of Administration

Les Mactaggart
Technical Consultant

John Pierce
Safety Consultant

Jim Reynolds
Manager of Fuel Services

Johnny Rutherford
Special Projects & Consultant

Al Unser
Driver Coach & Consultant

Chuck Whetsel
Manager of Timing & Scoring

CONTENTS

First published in 2001 by MBI Publishing Company, 729 Prospect Avenue, PO Box 1, Osceola, WI 54020-0001 USA

© IMS Corporation, 2001

All rights reserved. With the exception of quoting brief passages for the purposes of review,
no part of this publication may be reproduced without prior written permission from the Publisher.

The information in this book is true and complete to the best of our knowledge. All recommendations are made without any guarantee on the part of the author or Publisher,
who also disclaim any liability incurred in connection with the use of this data or specific details.

We recognize that some words, model names and designations, for example, mentioned herein are the property of the trademark holder.
We use them for identification purposes only. This is not an official publication.

MBI Publishing Company books are also available at discounts in bulk quantity for industrial or sales-promotional use. For details write to Special Sales Manager at
Motorbooks International Wholesalers & Distributors, 729 Prospect Avenue, PO Box 1, Osceola, WI 54020-0001 USA.

Edited by Paul Johnson
Layout by LeAnn Kuhlmann
Designed by Tom Heffron

Editorial Contributors: Tim Tuttle, Jonathan Ingram, Dick Mittman, Kris Palmer, and Michael Dapper

Printed in China   ISBN 0-7603-0974-4

Indy®, The Indy®, Indy 500®, Indianapolis 500®, The Greatest Spectacle in Racing®, Home of the 500®, Gasoline Alley®, Indy Racing League®, Indy Racing Northern Light Series®,
The Brickyard®, and Brickyard 400® are registered trademarks and used under license by the Indianapolis Motor Speedway Corporation.

Thank You

Indy Racing is without a doubt the most exciting form of motorsports, and that was demonstrated again and again in 2000. The battle for the Northern Light Cup went down to the final race of the season at Texas Motor Speedway where Buddy Lazier beat out Scott Goodyear and Eddie Cheever Jr. in a tight points battle. In nine races, the Indy Racing Northern Light Series produced eight different winners, and in June the closest finish in series history took place at Texas Motor Speedway when Scott Sharp nipped Robby McGehee by only .059 of a second.

Close competition was the hallmark of the practice and qualification days for the Indianapolis 500, exemplified by Greg Ray's banzai run on Pole Day to narrowly beat out Juan Montoya for the top spot by .061 of a second. Montoya came back on Race Day to win the 84th running of the Indianapolis 500-Mile Race, with Lazier and Eliseo Salazar rounding out the top three.

It was a great season that began in Orlando with new series sponsor, Northern Light, and a win by Robbie Buhl. Lazier was the only two-time winner in 2000, while Al Unser Jr. picked up his first Northern Light Series victory. Cheever and Goodyear both scored wins, as did Greg Ray and Scott Sharp. The Nissan Infiniti engine program recorded its first win, Kentucky Speedway inaugurated its new track, and we announced a 13-race schedule for 2001, including new events in Chicago, Kansas City, Miami, Nashville, Richmond, and St. Louis.

We expect the new season to be the best yet for Indy Racing as new and established venues showcase the men and women who dare to compete in the most exciting and most competitive open-wheel series on earth.

On behalf of my family, our staffs at the Indianapolis Motor Speedway and the Indy Racing League, our sponsors, crews, and drivers, thank you for supporting Indy Racing.

Sincerely,

Tony George

Tony George
President and CEO
Indianapolis Motor Speedway

2000 Indy Racing Northern Light Series

Rnd. 1 Delphi Indy 200/Walt Disney World® Speedway/January 29/Orlando, Florida/ Robbie Buhl, winner

Rnd. 2 MCI WorldCom Indy 200/Phoenix International Raceway/March 19/Phoenix, Arizona/Buddy Lazier, winner

Rnd. 3 Vegas Indy 300/Las Vegas Motor Speedway/April 22/Las Vegas, Nevada/Al Unser Jr., winner

Rnd. 4 Indianapolis 500/Indianapolis Motor Speedway/May 28/Indianapolis, Indiana, Juan Montoya, winner

Rnd. 5 Casino Magic 500/Texas Motor Speedway/June 11/Fort Worth, Texas/Scott Sharp, winner

Rnd. 6 Radisson Indy 200/Pikes Peak International Raceway/June 18/ Colorado Springs, Colorado/Eddie Cheever Jr., winner

Rnd. 7 Midas 500 Classic/Atlanta Motor Speedway/July 15/Atlanta, Georgia/Greg Ray, winner

Rnd. 8 The Belterra Resort Indy 300/Kentucky Speedway/ August 27/Florence, Kentucky/Buddy Lazier, winner

Rnd. 9 The Excite 500/Texas Motor Speedway/October 15/Fort Worth, Texas/Scott Goodyear, winner

by Tim Tuttle

Al Unser Jr.'s much-anticipated return to Indianapolis finally officially became reality. The two-time Indy 500 winner was cheered with unmitigated enthusiasm upon his arrival to the Galles ECR Racing pit by the opening-day crowd clustered in the Tower Terrace grandstands. Five hours later, they were cheering Unser again and it wasn't just for being there.

Unser supplied an exclamation point during the closing minutes with the fastest lap of the day, averaging 217.223 miles per hour in his backup Tickets.com 2000 G Force/Oldsmobile. "It's great to be back," Unser said. "This is the greatest race track in the world and the greatest race in the world. I can't tell you how much it means for me to be back here."

Car owner Dick Simon (left) was once again the first to send out a driver when the track opened. Driver Stephan Gregoire rolled out in the Mexmil/Tokheim/Viking Air Tools/Dick Simon Racing entry.
Jim Haines

Unser's last experience at Indianapolis was in 1995, when he failed to qualify. He spent the next four years with CART's Penske Racing, which didn't enter Indy. However, Unser returned to the Speedway on several occasions, including driving in the International Race of Champions (IROC) in late July, 1998 and for a private test with Galles a few weeks before the 2000 Indianapolis 500.

But this day was different. This was the very beginning of the competition.

"When I came out of Gasoline Alley, I started getting nervous," Unser said. "I wanted to make sure I got out of the pits. I thought, 'Don't stall it. Don't spin the car on the backstretch.' I didn't want to embarrass myself."

Next came the applause that bordered on adulation. "It was overwhelming," Unser said. "I saw that happen to my dad somewhat, but A.J. [Foyt] was the only one who really got that kind of stuff and it's special to get into that same type of category."

Unser wasn't thinking about going for the fastest lap. He'd been out in his primary G Force/Oldsmobile earlier in the day, with a best lap of 211.934 miles per hour. "We had a game plan to shake the cars down and get used to the track," Unser explained. "The primary car went off without a hitch. We went out in the back-up car to do the same thing. It was windy, really windy, around here in the afternoon, from two to four [P.M.]. When we put that [fastest] lap in, the conditions were perfect."

Stephan Gregoire's Mexmil 2000 G Force/Oldsmobile was first on the track, continuing a Dick Simon Racing tradition, and also had the second fastest lap, 217.035 miles per hour.

Hemelgarn Racing decided to park its 2000 Riley & Scott and purchase a 2000 Dallara for 1996 Indy 500 winner Buddy Lazier. Lazier had driven the Riley & Scott to victory at Phoenix International Raceway in March, but the chassis had struggled during pre-May testing. Lazier had finally gotten the Riley & Scott to 217 in late April. In his first day in the Delta Faucet/Coors Light Dallara/Oldsmobile with a seat that didn't fit as well as Lazier would have liked—he was third fastest at 216.810 miles per hour.

Eddie Cheever Jr. crashed his primary Excite@Home 2000 Dallara/Infiniti in Turn 2 when a half-shaft failed and spun him 360-degrees into the outside wall. Cheever had been warned on the radio by his crew that something was wrong and he had backed off the throttle. "I was already down to 180 [miles per hour]," Cheever said. "[Chief Mechanic] Owen Snyder had radioed the lap before for me to come in and I had not heard his urgency, so I thought I'd go one more." Cheever was uninjured and was back out practicing in his backup car an hour after the crash.

The new twenty-first-century look of the remodeled, historic Speedway was unveiled on opening day. The new Pagoda was partially operational, the 36 suites above the new pit-row Formula 1 garages were complete, and the infield section of the F1 circuit was in place.

From inside the cockpit, however, it was the same, beloved track Unser had remembered. "When you're out on the track, you don't see anything outside the walls, anything above the walls," Unser said. "It's the same track and if you're looking at anything over than it, you're not doing your job."

DAY-AT-A-GLANCE

Date: Saturday, May 13
Drivers on Track: 22
Cars on Track: 25

TOP FIVE DRIVERS OF THE DAY

Car	Driver	Speed (mph)
3T	Al Unser Jr.	217.223
7	Stephan Gregoire	217.035
91	Buddy Lazier	216.810
51	Eddie Cheever Jr.	216.773
17	Scott Harrington	216.471

At the end of the second day of practice, Eddie Cheever Jr. was full of smiles, and Tyce Carlson was full of sorrow. Cheever put Nissan's Infiniti on top of the sheets for the first time at Indy with a lap of 220.881 miles per hour in his #51 Excite@Home Dallara. He did it with only three minutes remaining and was ebullient upon exiting the car.

"What a good way to start," Cheever said. "We had a bad day yesterday, a drivetrain failure that put me into the fence. The Infiniti is great. You can't go fast down the straight here without horsepower. It was our intention to get everything out of the car. I'm surprised we went that fast, because the car was not perfect. We had a push in Turn 2."

Al Unser Jr. was up front for the second straight day, right behind Cheever at 220.686 miles per hour in his G Force/Oldsmobile. "I did get great pleasure in beating the redhead today," Cheever admitted. "He's an Unser and they're royalty at Indianapolis. Anytime you finish in front of Al at Indy, you feel good about it."

Unser was only concerned with what his Galles ECR Racing team was trying to accomplish. "We don't care what other people are doing, as long as we stick to our game plan and the car is doing what we want it to do," Unser said. "We feel very comfortable with the car, but every day everyone is going to go a little bit quicker."

Tyce Carlson hit the outside wall exiting Turn 1 in Hubbard-Immke Racing's Dallara/Oldsmobile with 32 minutes remaining. The impact sent his headrest flying. When Carlson slid across the track and made a second contact with the inside wall, he was knocked unconscious for about five minutes.

A native of Indianapolis, Carlson spent the night at Methodist Hospital. The concussion he suffered forced him to miss the remainder of practice, qualifying, and the race as well.

Carlson, who also suffered a bruised left ankle, was "probably the most devastated he's ever been in his life," commented team co-owner Jim Immke about Carlson missing a chance to drive in his third 500.

Carlson didn't know what caused him to lose control. "I went through the corner and the car came around on me," he said. "That's part of this track. You go around one time perfect. The next time, you go around on it. That's why only the best come here."

1998 Indy 500 winner Eddie Cheever Jr. slipped into the tub of his car prior to a practice run. He approached the race with great optimism based on the progress of his Infiniti engine development program. *Ron McQueeney*

DAY-AT-A-GLANCE

Date: Sunday, May 14
Drivers on Track: 33
Cars on Track: 35

TOP FIVE DRIVERS OF THE DAY

Car	Driver	Speed (mph)
51	Eddie Cheever	220.881
3T	Al Unser Jr.	220.686
5	Robby McGehee	219.780
8T	Scott Sharp	219.769
91	Buddy Lazier	219.453

by Tim Tuttle

As Robby Gordon practiced on Day 3 at the Speedway, he had to flash back to the 1999 race, when he ran out of fuel while leading on Lap 199 and dropped back to fourth. He posted the best time of the day—223.120 miles per day

Robby Gordon, Indy Car racing's prodigal son, dropped in unexpectedly at Indianapolis during the third day of practice. He hadn't driven a single-seater since the previous October, because he moved his Team Gordon CART operation into NASCAR's Winston Cup—his third career transition in four seasons.

In January, John Menard (a Team Gordon partner and the Midwest home improvement chain billionaire who also happens to own the best funded operation in the Indy Racing Northern Light Series) offered Gordon a chance to be Greg Ray's teammate at Indy. Gordon declined, saying he wanted to concentrate fully on the Winston Cup program.

After the Winston Cup's previous event at Richmond, Virginia, Gordon was 36th in the standings. Once considered cocky and a prodigy, Gordon has painfully learned a measure of humility in recent years. He's taken his lumps and his self-assuredness has waned. What better way—perhaps the only way—to regain some confidence than hopping into one of Menard's Indy entries?

Gordon asked Menard if the offer was still there and Menard said yes. On the third day of practice, Gordon went out during the closing minutes and ripped off a lap of 223.120 miles per hour, the best of the day. Gordon also left no doubt that this dose of driving an Indy Car has lifted his spirits and renewed his belief that he can run at the front. "Winston Cup is so competitive and we're a new team and you know all that," Gordon said. "But you start doubting yourself. It's so nice to be competitive. I have to thank John [Menard] for allowing me to drive such great equipment."

Gordon stepped into an operation expertly run by Team Manager and Engineer Thomas Knapp. He has a 2000 Dallara, and Menard's in-house Oldsmobile program is widely regarded as the best engine in the series. "I'm fortunate that Tom is on his game," Gordon said. "His mind is on the Indy 500 all year long. We have a very defined schedule. For the first two days, Greg was working on qualifying setup and I was working on race setup.

"And the end of the day [May 15], we'd decided to try each other's setup. Fortunately, Greg and I are able to drive each other's car. He didn't get out because we were out of fuel and I put that lap [223.120] in. If Greg had been able to get out, I'm sure he'd have gone faster. I have to give credit for that lap to Greg."

Al Unser Jr. was in the top two for the third straight day, lapping at 221.861. Ray was third fastest at 221.735. "We are right

there with everyone at the moment, but we are still going with our game plan of making sure that we get in the show," Unser said.

CART regulars Juan Montoya and Jimmy Vasser, who raced the day before in Japan, made their first appearances of the month. Montoya did a total of 21 laps in both his primary and backup Target/Chip Ganassi Racing G Force/Oldsmobile, with a best of 219.213; Vasser did a total of 17 laps between his two cars and posted a 220.146.

DAY-AT-A-GLANCE

Date: Monday, May 15
Drivers on Track: 36
Cars on Track: 41

TOP FIVE DRIVERS OF THE DAY

Car	Driver	Speed (mph)
32	Robby Gordon	223.120
3	Al Unser Jr.	221.861
32	Greg Ray	221.735
51	Eddie Cheever	221.506
17	Scott Harrington	221.397

by Tim Tuttle

For the fourth straight day, a different driver placed on top of the speed chart. The honor belonged to Scott Sharp who put together a lap of 223.936 miles per hour in Kelley Racing's Delphi Automotive Systems Dallara/Oldsmobile. He easily outdistanced Target/Chip Ganassi Racing's Juan Montoya, who was second at 222.102.

Sharp had not cracked the 221 barrier prior to Tuesday as the team focused its efforts on developing race setups. "The car's pretty good on the long runs," Sharp explained. "Then, we decided to see what the car could do. We took a little wing out, thinking we could get in the mid-222s. Then—wow!—I saw it pop up there [on his dash] and we decided to come in. It's only Tuesday and you have to put four of those laps together."

Sharp and teammate Mark Dismore also operated under a different system for the first time. "We have been trying to sort out our engineering program," Sharp said. "Just yesterday, we decided to truly work together to develop the car as a two-car team."

The track was under yellow conditions for 4 hours and 26 minutes of the scheduled 7 hours, including a nearly 3-hour rain delay.

Montoya had no complaints about his G Force/Oldsmobile. "The car is really good," he said. "I am happy with the speed that we got in the half day we ran. We made some changes, but didn't get a chance to get back out again. So, we'll see how they run tomorrow."

Target/Ganassi teammate Jimmy Vasser was third, at 221.773. Team Menard's Greg Ray was fourth and Dick Simon Racing's Stephan Gregoire fifth. Comptech Engineering built all the Oldsmobile engines of Sharp, Montoya, and Vasser.

Sarah Fisher, in Walker Racing's Dallara/Oldsmobile, had a busy and impressive day. The 19-year-old rookie ran 92 laps and was seventh fastest at 220.881. "It's great that we broke the 220 barrier," Fisher said. "That's good for a rookie to do. It gives us more momentum. I'm getting a lot more comfortable with running at the Indianapolis Motor Speedway. I'm comfortable in three out of the four turns now and we're working on breaking that last corner into segments so we can master that one, as well. [Breaking 220] is good for me, for Rob Edwards, our engineer, and for Derrick [Walker] and the team because they've all worked so hard."

Tony Stewart wasn't officially entered at Indianapolis, but he decided to take some laps in an effort to help Jeret Schroeder get up to speed. Stewart is a part owner of Tri Star Motorsports, which fields Schroeder's Kroger Dallara/Oldsmobile. Stewart, the 1996 Indy 500 Bank One Rookie of the Year and NASCAR Winston Cup regular, ran 11 laps with a best of 218.124. Schroeder's best in four days and 138 laps had been 217.402.

"I wanted to play a bit," Stewart said. "And I also felt that I was not working enough with Jeret. I wanted to get a feel for the car and feed that back to Jeret. We're not where we want to be, but Jeret is doing a good job. He is giving the same info to [team manager/engineer] Larry [Curry] and that should give him confidence that what he is feeling is accurate. "Jeret had questions, Larry had questions, and I had questions. And we wanted to get answers."

Scott Sharp's crew fueled his car for a practice run. Drivers test their cars with light fuel tanks to find the fastest possible qualifying setup, and with full tanks to simulate race day setups. *Roger Bedwell*

DAY-AT-A-GLANCE

Date:	Tuesday, May 16
Drivers on Track:	34
Cars on Track:	36

TOP FIVE DRIVERS OF THE DAY

Car	Driver	Speed (mph)
8T	Scott Sharp	223.936
9	Juan Montoya	222.102
10	Jimmy Vasser	221.773
1	Greg Ray	221.740
7	Stephan Gregoire	221.397

WHY DO INDY WINNERS DRINK MILK? **Search**

Witness the 85th Indy 500 by entering the Fantasy Weekend Sweepstakes at www.NorthernLight.com/fantasy.
NorthernLight.com, the world's most comprehensive search engine. Proud sponsor of the Indy Racing™ Northern Light Series.

NorthernLight.com
Just what you've been searching for.

PHOTO FINISH!

(DOUBLE-LENGTH SEQUENCE IIIE TEST USING CONVENTIONAL 5W-30 MOTOR OILS)

CASTROL

MOBIL

PENNZOIL®

VALVOLINE

HAVOLINE

Protection so strong, you can see the difference.

Unenhanced photographs allow the whole world to see how well Pennzoil® with PureBase® performed in a grueling double-length Sequence IIIE test. Unenhanced photographs also allow the whole world to see how the other leading brands performed. And as you can see by the oil pans alone, it wasn't even a photo finish. Check out the photographs for yourself at pennzoil.com. And make sure your engine gets Pennzoil® with PureBase® every 3,000 miles. It's protection so strong, you can see the difference.

Stop. Go. Pennzoil.

PENNZOIL

To see the complete results, log on to www.pennzoil.com

TRACKSIDE FILES
DAY 5
WEDNESDAY, MAY 17

PRACTICE

by Tim Tuttle

Because of rain the track opened 24 minutes late on the fifth day of practice and closed only 33 minutes later. However, Juan Montoya and Buddy Lazier made very impressive use of the short amount of time they had.

Montoya burst out of the gate to run 221.566 miles per hour on his sixth lap for the fastest of the day in Target/Chip Ganassi Racing's G Force/Oldsmobile. The rookie from Colombia turned only nine total laps. "We got about four flying laps wide open and that was it," Montoya said. "It felt good, but we've got to keep improving it."

Lazier put the day's second fastest lap, 221.510, on the board on his sixth lap and did eight total in Hemelgarn Racing's Delta Faucet/Coors Light Dallara/Oldsmobile. "You know, we had a feeling the rain was coming," Lazier said. "Ron Dawes, my engineer, said I'd only have about 10 minutes on the track. We ran four or five laps at speed. We had the new practice motor and it ran really good. The car ran good. We're happy with that speed. It was funny. It was so dark in Turns 3 and 4. It felt like about seven at night and [Turns] 1 and 2 were really bright."

Kelley Racing teammates Scott Sharp and Mark Dismore were the only others to crack the 220 barrier. Sharp ran 220.886 on his fifth lap of 11 total, and Dismore 220.395 on his 16th, of 17. "Luckily, the Delphi car has gained a lot of ground the last two days," Sharp said. "If we do get rained out [for the rest of the week], I don't think it's going to have any effect on us. We're in a good position. We're pretty well dialed in."

Dismore didn't share Sharp's attitude. "The rain is going to make for some catch-up the next two days," he said. "We're a little behind on our qualifying setup. The next two days will be a total focus on the qualifying setup."

Jimmy Vasser, Montoya's teammate, also wasn't happy to see the rain. He ran 18 laps, the second most of the abbreviated session, and was fifth at 219.800.

"It's tough waiting around because we would really like to be out there running," Vasser said. "You can get everything done in the time allotted, but we haven't gotten much time yet, so I really want to get on the track."

Four-time Indy 500 winner Rick Mears, participating in the Legends of the Speedway week, provided the highlight of the afternoon when he took two laps around the Speedway in the Gould Charge PC6-Cosworth, which he drove to victory at Indy in 1979. "It felt great," Mears said. "There's a lot of fond memories in this car. This is a style of car I started out [in Indy cars] with in '78 driving for Roger [Penske]. We kept the car in '79 and the car was good to us."

Mears remains one of the most popular drivers in Indianapolis history and the fans let him know when he appears on the track. "The fans here are race fans and that's why they're here," Mears said.

Despite having several years of professional racing and the CART Championship under his belt, Juan Montoya was an Indy 500 rookie in 2000. Racing experience on superspeedways such as Michigan International Speedway and California Speedway at Fontana certainly helped him adapt to Indianapolis.
Jim Haines

DAY-AT-A-GLANCE

Date:	Wednesday, May 17
Drivers on Track:	17
Cars on Track:	17

TOP FIVE DRIVERS OF THE DAY

Car	Driver	Speed (mph)
9	Juan Montoya	221.566
91	Buddy Lazier	221.510
8T	Scott Sharp	220.886
28T	Mark Dismore	220.395
10T	Jimmy Vasser	219.800

by Tim Tuttle

Jimmy Vasser, the veteran half of Target/Chip Ganassi Racing's potent one-two punch, won a close decision over teammate Juan Montoya in round six. The 34-year-old had the day's fastest lap at 221.681 miles per hour, an eye-blink ahead of Montoya's 221.555. The speed wasn't Vasser's best of the week—he ran 221.773 on Tuesday—but it was a real dandy considering the windy conditions. Gusts near 40 miles per hour were recorded. "It was pretty windy, but we spent all day out there because it could be windy on race day," Vasser said. "The wind was blowing down the straightaways, so it wasn't that bad."

Under the finest of conditions, it isn't easy to go fast at Indianapolis. "You're just trying to get the most out of the race car, trying to trim it out," Vasser explained. "These cars are not planted by no means. To make them go fast, you have to loosen them up, you've got to take all the things that make downforce and drag off that you can. Not to give the other guys any hints, but just from my seat, it is an edgy car when you want to go fast . . . you have to put it on that ragged edge. When you go around here, you try to get the car balanced, trimmed out, and working right."

It was the Ganassi team's fourth day of practice and by far its busiest. Vasser did 44 laps in his primary G Force/Oldsmobile and 38 in his backup; Montoya did 42 in his primary and 44 in his back-up. "We have a very methodical approach to what we're doing this week," Chip Ganassi said. "You have to have your act together quickly here. In years past [when there was an additional five days of practice], you could run your race motor, take it apart, and then bring it back two weeks later. We don"t have the luxury of time any more."

Treadway Racing's Robby McGehee had the third-fastest time of the day and his best of the week at 220.964. The 1999 Bank One Indy 500 Rookie of the Year ran a total of 85 laps. Fresh Firestone rubber made the difference for McGehee's Mall.com G Force/Oldsmobile. Rain had denied him the chance to run on sticker tires for the previous two days.

"Our speed problem was the fact that we were running on old tires," McGehee said. "Every time we put stickers on, it started to rain. So, today we actually got lucky and ran several laps with stickers, and that made all the difference in the world."

Team Menard's Greg Ray and Robby Gordon didn't run in the sixth practice session. A 64-minute rain delay in the late afternoon caused the team to alter its plans. "We were going out to run when it started raining," Menard team manager/engineer Thomas Knapp said. "Then, we decided to change engines and prepare for the weekend."

Mario Andretti, the 1969 Indy 500 winner, was honored as part of the Legends of the Speedway program. When Andretti, who failed to finish 20 of his 29 Indianapolis 500s, went out in the car he drove in 1967, a Brawner-Hawk, it stalled on the back straight and stopped before making it back to the pit lane. One more time, the crowd heard public address announcer Tom Carnegie say, "Mario is slowing down." Added Andretti, with a smile, "I didn't think I'd ever hear that again."

Jimmy Vasser drove through the south-end short chute during a practice run. He would eventually earn the seventh starting position in his Target G Force/Oldsmobile.
Ron McQueeney

DAY-AT-A-GLANCE

Date:	Thursday, May 18
Drivers on Track:	33
Cars on Track:	39

TOP FIVE DRIVERS OF THE DAY

Car	Driver	Speed (mph)
10T	Jimmy Vasser	221.681
9T	Juan Montoya	221.555
5	Robby McGehee	220.964
28T	Mark Dismore	220.896
8T	Scott Sharp	219.922

by Tim Tuttle

Indianapolis 500 veteran Eliseo Salazar awaited the signal to leave the pits. The Chilean driver would enjoy his most competitive Indy 500 ever in 2000.
Jim Haines

Greg Ray had barely been heard from all week, but on the final day of practice prior to Pole Day, he roared from the top of the mountain. Ray's 223.948-mile-per-hour lap in the final hour was the fastest of the week and a more than 2-mile-per-hour improvement of his previous best in Team Menard's Conseco Dallara/Oldsmobile.

The 33-year-old Texan had dominated practice in 1999, leading five of the seven days. This year, through six practice sessions, he'd only been in the top five twice.

Ray pointed to two factors that had prevented him from showing what he could do. "We've been running two drivers out of one stable, which has limited us on track time and it's been a bit of an issue," he explained. "Between the weather and some of the timing, we haven't had much on-track time. I think there were a couple of times this week we could have posted the top time.

"We've been out of sync somehow. We'd get a good lap going and then we'd hit a yellow. Finally, we got a little bit of open track space. I was just trying to post a time and get a feel for the car driving totally flat out in all four corners."

Team Menard had operated as a one-car team in 1999. Robby Gordon had used one of Ray's backup cars to qualify and race, but he did it with Team Gordon personnel. This year, Gordon tapped directly into the Menard team.

Ray ran 39 laps on the seventh day of practice and only 195 for the week.

Jeff Ward popped into the top five for the first time, ranking second along with Kelley Racing's Scott Sharp 222.949 miles per hour in A.J. Foyt's Harrah's G Force/Oldsmobile.

Foyt never runs many laps or shows significant speed early at Indy. Ward had run only 117 laps between his primary and backup cars prior to the final practice, when he added 38 more. Ward's lap of nearly 223 was the fourth fastest of the week. "It feels pretty good," Ward said, "but I didn't get a real clean lap, so I don't know how I'll run by myself."

Sharp was doing some fine tuning on the final day in the Delphi Automotive Systems Dallara/Oldsmobile. "We're basically working on our qualifying setup," he said. "The Delphi car is very balanced and we're trying to do some final tweaking of the chassis. Right now, we don't want to show our full hand."

Like teammate Ward, Eliseo Salazar hadn't done extensive running—119 total laps through six days—prior to the final practice. The Chilean did 40 on Friday and was fourth at 222.921, elevating him to the fifth-fastest driver of the week. Salazar didn't do it with a speed-enhancing tow. "There was no one in sight," he said, "and I was on used tires. New tires and a little tow, it would have been a 224 easy."

Pole Day was next.

"The last couple of years have been very competitive up front, but this year it's going to be bloody tight," Ray said. "It's going to be tight, tight, tight."

His assessment was right on the money.

DAY-AT-A-GLANCE

Date: Friday, May 19
Drivers on Track: 39
Cars on Track: 47

TOP FIVE DRIVERS OF THE DAY

Car	Driver	Speed (mph)
1T	Greg Ray	223.948
14	Jeff Ward	222.949
8T	Scott Sharp	222.949
11	Eliseo Salazar	222.921
32	Robby Gordon	222.901

by Tim Tuttle

For Greg Ray, winning the pole for the 84th Indianapolis 500 wasn't about out-dueling CART champion Juan Montoya, the $100,000 and other assorted goodies that go along with it, or the glory. Primary motivation was derived from a year-long wait to succeed where he had failed.

The Texan had been the favorite in 1999 to take the most-prized qualifying award in auto racing, but he took the second spot to Arie Luyendyk. Ray had been fastest in five of the seven days of practice prior to qualifying and had the top practice lap at 227.192 miles per hour. But he fell off to a four-lap average of 225.073 miles per hour, .106 miles per hour short of Luyendyk in qualifications. And although Ray went on to three victories and the Indy Racing League championship, the hurt of that lost pole was not forgotten.

Ray had Team Menard's Conseco 2000 Dallara/Oldsmobile on the ragged edge in averaging 223.471 miles per hour to edge Montoya's 223.372-mile-per-hour effort in Target/Chip Ganassi Racing's 2000 G Force/Oldsmobile.

"I'd be lying to you if I didn't say the pole was a big focus for us," Ray said. "There's no question we wanted to put the car on the pole. I'd have soon as qualified 33rd as been second again. The four laps of qualifying here are the ultimate speed event. You've got to drive it for all it's worth. Qualifying day is an event all by itself and you do everything you can to go fast."

Ray had aborted his first attempt. He had gone into Turn 1 at 233 miles per hour. "I was committed at the turn-in and the car went straight," Ray explained. "I had to back off to keep it off the wall, and there was no point to continuing the run at that point."

Ten minutes later, Montoya threw down the gauntlet with his 223.372 four-lap average. "I tried setting the [IRL] car up similar to the [CART] Champ Car," Montoya said. "I like the car. It's a really friendly car . . . fast and friendly. We had a bit of understeer in Turn 1, but the car was good. We tried a lot of things all week; try this, try that. All week we've been pretty fast and we just started trimming it out [for qualifying]. I was very happy with that."

It was an unseasonably cool day for mid-May in Indianapolis, around 60 degrees for most of the afternoon. Drivers had to be careful getting heat into the tires on the warm-up lap—several weren't and ended up in the wall—but once that was accomplished, the conditions were ideal for both horsepower and grip.

When the track was opened for practice, because no cars were in the qualifying line, Ray went out and did 10 laps, topping out at 223.988. It was time for his second attempt, nearly three hours after his first. "To be fast for qualifying here, you have to take

all the downforce out of the car," Ray said. "The car was definitely on the edge. The Firestone tires were great, but I think I slung a [wheel] weight on the backstretch. I knew I had to keep my foot in it because it was my second attempt."

Ray says he wasn't thinking about Montoya as a CART champion, only as a tough competitor. "I haven't thought about that issue," Ray said. "As a driver or an athlete in any sport, you want to measure yourself against the very best. Everyone holds Chip [Ganassi] and Juan and Jimmy [Vasser] in high regard. It just shows there's a lot of good teams here. You want to play with the best, and it's great to have Robby [Gordon] coming over from NASCAR and Juan and Jimmy over from CART. It's great for the fans and the media."

Montoya settled for the inside of the front row. "It's really good," he said. "It's the front row. The only place to go low is Turn 1. You have to be aggressive to make the car rotate."

Chile's Eliseo Salazar took the outside of the front row in A.J. Foyt's Rio 2000 G Force at 223.231. When Salazar, a veteran of Formula 1, CART, and the Indy Racing League, signed with A.J. Foyt in January, he knew it was A.J.'s way or the highway. He has no complaints about the arrangement. Salazar would have preferred to practice more in the week leading up to Pole Day. Foyt is a legend at Indy and legendary for restricting the laps his drivers run in practice. Salazar ran only 61 laps in the opening five days of practice.

"You know my boss," Salazar said. "As soon as we got in the top five, he'd say, 'OK, that's it.' He wouldn't let me practice

Driver Greg Ray (center) and car owner John Menard (left) were glad to accept the lucrative PPG Pole Award money for winning the pole of the 2000 Indianapolis 500. *Jim Haines*

The crew of Floridian Stan Wattles made some major adjustments to the car before rolling it into line for a qualification run on Pole Day. Their efforts paid off with an eighth-best qualifying speed.
Ron McQueeney

anymore because you know he doesn't like to show speed early. From the beginning, he said we'd peak on Saturday."

Salazar did just that. He ran a blistering 223.964-mile-per-hour lap in the Pole Day morning practice, the fastest of the week to that point. Then, Salazar qualified on the outside of the front row, at 223.231 in the 2000 G Force/Oldsmobile. He was .241 miles per hour slower than Ray, a .173-second difference after 10 miles. The gap between pole and third was the narrowest in 500 history. "On the last lap, I made a slight mistake and it cost us," Salazar said.

"I went too deep into [Turn] 1, at close to 230, and went too far to the inside and touched the rumble strips."

They weren't up front at the end of Pole Day, but the fact that Al Unser Jr. and Sarah Fisher were solidly in the field created plenty of excitement at the Speedway. Unser was the first to complete an attempt, averaging 220.293 in Galles ECR Racing's Tickets.com 2000 G Force/Oldsmobile. He would line up for the race on the outside of the sixth row, 18th position. Unser had not tried to qualify for the 500 since 1995, when he failed to make the race as the defending champion. After his experience in 1995, Unser admitted he was concerned about qualifying this year. "I never thought that could happen, but it did [in 1995]," he said. "Was I worried? The answer is definitely yes. Anything can happen here. Unser's first lap was 218.187. He went faster with each lap, topping at 221.440.

Fisher became the third woman to qualify at Indianapolis. At 19, she was the youngest in the field. Fisher took the 19th spot on the grid, averaging 220.237 in Walker Racing's Cummins Special 2000 Dallara/Oldsmobile. Her performance capped off an impressive mistake-free week in which she completed 407 laps in practice, the most of any driver prior to the start of qualifications. "I was flat all the way around," Fisher said, "and ducking on the straightaways. That was all she had. So far, it's been a tremendous thrill. It's really cool to run around this track. It's so unique, not stamped out like others, and it takes a different technique."

Pole Day's most surprising performance was turned in by veteran Stan Wattles. Wattles didn't get his Dallara/Oldsmobile on the track for practice until Tuesday's fourth day and had only 13 laps in it through Wednesday. Then, Wattles started putting in the miles and finding the speed: He did a combined 127 laps in practice

Jeff Ward has come close to winning at the Speedway in the past. As he rolled onto the track to qualify, he was counted among the favorites to win the 2000 race.
Ron McQueeney

Fans kept popular 1996 Indy 500 winner Buddy Lazier busy signing autographs and posing for photos during Pole Day. He qualified in the 16th position and had a great run on race day.
Roger Bedwell

on Thursday and Friday, another 29 in Pole Day's morning practice including his fastest of the week, 221.251.

In his four-lap qualification attempt, Wattles averaged 221.357. Three of the laps were his fastest of the month and he'd put them together to take eighth in the lineup. "I can't tell you how excited I am," Wattles said. "We've been playing catch-up since we got here and it finally paid off. I knew in my heart that the car was capable. I just need to focus and let the qualifying run come to me. On the second lap the oil alarm went off. I kept asking my crew if I should back off, but they told me everything was fine, just keep my foot in it."

The Riley & Scott chassis that Wattles ran in practice proved to be uncompetitive—none made the field—and that sent the Hemelgarn team looking for another car. "When [Metro team manager] Greg [Wattles] told me he found a 2000 Dallara to purchase, it all started to come together," Wattles explained. "We bought the car from Kelley Racing and my guys put it together in less than a week. We were forced to miss the first four days of practice, but we made up for it."

Team Menard's Robby Gordon waved off twice before qualifying the Turtle Wax/Burger King 2000 Dallara/Oldsmobile into the fourth position at 222.885. "The front row would have been great,

but this isn't that bad," Gordon said. "I was flat the whole way around, from the warm-up lap on."

Gordon stopped his first attempt after one lap and his second after two because he couldn't run flat. "The first time, the car pushed and we knew we weren't going to be quick enough," he explained. "I did a 221.7 on my warm-up lap on the second one, but still had understeer. I tried to get low in Turn 1 and got on the rumble strips. I got a bit sideways. I guess that's what you call one of those death wiggles here at the Speedway. I was fortunate to save it, bring it back in and think about it."

Scott Sharp had a smooth first attempt, qualifying in fifth position in the Delphi Automotive Systems 2000 Dallara/Oldsmobile. "We're pleased," he said, "particularly with that 223 [.447, on his second] lap," he said. "The car ran flawless, flat all the way around. I didn't have a dash because our battery died. I held the pedal down and hoped the car turned."

Jeff Ward had an uneventful, fast run to sixth position, averaging 222.639 in the Harrah's A.J. Foyt Racing 2000 G Force/Oldsmobile. "The run was simple, pretty easy," he said. "The car was perfect. We probably ran too short a gear. I told Eliseo [Salazar, who went out 14 minutes later] he needed to go up a gear. There was a lot of grip in the track and no wind. It's a perfect day for qualifying."

With 5¢ Everyday Savings, you can afford to take the time to explain chassis adjustment . . .

and why it's not rude to do in public.

Now you don't have to race to finish your long distance conversations. The WorldCom 5¢ Everyday Savings plan lets you talk for just 5 cents a minute—every weekday evening and all weekend long. 5¢ Everyday Savings is just $1.95 per month. Call 1-800-EVERYDAY.

WorldCom is the Official Long Distance and Local Service Provider of the Indy Racing League. **www.worldcomracing.com**

Winner's Choice!

Actual size.

The Preferred Mobile Phone of the Indy 500 & the Brickyard 400

www.NokiaUSA.com

Indy 500 rookie Sarah Fisher (back to camera) welcomed the advice of four-time Indy 500 winner Al Unser (in sunglasses) and three-time winner Johnny Rutherford (right).
Roger Bedwell

Mark Dismore, forced into his backup On Star/GM Buy Power 2000 Dallara/Oldsmobile when he crashed his primary late on the previous day, qualified for the 11th spot in the lineup at 220.970. It took Dismore two attempts to make the show. "We qualified with a motor that had 400 miles on it," Dismore said. "We had the bull by the horns and were going for the front row. We had a shot at the front row and I made a mistake. We'd run over 222 in practice."

Other previous Indy 500 starters who qualified on Pole Day were Robby McGehee, 12th in the Meijer/Energizer 2000 G Force/Oldsmobile; Scott Goodyear, 13th in the Pennzoil 2000 Dallara/Oldsmobile; Donnie Beechler, 15th in Cahill Racing's 2000 Dallara/Oldsmobile; Buddy Lazier, 16th in the Delta Faucet/Coors Light 2000 Dallara/Oldsmobile; Stephan Gregoire, 20th in the Mexmil 2000 G Force/Oldsmobile; Buzz Calkins, 22nd in the Bradley Motorsports 2000 Dallara/Oldsmobile; and Richie Hearn, 23rd in Pagan Racing's 2000 Dallara/Oldsmobile.

Target/Chip Ganassi's Jimmy Vasser, competing at Indy for the first time since 1995, took the inside spot on the third row by averaging 222.107 on his first attempt. "I'm not happy about it, but we'll take it," Vasser said. "I had a notion to turn in after those 222s [on his opening two laps], but [Ganassi Managing Director] Tom Anderson said, 'Let's get in the race; this place can turn on you.'"

The outside of the third row went to Robbie Buhl, in the Team Purex 2000 G Force/Oldsmobile, at 221.357. He was fifth out in qualifying and the third to put it in the show, a solid run that went as smoothly as the rest of the week had gone. "It really has been a pretty good week," Buhl said. "We did a lot of full tank stuff early and started to trim the car out yesterday."

Eddie Cheever, Jr. had the lone Nissan Infiniti-powered car among the 23 Pole Day qualifiers. He put the Excite@Home 2000 Dallara into the 10th starting position by averaging 221.270. Cheever went out for his attempt 36 minutes before Ward and didn't share his assessment of the conditions. "The conditions were strange," Cheever said. "We had to make a choice on aero[dynamics package]. There's nothing worse than a loose car and we went conservative. That's all we had."

Lazier had run 222.363 in the morning practice on Pole Day and qualified at 220.482. Hemelgarn Racing had switched from Riley & Scott to Dallara just prior to Indianapolis. Lazier had mixed emotions about his starting position. "We're elated to make the race," he said. "It's a hard race to make. We've only had the car for seven days and other teams have had it for seven months. We ran wide open and that was it. But I'm always disappointed when we don't get the most out of the car."

Hearn was the slowest of the 23 qualifiers on Pole Day, at 219.816. He had been third at Indy as a rookie in 1996 and hadn't competed at the Speedway again until this year. The 500 was the first race of the season for the Pagan team and Hearn struggled most of the week to find the speed required to make the race. Hearn's fastest lap through Thursday was 213.935.

Pagan hired Derrick Walker's CART personnel [who were a separate group from Walker's Indy Racing team]. "We were fortunate to get some help from Derrick Walker," Hearn said. "We got the best guys from his CART team, five of them. I wish we'd gotten them a little earlier. My run was OK, flat out, but I'm disappointed we didn't qualify better."

Scott Harrington of Indianapolis is a popular driver who has earned outstanding fan support because of his never-say-die efforts to succeed.
Ron McQueeney

In addition to both Montoya and Fisher, rookies who qualified on Pole Day were Sam Hornish Jr., 14th in PDM Racing's 2000 Dallara/Oldsmobile; Jason Leffler, 17th in the UnitedAuto Group 2000 G Force/Oldsmobile; and Airton Dare, 21st in the TeamXtreme USA Credit.com 2000 G Force/Oldsmobile.

Hornish, only 20, was the second fastest rookie to Montoya. "I'm real happy," Hornish said. "I'm happy for the guys at PDM Racing. It's great to be here."

Leffler, driving for Treadway Racing, was sponsored by a company controlled by Roger Penske. Penske's involvement in the program didn't end there. He loaned Marlboro Team Penske President Tim Cindric and engineer Ian Reed to Treadway to assist in Leffler's effort.

Jimmy Kite, Scott Harrington, Memo Gidley, Hideshi Matsuda and Lyn St. James crashed during qualifications on Pole Day. They were all cleared to drive, but rookie Gidley would not have another opportunity. He had only one car, a 1999 Dallara, and one Oldsmobile, both loaned to him by Dale Pelfrey, and it could not be rebuilt in time for MBNA Bump Day. Johnny Unser, Billy Boat, Jeret Schroeder, Roberto Guerrero, Raul Boesel, Jaques Lazier, and Doug Didero waved off qualification attempts on Pole Day.

Both Ray and Montoya had downplayed the political significance of the defending Indy Racing champion edging the defending CART champion for the pole. John Menard, Ray's car owner, viewed his team's accomplishment as defending his series' honor. "I'm glad they [Ganassi team] came and I'm glad they're not going home with all of the pie, either," Menard said. "They may still. The race will be a real battle. This [competition] is as good as it gets and we'll see how it plays out. We defended the IRL's honor today. Team Ganassi came to play in our backyard and we did a little better."

DAY-AT-A-GLANCE

Date: Saturday, May 20
Qualification Attempts: 46
Qualifiers: 23

POLE DAY QUALIFIERS

Car	Driver	Speed (mph)
1	Greg Ray	223.471
9T	Juan Montoya	223.372
11	Eliseo Salazar	223.231
32	Robby Gordon	222.885
8T	Scott Sharp	222.810
14	Jeff Ward	222.639
10T	Jimmy Vasser	221.976
92	Stan Wattles	221.508
24	Robbie Buhl	221.357
51T	Eddie Cheever Jr.	221.270
28T	Mark Dismore	220.970
5	Robby McGehee	220.661
4	Scott Goodyear	220.629
18	Sam Hornish Jr.	220.496
98	Donnie Beechler	220.482
91	Buddy Lazier	220.482
50	Jason Leffler	220.417
3T	Al Unser Jr.	220.293
15	Sarah Fisher	220.237
88T	Airton Daré	219.970
7	Stephan Gregoire	219.970
12	Buzz Calkins	219.862
75	Richie Hearn	219.816

WHY DO INDY WINNERS DRINK MILK? Search

Witness the 85th Indy 500 by entering the Fantasy Weekend Sweepstakes at www.NorthernLight.com/fantasy.
NorthernLight.com, the world's most comprehensive search engine. Proud sponsor of the Indy Racing™ Northern Light Series.

 NorthernLight.com
Just what you've been searching for.

© Copyright Delco-Remy ™

We start the world...

Starters

Alternators

Road Gang™ Premium
Electrical Systems

Remanufactured Engines

"Pro-Net"™ Drivetrain
Transmission Technology

Diesel Fuel Systems

Intelli-Check™ and Bench Top
Diagnostic Systems

Intelli-Scan™ Ultrasonic Obstacle
Detection Systems

Integrated Starter Alternator
Dampers

Zeus™ "Smart-Start" Cranking
Motors

Axial Gap Motor Generators

Integrated Solenoid Cranking
Motors

SuperCapacitor power storage

Delco Remy

...and keep it running.

For complete information, contact The Delco Remy Technical Support
Service Representative at 1-800-DRA-0222 or check our web
pages at www.delcoremy.com

RMY
Listed
NYSE
THE NEW YORK STOCK EXCHANGE   Listed on the New York Stock Exchange

by Tim Tuttle

Billy Boat bounced off the Turn 1 wall, his Indy 500 hopes in tatters, but rebounded to make a rousing run into the 33-car field during the final minute. Lyn St. James, knocked down only 24 hours before, picked herself off the deck and bolted into the show. Andy Hillenburg squeezed in, bringing tears of joy to his eyes. Steve Knapp succeeded in the most unlikely of comebacks.

Some went away empty handed. Dr. Jack Miller, Scott Harrington, Robby Unser, and Davy Jones were bumped in the final 21 minutes. Roberto Guerrero and Danny Drinan didn't have the speed and waved off. Doug Didero and Hideshi Matsuda smacked the wall.

When Billy Boat smacked the wall with his Team Pelfrey Dallara on Pole Day, his prospects for qualifying for the Indy 500 looked grim. With luck on his side, he found a great ride with his former boss, A.J. Foyt. It took two qualifying attempts, but Boat averaged 218.872 miles per hour to take the 31st starting position.

This was MBNA Bump Day 2000, replete with the high dramas that have characterized so many of them in the past. Boat had waved off on Pole Day after three straight laps in the 218s. He went out for his second qualifying attempt in Team Pelfrey's 2000 Dallara/Oldsmobile seven minutes into Bubble Day, but spun and hit the outside wall in Turn 1 on his second lap. Boat's car had substantial rear damage that was unrepairable in the nearly six hours that remained. Pelfrey's backup car was a 1999 Dallara, not a competitive option. Boat began searching in Gasoline Alley for an available 2000 and found one in the garage of A.J. Foyt. Boat had driven for Foyt for the previous three seasons.

Foyt's regular drivers, Eliseo Salazar and Jeff Ward, had qualified on Pole Day. Roberto Guerrero, a veteran of 15 Indy 500s, had been hired to drive Foyt's No. 41 entry on Friday. He'd tried to qualify twice on Pole Day, but waved off after three laps that averaged in the mid-218s on both occasions. Guerrero couldn't get the 2000 G Force/Oldsmobile above 207.763 in practice—it turned out the car had an undetected ignition problem—on Bubble Day. Foyt decided to take him out and put Boat in the car.

Boat took the third attempt in the No. 41 car with 42 minutes remaining. His first two laps averaged 218, but the car lost power from the ignition and he averaged 192.105 for the four laps. With nothing to lose, the team accepted the run and Boat became the 31st qualifier in the field.

They knew it wasn't going to stick. Foyt ordered the team to prepare Salazar's backup No. 11, a 2000 G Force that had never turned a wheel. Boat barely beat the gun signaling the end of qual-

ifications. It went off as he completed his second warm-up lap. Boat averaged 218.872 for his four laps, knocking Miller's 216.154 out.

Foyt sets all his cars up the same and Boat knew what the car would do from his previous time with the team. "It actually was like a shakedown run," Boat said. "I really have to give a hand to the A.J. Foyt crew. A.J. said, 'It's going to be the same as the other ones. Go out and stand on it.' "

Boat, who would line up on the inside of the 11th row, had maintained his friendship with Foyt despite the fact they had parted company. He was grateful for a second chance to drive for Foyt. "It means a tremendous amount to me," Boat said. "A.J. and I always had a great relationship. We didn't really part ways for any particular reason. We just weren't going anywhere." Foyt had confidence that Boat could do the job. "I've got a lot of respect for Billy and he's a good racer," he explained. "But I know that or otherwise I'd have never had him as a driver. He's done a hell of a job and I'm real proud of him."

St. James had whacked the wall hard Saturday during a qualification attempt. The contact, which demolished her Dick Simon Racing 2000 G Force/Oldsmobile, didn't hurt nearly as badly as missing the 500 the previous two years. St. James raced in six straight Indy 500s from 1992 to 1997. She was bumped from the field last year and didn't go fast enough in 1998. "The last two years not making it tore me up inside," St. James said. "It was the strongest test I've had in knowing who Lyn St. James is."

She is both resilient and determined. At 53, St. James was the oldest driver trying to qualify for the 500, but she didn't have a backup car that was ready. A 2000 G Force was entered as teammate Stephan Gregoire's backup and had been leased to Jonathan Byrd/McCormack Motorsports for Robby Unser the previous day. When St. James crashed, Simon had the G Force returned. The Simon crew went to work on changing the steering and setup and completed it by about 2 P.M. Sunday.

She went out to qualify at 5:34 P.M., 26 minutes before the ending of qualifications. With a long line waiting to qualify, St. James couldn't make any mistakes. Her four-lap average was 218.826 miles per hour. St. James started with laps of 219.464 and 219.518 before dropping down to 218.664 and 217.670. She was in her seventh Indy 500. "These last two years are something I would not want anyone to go through," St. James said. "I know what it is to be on the board and get bumped. I am elated. I have an incredible feeling inside to be in the show."

For the first time, there would be two women in the Indianapolis 500.

Hillenburg may have been the slowest qualifier in the field at 218.285, but he was likely the most emotional. He was raised in Indianapolis, but had abandoned an open-wheel career in the 1990s to move into stock cars.

He crashed his 2000 Dallara/Oldsmobile in the morning practice the previous day. The car was repairable and he had 10 laps of practice on Bubble Day morning. With slightly more than an hour remaining, he qualified. Climbing out of the car, he cried. "This is probably one of the most wonderful feelings a race driver can have," he said. "This has been the most nerve-racking week of my life and this is a day I'll remember for the rest of my life. I've worked on this forever. Every book report I ever did, even in grade school, everything has always been about being here. This is something I've wanted ever since I can remember."

Prior to Bubble Day, Knapp hadn't been in an Indy Racing League Car since breaking his neck in a crash at Atlanta Motor Speedway the previous July. Less than a month before the festivities at Indianapolis began, Knapp wasn't sure he ever wanted to be in an Indy Car again.

In a remarkable rejuvenation of his career, Knapp changed his mind, put together a deal with Dreyer & Reinbold Racing in the final days leading up to qualifications and drove it into the race with 34 minutes remaining. Knapp had 27 laps of practice in a 2000 G Force/Infiniti before averaging 220.290 miles per hour in his four-lap qualifying attempt. It placed him on outside of the ninth row.

"I was pretty close to retiring," Knapp said. "I went to Phoenix [for the Indy Racing Northern Light Series event in March] to see if the spark would come back and left with the attitude that I was really done. I'd had a few crashes and thought if I was doing that, I really shouldn't be out there."

Knapp was Indy's Bank One Rookie of the Year in 1998, finishing third with ISM Racing. The team had been run by Team Manager/ engineer Mitch Davis. A few weeks prior to the May 13 opening of practice at Indianapolis, Davis called Knapp to see if he was interested in driving at Indianapolis. Davis is now running Dreyer & Reinbold Racing, which has Robbie Buhl (a partner in the team) as its regular driver.

"Mitch talked to me and turned me around on my thinking of the accident at Atlanta," Knapp said. Mitch had bought the actual car I had crashed from the insurance company, to make it into a show car. When he took it apart, he found the right rear wheel bearing had failed. All along, I thought the crash was my fault."

Davis told Knapp there was a possibility his team would run Buhl's backup 2000 G Force/Infiniti if all went well in practice and qualifying and wanted Knapp to drive it. He would have to bring partial sponsorship to close the deal. He wasn't sure if he wanted to do it. A few days prior to the opening of practice at Indy, his close friend Bruce May, a Formula Ford driver who lived in the Indianapolis area, died of a heart attack at age 46. Steve came to Indy for the funeral on May 14, and then went to the Indianapolis Motor Speedway.

"I was so depressed over Bruce that the only people I talked to were Mitch and my cousin Tom [team manager/engineer of Team Menard]," Knapp said. "I went home. I got home and I started hearing Bruce's voice in my head. He said, 'You had better get back down there.' I knew he wanted me to be in the race. Bruce actually spotted for me at Indianapolis last year.

"I called Mitch on Wednesday to see what was going on. He told me there was a chance and what would have to take place in order for it to come together." Knapp needed to find some sponsorship, in a hurry. He called a friend at Beatrice Foods, Russ Sprague. "I told him, 'I need your help and this is what is available if I get it,' and he put together a sponsorship for me with Reddiwip," Knapp explained.

Knapp also had to clear his return with wife Bobbi and their nine-year-old son Logan. Everything in Indianapolis was falling into place for Knapp. Buhl had a smooth week and qualified solidly on Saturday. That opened up the backup for Knapp, who signed his deal with Dreyer & Reinbold Racing at 4 P.M. that afternoon. "It was like my dad [Jerry] and Bruce were up there in heaven pulling strings to get this done," Knapp said.

Knapp got on the track a few minutes past 2 P.M., four hours before the end of qualifications. Buhl had set the car up with 14 laps in the 1-hour, 15-minute morning practice and reached 214.774 miles per hour. It was the first laps the car had ever run.

In 27 laps of practice, Knapp was up to 219. He got into line to qualify. The idea was to make an attempt, see how the car was, and wave off if necessary. "About six cars pulled into [qualifying] line behind us and we decided we had to take it, because we didn't know if we could get back out again," Knapp said.

Knapp's four-lap average of 220.290 was plenty to assure him a spot in the field. "If you make it through Turn 1 on the green-flag lap, the rest is pretty easy," Knapp said. "I just ran flat out for four laps." Knapp was full of emotion as he came down the pit lane.

After Jimmy Kite's Pole Day crash, Blueprint Racing bought a Team Ganassi G Force in order to make a Bubble Day qualifying attempt. With the new chassis, Kite was able to post a 220.718 mile per hour average, which was good enough for 25th on the starting grid.

"I started crying," Knapp said. "Then, I saw Al Unser Jr. clapping and giving me thumbs up. That meant a lot to me, that somebody like him would recognize me for getting into the 500. I haven't even met him yet, but he's one of my heroes."

Raul Boesel was Bubble Day's fastest qualifier at 222.113, a speed that would have put him on the inside of the third row if he had done it the previous day. The Brazilian was driving a third G Force/Oldsmobile for Treadway Racing, which was short on manpower. Boesel didn't start practicing until Thursday. On Pole Day, the team waved off after three laps that averaged 218.

Boesel went out late in the day, but pulled in the pits following a warm-up lap. "The engine wasn't running right," Boesel said. "We went back to the garage, put the engine from [teammate] Robby McGehee's backup car in mine and qualified on Sunday. We didn't change anything else."

Jimmy Kite had crashed on Pole Day and didn't have a 2000 backup car. Blueprint Racing purchased a new G Force from Target/Ganassi Racing. It had been Jimmy Vasser's No. 10 car, which had practiced at 220.589. "I've got to thank Chip Ganassi and everybody at Ganassi Racing for giving us the opportunity that they didn't have to give us, especially with them coming in here from CART," Kite said. "It shows what a class act they are."

Rookie Jaques Lazier and Truscelli Racing had originally entered a 1999 G Force. When it became obvious that a 2000 car was needed to make the race, the team leased a 2000 G Force from TeamXtreme. Lazier didn't get out in the new car until Friday. The team waved off a three-lap attempt on Pole Day that 23 averaged 218.8.

Lazier went out twice on Bubble Day. He pulled in after his first warm-up lap on the initial run, then returned 11 minutes later. Lazier averaged 220.675 and qualified for the inside of the ninth row. "It really feels great to finally make the race," Lazier said.

Davey Hamilton had fuel pressure problems on his first attempt on Bubble Day and waved off after one lap. He qualified TeamXtreme's 2000 G Force/Oldsmobile nearly three hours later at 219.878, putting him on the inside of Row 10. Hamilton had struggled to find speed all week and didn't crack the 220 barrier in practice until the morning practice on Bubble Day.

Jeret Schroeder had waved off twice on Pole Day, then lost an engine in midday practice on Bubble Day in Tri Star Motorsports' 2000 Dallara/Oldsmobile. The Larry Curry-run team leased an engine from Dreyer & Reinbold Racing and Schroeder qualified at 219.322 on his third attempt.

Johnny Unser also made it in his third attempt in the Delco Remy 2000 G Force/Oldsmobile, averaging 219.066. "I can't take too many more days like this when I qualify on my last attempt," he said. "We found our real speed during qualifying, a great time to peak."

Dropped by Foyt that afternoon, Guerrero made a last-gasp effort by climbing into Hubbard-Immke Racing's backup 1999 Dallara/Oldsmobile. He waved off after a lap of 206.996.

Drinan jumped into the Hillenburg team's backup 1999 Dallara/Oldsmobile, but aborted his qualifying run after one lap at 213.265. He stopped with one minute remaining, allowing Boat to get on the track.

With no other choice, Robby Unser had returned to Byrd/McCormack's 2000 Riley & Scott/Oldsmobile on Bubble Day. The team had parked the car on Friday after failing to exceed 214.684 in practice.

There were spots available in the field with two hours remaining and Unser qualified at 212.678. Unser was bumped by Davy Jones with 18 minutes remaining. Jones was driving an Indy Racing League Car for the first time since 1997, when he was seriously injured at Walt Disney World Speedway. Jones didn't get into the Team Coulson 1999 G Force/Oldsmobile until the Bubble Day morning practice.

Jones, runner-up at Indy in 1996, extracted a 214.932 average, impressive considering the equipment and time in the car, and was in the field for five minutes. Harrington went out next and averaged 215.971 in Nienhouse Motorsports' 2000 Dallara/Oldsmobile. He'd crashed on Pole Day and the team never got the car back up to speed. Harrington bumped Jones and was in the field for eight minutes. Schroeder knocked him out. Dr. Jack Miller was in the field when the gun went off and out of it when Boat completed his run.

Didero hit the outside wall in Turn 1 with 55 minutes remaining. He wasn't hurt, but Mid America Motorsports did not have a 2000 backup car. Hideshi Matsuda crashed hard in midday practice in Turn 3 in Hubbard-Immke's 2000 Dallara/Oldsmobile. It was the third straight day Matsuda had hit the wall. The Japanese driver suffered a broken right wrist and left knee and spent four nights in the hospital before being released.

It had been a wild Bubble Day.

DAY-AT-A-GLANCE

Date: Sunday, May 21
Qualification Attempts: 21
Qualifiers: 15
Bumped: 5

BUMP DAY QUALIFIERS

Car	Driver	Speed (mph)
55	Raul Boesel	222.113
27	Jimmy Kite	220.718
33	Jaques Lazier	220.675
24T	Steve Knapp	220.290
16	Davey Hamilton	219.878
6	Jeret Schroeder	219.322
22	Johnny Unser	219.066
11T	Billy Boat	218.872
7T	Lyn St. James	218.826
48	Andy Hillenburg	218.285

by Tim Tuttle

Juan Montoya flexed his muscles on Coors Carburetion Day, the final on-track activity prior to the running of the 84th Indianapolis 500. Pennzoil Panther Racing won the day's real competition, taking the Coors Pit Stop Challenge.

Montoya averaged 218.257 miles per hour on his 13th of 14 laps in Target/Chip Ganassi Racing's G Force/Oldsmobile to post the fastest time of the day. Eddie Cheever Jr. was second at 217.909 in his Excite@Home Dallara/Infiniti, and Buddy Lazier logged in the third-fastest lap at 217.728 in the Delta Faucet/Coors Light Dallara/Oldsmobile. Cheever completed 18 laps, just enough to make sure everything was functioning properly.

Lazier was happy with his race setup after running 25 laps.

Raul Boesel, running with full tanks for the first time in the month, was fourth in the Treadway Racing's EPSON G Force/Oldsmobile at 217.303.

All 33 qualified cars and 32 drivers were on the track. Jimmy Kite drove two: his regular Blueprint Racing Founders Bank G Force/Oldsmobile and Jason Leffler's Treadway Racing UnitedAuto Group Special G Force/Oldsmobile.

Leffler was at Lowes Motor Speedway preparing for a NASCAR Busch Grand National race. "Jason is a buddy," Kite said. "We were just doing those guys a favor. We were mostly just leak checking." Kite and Leffler had developed their friendship competing in USAC, and Kite was a perfect fit for Leffler's seat and belts.

Carb Day's primary purpose is to make sure everything is working and the race engine has been installed properly. Several teams encountered problems. Scott Sharp's Delphi Automotive Systems Dallara/Oldsmobile had its clutch fail before leaving the pits. The Kelley Racing crew spent nearly two hours replacing it, getting him out for three laps just before the session ended.

Buzz Calkins had a misfire in the Bradley Motorsports Dallara/Oldsmobile. He ran 212.429 and completed 23 laps.

Target/Chip Ganassi Racing's Jimmy Vasser had the fifth-fastest lap in his G Force/Oldsmobile at 216.1845, but the day wasn't trouble free.

TeamXtreme's Davey Hamilton ran 45 laps, the most of the session. His fast lap in the FreeInternet.com G Force/Oldsmobile was 213.083, 17th fastest.

Robbie Buhl also had a clutch failure in his Team Purex G Force/Oldsmobile, but not until he had run 31 laps.

Stan Wattles had crashed his qualified Hemelgarn/Metro Racing Dallara/Oldsmobile on Bubble Day, forcing his crew to repair it to maintain the No. 8 starting position in the field. He ran 19 laps, with a best of 213.324.

Panther won the $80,000 pit stop contest for the second time in three years with four fast and mistake-free victories. The team earned $37,500, plus $5,000 donated to the American Red Cross of Greater Indianapolis in Panther's name. The contest requires a four-tire change and simulated fueling and is timed from when the car enters the pit box until it leaves.

Panther's final stop of 11.19 seconds was its slowest, but beat the 12.72 seconds by Robby McGehee's Treadway Racing crew. The Treadway time included a three-second penalty for allowing a tire to roll outside of the pit box. "We had four pit stops today and no mistakes," Goodyear said. "They practiced, they train, and look forward to it every year."

Panther chief mechanic Kevin Blanch said the competition gives the team a psychological lift going into the race. "We don't like to give away seconds in the pits and I think we showed again that we're pretty good at doing that," Blanch said. "We've got a great group of guys and we don't beat ourselves.

Galles ECR Racing had won three of the previous four pit stop challenges, but was eliminated by nearly two seconds, 9.99 to 11.90, by Panther in the second round. Panther defeated Mark Dismore's Kelley Racing crew 10.28 to 18.13 (including a five-second penalty for an air gun being incorrectly passed) in the first round and Sharp's Kelley Racing crew 9.69 to 10.11 in the third.

Other participants in the pit stop challenge were Buhl's Dreyer & Reinbold Racing, which defeated Buddy Lazier's Hemelgarn Racing crew 12.86 to 18.86 (including a five-second penalty for a loose wheel lug) in the first round; Greg Ray's Team Menard crew, which defeated Jeff Ward's A.J. Foyt Racing crew 10.62 to 11.22 in the first round; Billy Boat's Team Pelfrey crew, which lost 10.03 to 13.37 to Treadway in the first round; Juan Montoya's Target/Chip Ganassi Racing crew, which lost to Treadway's 10.27 because their G Force failed to leave the pit box under power in the second round; and Team Cheever's Eddie Cheever, Jr. which lost 10.43 to 15.18 to Team Menard in the second round. Treadway defeated Team Menard 9.49-16.04 (including a five-second penalty for a wheel coming off exiting from the pits) in the other third-round contest.

The Coors Pit Stop Challenge brought the on-track prerace race to a close. The most grueling 500 miles in racing remained.

Scott Goodyear's crew provided rapid service during the annual Carburetion Day Pit Stop Contest, in which crews get to practice their duties and compete for bragging rights and bonus pay. *Walt Kuhn*

DAY-AT-A-GLANCE

Date:	Thursday, May 25
Drivers on Track:	32
Cars on Track:	33

TOP FIVE DRIVERS OF THE DAY

Car	Driver	Speed (mph)
9	Juan Montoya	218.257
51	Eddie Cheever Jr.	217.909
91	Buddy Lazier	217.728
55	Raul Boesel	217.303
10	Jimmy Vasser	216.845

A Razor's Edge Ride to *INDY 500* Glory

JUAN MONTOYA AND GANASSI RACING DOMINATE

By
Jonathan
Ingram

A better race day omen could not have occurred for the Target/Chip Ganassi Racing team upon its return to the Indy 500 for the first time in five years. The 84th running of the "Greatest Spectacle in Racing" was unable to begin at its usual time of 11 A.M. because a curtain of rain had moved across the Indianapolis Motor Speedway causing a three-hour delay. In their Gasoline Alley garage, the Ganassi team's race day crew embraced nature's fate.

Having just completed a three-day stretch of dashing from Coors Carb Day at Indy to the Championship Auto Racing Teams (CART) race at Nazareth Speedway and back again, the Ganassi race team lapped up the down time. Ganassi's test crew had handled the chores of car preparation during practice, then qualifying, and simply had to roll the two Target-backed G Force/Oldsmobiles into the pits on Sunday. But for the race day crew, it had been a hectic 24 hours.

The team worked until the wee hours to transfer all the equipment from Nazareth, Pennsylvania to Indy for the 500-mile event and

Rookie? Hardly! Although Juan Montoya (9) was listed as an Indy 500 rookie, his racing savvy and experience showed as he dominated the 2000 race and won in convincing fashion. This photo shows second place finisher Buddy Lazier chasing Montoya in the waning stages of the race.
Steve Snoddy

The field of 33 cars takes the green flag and funnels into Turn 1. Robby Gordon (32) dove inside of pole-sitter and Menard teammate Greg Ray (1) in Turn 1 of the first lap while Eliseo Salazar (11) and Juan Montoya (9; behind Ray) joined the fight. *Walt Kuhn*

had to gear up for its second race in as many days. At Indy, the eyes of the world would be upon them. Directed by Tom Anderson and Mike Hull, they would be working the pit strategy and pit stops for drivers Juan Montoya and Jimmy Vasser. Along with the Ganassi team itself, their arrival had been awaited with greater anticipation than any entries at Indy in five years.

Some spectators had booed the team, which had won four straight CART championships, during the days of practice and qualifying. The team was even taunted during the pit stop contest on Coors Carb Day. Others were eager to see the return of one of the leading CART teams to the Speedway for the first time since 1995. In 1996, the Indy Racing League was born, and CART chose to continue with its own engine and chassis formula, taking a separate path from the Indy Racing League. Montoya, winner of the 1999 CART title, was reckoned to be one of the best to ever don a helmet and gloves at the track before even setting foot in it. Vasser was an old favorite coming back after conquering CART for a title in

1996. The entire team, including its savvy, mercurial owner, gave the massive facility an air of anticipation; a newness befitting the modern Pagoda, press center, and pit suites that had been erected since the 1999 version of the world's most famous 500-mile race.

Within the quiet walls of their garage amidst the dewy smell of fresh rain, the Ganassi crew got one last chance to relax backstage before the big show. It was an opportunity to let go of the frustrations and forget the snafus of the previous days. Montoya had blown his start in the pit stop contest in an embarrassing display on

Robby Gordon's racing career is now focused on stock cars, but he made the most of his lone open wheel race of 2000, running strong and finishing sixth in the 2000 Indy 500. Gordon reduced the downforce as much as comfortably possible, but he didn't have the speed to get on terms with the leaders. *Ron McQueeney*

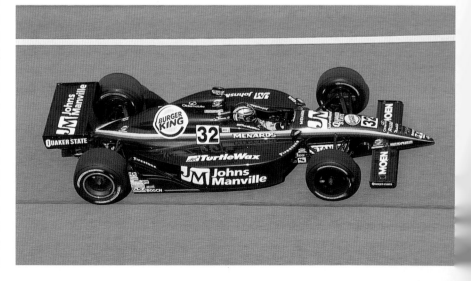

Carb Day, drawing chants of "I-R-L!" from those in the crowd who favored the Indy Racing Northern Light Series, its teams, and drivers. In addition the crew had flubbed one pit stop at Nazareth the day before, costing Montoya a clear shot at victory. The rain was like a baptism of renewal before the fire. "With our situation, I think the delay was positive for the team," said Ganassi. "It gave us a chance to loosen up, get together, tell jokes. It could have been a negative for other teams, but for us it was positive."

By the time the race was over, the Ganassi team and Montoya had measured up to their day of destiny. On a day when Indy 500 speed records were set for the first seven 10-lap intervals, Montoya and the Ganassi team performed with eye-popping precision. In a race where cars and engines were as evenly matched as ever seen in Indy 500 history thanks to the Indy Racing League formula, Montoya and his team left no doubt about their conquest. "When you win this race, you deserve it," said runner-up Buddy Lazier, the winner in 1996. It was Lazier's chase in Hemelgarn's Delta Faucet entry, in fact, that confirmed Montoya's incredible ability.

With a verve that had many fans standing and applauding at race's end, Montoya littered the landscape with records. The first rookie to win since Graham Hill in 1966, the Colombian set marks for laps led by a freshman (167) and consecutive laps led (143). His average winning speed of 167.607 miles per hour was the fourth-fastest in Indy 500 history.

Montoya made it look easy while living on the edge of his Firestone tires' adhesion. When the checkered flag fell, the favorable

response from what had been an occasionally antagonistic crowd confirmed his brilliant performance.

"I was pushing it every lap as hard as I could," said Montoya, rising to the occasion on six restarts as well as in an early race duel with pole-starter Greg Ray and a late-race match-up with second-placed Lazier. The quiet, extremely confident, and occasionally aloof Colombian won over some fans along the way. When he first saw the front-straight stands filled with spectators on race day morning, Montoya was stunned. "I looked at my girlfriend and said, 'This is unreal.'" Later that afternoon, many of those same fans were standing to applaud him on his victory lap, having watched him

Hopes were high for pole-sitter Greg Ray (1). A low downforce aerodynamic setup contributed to Ray's crash in the Turn 2 wall while chasing Ganassi Racing's Juan Montoya. The Menard crew hastily repaired the car and Ray returned to the race, but he once again crashed in Turn 2, relegating him to a 33rd-place finish.
Ron McQueeney

Indy Racing League veteran Scott Sharp (8) didn't have his best day in the Delphi Automotive Systems/ MCI WorldCom Dallara/ Oldsmobile/Firestone. Sharp and the Kelley Racing team tried to find the right aerodynamic combination, but they simply couldn't find the straightline speed to run up front.
Ron McQueeney

The close racing, for which the Northern Light Series is known, thrilled fans at the Indy 500. Scott Sharp (8) led a tight pack that included Robby McGehee (5), Mark Dismore (28), and Al Unser, Jr. (3). Sharp eventually finished 10th, McGehee 21st, Dismore 11th, and Unser Jr. 29th.
Bret Kelley

flawlessly four-wheel drift through the corners at the front for most of the three-hour race. "I saw a lot of people standing," he said in a rare moment of emotion. "It means a lot to me."

Ray, the defending Indy Racing League champ, once again failed to finish after starting on the front row for the third straight year, racing for the second straight year under hard-luck team owner John Menard. In fact, Ray demonstrated just how difficult it was to maintain the pace of Montoya. The Texan skated into the Turn 2 wall on the 66th lap, after his team adjusted downforce a second time during his second pit stop in search of more pace since he had faded to seventh. Thus, the defending Indy Racing League champ finished last for the second time in three years. (Tony Stewart finished last in 1998.)

For his part, Montoya controlled the race from his second-place starting position. He got the lead from Ray on the 27th lap, lost it for three laps during the first round of pit stops, and then reeled off his string of 143 circuits at the front. He worked traffic better on a day when all drivers complained of the diffi-

culties of passing with the new, sleek, aerodynamic 2000 chassis of G Force and Dallara plus the smaller, 3.5-liter V-8 engines from Oldsmobile and Infiniti. "You had to decide where to pass because you would lose the momentum if you made a mistake," said Montoya. The winner modulated the wheel in the corners to control his understeer and the fuel pedal to time his overtaking in traffic, thus taking advantage of what was usually a healthy lead.

The start was a different story. Once the 2001 Oldsmobile Aurora Pace Car had pulled off, pole-sitter Ray "wasn't going flat out

Two-time Indy 500 winner Al Unser, Jr. (3), was ecstatic to be back at the Brickyard. His results didn't match his delight, however, as he finished 29th with an overheating engine.

Jeff Ward's Harrah's A.J. Foyt Racing crew provided quick service during an early pit stop. The motocross veteran has logged in some spectacular drives at the 500. He led the 1997 Indy 500 and eventually finished 3rd, in 1998 he finished 13th, and last year he was rewarded with a 2nd-place finish. In the late stages of this year's race, Ward wasn't in touch with the leader and couldn't challenge for victory, but another solid drive netted him a fourth-place finish.

so no one could get a run on him," said Montoya, who was slightly balked, enabling Robby Gordon to get past. Gordon dove down the inside from his second-row position and attempted to pass pole-starter and Menard teammate Ray at Turn 1, almost making it. Montoya then reclaimed second from Gordon in the short chute between Turns 3 and 4, before the first lap had even been completed.

Pre-race speculation centered on whether Montoya would lead or chase Ray. Would one try to press the issue early on with the other? As it turned out, veteran Ray led the way for the first 26 laps while Montoya followed a respectful distance, about one second behind. Gordon, destined to finish sixth, exchanged second place with Montoya on Laps 13 and 14, but that turned out to be his last hurrah. As the day progressed, Gordon would complain of not enough "steam" in his engine, a situation confirmed by team owner Menard. "But it might be something we've done with the car," said Menard. "One can affect the other." The gangway start by a determined Gordon would be the closest he would get to the lead all day.

As would be crucial during this overcast and cool day, lapped traffic proved pivotal. Montoya smoothly scythed through it, while rarely getting balked enough for anybody to pass him. Gordon had slipped by due to lapped traffic, but Montoya made traffic work in

Scott Goodyear was poised to win the Indy 500 in 1992 and 1995, so this year's ninth place was a big disappointment. "We came here to win, so we're not happy with ninth," he said. "But at least we have points toward the Indy Racing Northern Light Series championship." Like others, Goodyear wasn't able to find a low downforce setup to give his car the necessary speed to challenge the leaders. *Ron McQueeney*

1998 Indy 500 winner Eddie Cheever Jr., pushed his Infiniti engine hard all day and finished fifth. Cheever's efforts to capture another Indy 500 victory weren't helped by a transmission that stuck in neutral for half a lap. *Steve Snoddy*

Tickets.com entry when debris holed his radiator after he had moved from his 18th starting position to 9th. (Ray would later return after repairs to his right front suspension plus a new nose assembly and rear wing. When something in the suspension or steering apparently failed, he crashed at Turn 2 again, ruining any chance of gaining Indy Racing Northern Light Series points.)

Long before the halfway mark, control of the race fell in the mesmeric hands of Montoya and his Ganassi pit crew. Although they lost crucial track position the previous day at Nazareth on a pit stop, the crew got Montoya out without losing position on his first stop and every one thereafter during the 500. Once he reclaimed the lead after the first round of green stops, Montoya would hold it until teammate Vasser's fuel strategy put him in front late in the race.

The early pace of Ray and Montoya had put Kelley Racing teammates Mark Dismore and Scott Sharp (whose crew had a problem with its fuel nozzle that cost it seven seconds) a lap down, along with Scott Goodyear and rookie Jason Leffler. Until the race's midpoint, the remaining contenders—Vasser, Jeff Ward, Eliseo Salazar, Lazier, Gordon, Cheever, and rookie Airton Daré—fought like cats in a bag to get around the lapped cars on the restarts, and then one another. Former two-wheel champion Ward felt as if he might be back in a supercross due to the wind. "Every time you'd pull out to pass, it was like hitting a wall," he said. Montoya, meanwhile, waltzed his car through the corners at an unchallenged distance in the lead.

his favor a lap later, even though the car of Lyn St. James almost forced him into the grass in the chute between Turns 3 and 4. On the 27th lap, Montoya made a clean pass for the lead on the inside of Turn 1, after cars went four abreast on the front straight. Ray reclaimed the lead in traffic in Turn 1 on the next lap, and then headed for the pits. That would be the end of the duel of the champions, and the last time any driver was able to use traffic to get by Montoya.

When the first green flag stops ended, Ray was fifth, 20 seconds behind Montoya and trailing Gordon, Salazar, and Eddie Cheever, who was up from 10th in his Infiniti-powered Dallara. Cheever would be a contender until gear selection problems hampered him in the last 70 laps. But including the Dreyer & Reinbold Racing entry of Steve Knapp, two Infiniti-powered cars would finish the race for the first time.

During the first round of pit stops, Ray and his team tried to get more straight-line speed by taking out downforce. "That's what cost us," said Ray of his fade. During the second round of green flag stops, the team added downforce, in an effort to get the gearing right. "I just didn't have enough gear, so they put more downforce on."

It just wasn't to be Ray's day. His Conseco Dallara sailed into the marbles and crashed at the exit of Turn 2 on the 66th lap, bringing out the first yellow. The crash also took out Al Unser Jr.'s

The 1999 Indy 500 Rookie of the Year Robby McGehee led once for two laps but was slowed by engine problems. "I think we easily had a top-three car, it's just hard with seven cylinders. The car was awesome at the start." *Walt Kuhn*

An incident at Turn 1 on Lap 74 knocked out the women drivers from a field that contained a record number of two, and underscored the difficulties of working traffic. When rookie Jaques Lazier drove his G Force/Oldsmobile inside the Dallara of Sarah Fisher, who in turn glanced off the G Force of Lyn St. James, the worst case scenario evolved for those pulling for the female drivers. After Fisher tangled St. James, both ended up in the wall. The younger Lazier, the highest finishing rookie after Montoya, carried on.

"It's not my fault. I was stuck in the middle. I was a sitting duck in this case,'" said Fisher. St. James admitted that her G Force was not handling well and that she had been driving with her mirrors all day. But she took exception to the situation. "I'm surprised they would try to force a pass at that point," she said.

After that two-car incident brought out the second yellow flag, virtually the entire field took its third round of stops during the next caution for debris. It was preceded by a spectacular outside pass of Vasser by Daré (pronounced dar-ay) at Turn 3, which put the freshman up to third behind sophomore Robby McGehee, who had made a pilgrim's progress from eighth place in Treadway's Meijer G Force.

When the field restarted on Lap 102, Montoya had the best of both worlds. He had three slower backmarkers ahead of him that he easily dispatched. Behind him came the faster contenders, still hoping to get their laps back—Goodyear's Pennzoil Dallara, Sharp's Delphi Automotive Systems Dallara, and Stephan Gregoire in the Mexmil G Force. That gave Montoya plenty of traffic between himself and the other contenders.

Eventual winner Juan Montoya (9) led Mark Dismore (28) and the field through Turn 4. Montoya's performance was nothing short of stunning, and it demonstrated a genuine and rare talent. The last rookie to win the 500 was Graham Hill, who took a Lola to victory in 1966.

Jimmy Vasser (10) led twice for a total of five laps, but a late fuel stop cost him valuable track position. Vasser and Team Ganassi gambled and stayed out when the leaders pitted with 25 laps to go. He hoped rain would prematurely end the race, but the strategy didn't work out and he settled for seventh place.

Chilean Eliseo Salazar had a great run in his Rio A.J. Foyt Racing G Force/Oldsmobile. He started and finished third, his best Indy 500 finish. When teammate Jeff Ward jumped on his brakes to avoid Jimmy Vasser, who swung out in front of Ward on his way to the pits, Salazar nipped past Ward for third and held the position to the flag. *Ron McQueeney*

restarted second on the board and eighth on the track. Third-placed McGehee began having engine trouble due to a faulty ignition coil, and he would have to nurse his G Force/Olsmobile home.

All this led to a spectacular display by Daré, who split the cars of Salazar and Cheever into Turn 1 on the 118th lap and then passed the slipping Vasser's G Force in Turn 3 on the same lap. That put Daré in fourth behind Montoya, Buddy Lazier, and Ward. Unfortunately, the Brazilian's engine blew up eight laps later.

By then, Lazier had made his presence known. Having started 16th, the Hemelgarn team had taken out the excessive downforce that hampered the qualifying effort. Only Lazier, it seemed, could handle a car trimmed out for straight-line speed and the subsequent understeer in the corners with the same aplomb as Montoya. Gutsy as usual in traffic, Lazier

Three contenders fell back during the subsequent segment of green, giving Montoya even more breathing room. Vasser's crew had attempted a change to the rear wicker, but debris from the track clogged the groove in the rear wing and he left the pits without any wicker! That meant a very scary, loose condition for the guy who

Billy Boat (41) ran a smart race, finishing 15th after starting 31st. Boat reunited with A.J. Foyt to run the Harrah's G Force/Oldsmobile. He passed more cars than any other driver in this year's 500 and proved that he deserves a full-time ride. *Dan Boyd*

emerged from the catfight as the leading contender, just four cars behind Montoya on the restart, following the clean-up for Daré's blown engine.

Again, Montoya used the four lapped cars ahead of him to his advantage by quickly dashing around at the green. After slicing down the inside to get second-placed Ward's Harrah's G Force on Lap 134, Lazier began reeling in Montoya—the first time anybody had seen that on this day. He whittled down the margin from 5.4 seconds to 3.23 seconds after clearing Ward and traffic.

As would be Lazier's fate all day, however, he would continue to fight traffic. The yellow for Ray's second crash sent all the leaders to the pits on Lap 145. Despite a good stop of 14 seconds, Lazier's pit location in the middle of the pit road meant both Montoya (13 seconds) and Ward (14 seconds) beat him out. "It would have been different if we hadn't started 16th," Lazier would confess later of the constant demands of fighting traffic.

Ninth in line, and third behind Montoya, Lazier made it into second with a daring outside pass of Ward on the front straight, giving the team Foyt driver something to remember. The next yellow for rookie Sam Hornish's spin at Turn 1 played into Lazier's hands. He and the Colombian started at the front of the field with nothing but clear track ahead of them.

On the first lap of green, Lazier began making his inside runs at Montoya at Turn 1, hoping to gradually push the leader into a wider parabola as he struggled with the inevitable understeer resulting from

a car trimmed for the straights. By the end of the second lap under green and the 163rd circuit, Lazier pulled within 0.137 seconds. The 1996 Indy 500 winner thought he had the Colombian in his crosshairs. "He kept moving up the track a little bit each lap and I thought I would get by him," said Lazier. "I felt like I was in control."

1996 Indy 500 winner Buddy Lazier (91) was among the few drivers who had the speed to challenge winner Juan Montoya. Lazier started 16th and ran a smooth, fast race. He was gaining on Montoya in the last five laps, but a slower car thwarted his attempt to overhaul Montoya and he had to settle for second.
Ron McQueeney

Mark Dismore (28) powered through Turn 4 onto the front straight with Davey Hamilton (16) and a quartet of challengers close behind. Dismore took 11th place while Hamilton came home 20th.

The day's last yellow for the smoking engine of Stan Wattles bunched the field and gave contenders one last shot at Montoya, first on pit road and then at the restart. Vasser had already anticipated that speed would not be the best methodology and opted for a fuel strategy by staying out during the yellow. He had pitted during the previous yellow in anticipation of just such a strategy, which the driver had endorsed along with his team.

"I think we tried to get a little tricky with our pit strategy," said Vasser afterward. "I have to take some of the responsibility." As it turned out, Montoya came past his teammate within three laps of the green. At first Montoya, who again led all cars off pit road, did not realize that Vasser was leading by virtue of not pitting. "Juan radioed me and asked me to tell Jimmy to move over," said Ganassi. "'I told him, 'Juan, this is for position.'"

After the final restart, there wasn't much of a battle as the No. 9 Target car dove under Vasser at Turn 3. The hullabaloo concerned the fight for second among Vasser, Ward, Salazar, and Lazier, whose

Indy 500 rookie Airton Daré ran with the leaders in the first half of the race, but succumbed to engine failure after 126 laps and ended up 25th. "It's too bad. I had a little bit of understeer, but things were going well." Dan Boyd

Dick Simon Racing's Stephan Gregoire was pleased with his eighth-place finish: "I am delighted . . . My car was handling well all the race and was easy to drive in traffic. Aside from my gear selection troubles, it was an easy race for me." Dan Boyd

But Montoya had other plans. "I had led too many laps, so I wasn't going to make it easy," he said. "I went deeper into Turn 1 one time and that made the difference."

On Lap 165, the gap widened to 0.199 seconds as Montoya fought off the challenge. The gap then widened to 0.529 seconds, then 0.554 seconds, as the Colombian transcended the challenge. Finally, the duel ended when Montoya slipped by the ailing G Force of McGehee entering Turn 1 and Lazier caught the slower car midway in the short chute. That bumped the gap to 1.573 seconds, but more importantly brought Lazier within range of Salazar. The Chilean's Rio G Force passed Lazier four laps later for second, effectively ending any hopes that anybody would catch Montoya on this day.

Through it all, no one be-grudged Montoya his pace enough to block him and give the pursuing Indy Racing League drivers an easier shot at the leader. Instead, the Indy Racing League regulars fought for position wherever they could. "All I needed to get by him was for somebody to box him in," said Lazier. "But there was no poor sportsmanship."

Juan Montoya crossed the fabled yard of bricks for the final time as he won the 84th running of the Indianapolis 500. Montoya earned $1,235,690 from the record purse of $9,476,505.

last 16-second pit stop was on par with the others but he lost two track positions. Salazar had brought back memories of his body slam on Davy Jones in the 1996 race on a late restart when he pinched Lazier at Turn 1 on the final restart. "Eliseo drove me into the fence, which was really disappointing," said Lazier. "I didn't dare [go low] or we would have wracked up a bunch of cars."

The runners-up trailed the leader by 10 seconds in a gaggle with 10 laps to go and Lazier was once again leading the group by working traffic on the straights and holding on in the corners. The issue for third was decided when Vasser pitted with four laps to go, balking Ward and allowing Salazar to slip by on the inside down the front straight.

Therefore, the 1999 winning team owner, A.J. Foyt, ended up 3rd (Salazar), 4th (Ward), and 15th (Billy Boat, who had started 31st as the last driver to qualify). "Any time you get three cars to the finish here you're doing good," said the four-time Indy winner, who had nothing but praise for Montoya. "He's one helluva race car driver," said "SuperTex."

Track position counted for a lot in a race for such evenly matched cars. Lazier set the race's fastest lap of 218.494 miles per hour two circuits from the end. Montoya was hardly slowing down, setting his fastest lap of 217.691 miles per hour while in the lead one lap later. He did back off down the front straight as his team congratulated him by radio on the way to a well deserved checkered flag. "You're world famous now," said his team owner.

Less than 10 minutes later, a light rain began to fall. It was a fitting benediction to a hard-fought race and another big chapter in Indy 500 history.

2000 Indy 500 Winner Juan Montoya celebrated with the traditional bottle of milk. Sharing in his joy was team owner Chip Ganassi (white cap).
Roger Bedwell

1

JUAN MONTOYA

#9 Target
Entrant: Target/Chip
Ganassi Racing
Crew Chief: Steve Gough

Calm and focused throughout practice, qualifying, and the race, Juan Montoya enjoyed one of the most impressive Indianapolis 500s in its storied history. It was an extraordinary performance for a rookie. The Colombian led 167 laps; the most ever for a rookie and the most by a winning driver since Al Unser Sr.'s 190 in 1970. He was the first rookie to win the 500 since Graham Hill in 1966, and the second since George Souders in 1927.

Montoya won by 7.184 seconds over Buddy Lazier. If it sounds like Montoya had an easy race, he assures that it wasn't. "I had to push it," Montoya said. "I wasn't going to back off. It's not easy . . . I can tell you it was tough." Defining the difficulty, Montoya said: "Oh, just keeping everything together, trying to keep cool while at the same time you've got to be aggressive. You know, I had a couple of moments that it was close and I was pushing it, I can tell you. Every lap today, I pushed it as hard as I could."

It was Montoya's incomparable car control that carried him to victory in the 84th Indianapolis 500. Montoya went for a low downforce setup, which gave him straight-line speed, especially in clean air. But Montoya was playing Russian roulette with the turbulence created by traffic entering the turns, running at 230 miles per hour in a gale-force wind where the slightest loss of control would have planted him in the fence. There were, undoubtedly, brief moments when Montoya had to make those infinitesimal adjustments with the steering wheel that kept him moving to the left when his car wanted to go straight. Montoya never slipped.

"Juan went for low downforce and relied on his talent," third-place finisher Eliseo Salazar said. "That wasn't easy." Montoya, however, was modest about his ability. "The car was perfect," he said. "You know, we didn't risk anything." Montoya didn't win Indianapolis on his own. Target/Chip Ganassi Racing prepared him a 2000 G Force and contracted with Comptech to build its Oldsmobile engines; neither missed a beat. The pit stops were superior, fast, and efficient. The Indy victory was the type of performance that the Ganassi team has become known for in winning four straight CART championships, and the triumph at Indianapolis affirmed Ganassi's status as the finest open-wheel operation in the United States.

At the learning-stage age of 24, Montoya won the European Formula 3000 championship, CART's FedEx championship, and the Indianapolis 500 in successive years. "A lot of people compare him to Ayrton Senna," Salazar said, "and maybe he will be. He's obviously an awesome race car driver."

Montoya had been a rookie in CART the previous year. He won in his third start, at Long Beach, and proceeded to win at Nazareth and Rio de Janeiro for three straight victories on three different types of circuits. It was the greatest start for a rookie in CART history. Nigel Mansell, the previous year's Formula 1 world champion, won three races in his first 10 starts in 1993; and Alex Zanardi, the 1997 and 1998 CART champion, needed 16 starts to win three races in 1996. It took Montoya only five starts.

Montoya won seven races and the CART crown in 1999. He also had seven poles in 1999. In 1998, Montoya won 4 of 12 races to capture the European Formula 3000 title. He also logged thousands of miles as the test driver for the F1 Williams team. Montoya won three races and was runner-up for the F3000 championship in 1997.

A native of Bogota, Montoya began racing karts at age five. He was the junior Colombian national karting champion in 1986. Montoya spent several years competing in world karting competition before moving into cars in 1992. Montoya honed his skill by attending the Skip Barber Racing School in the United States in 1992 and continued to win races in his native country. By 1994, he was ready to go against international competitors. Montoya won twice in the pro Barber Saab Championship in the United States and won four Formula N races in Mexico.

Moving to England, Montoya won four races and four poles with Paul Stewart Racing in the British Formula Vauxhall Championship in 1995. Montoya moved up to British Formula 3 the next year, winning twice and adding three other podium finishes. F3000 was next.

He advanced quickly to the highest echelons of open-wheel racing and had tremendous success when he got there. "Winning the [CART] championship meant a lot of me," Montoya said. "The win [in the 500] did as well. And I think those are the two biggest things that have ever happened in my life so far. It's not one or the other. They both are just massive."

There were those who saw this race as a CART versus Indy Racing Northern Light Series battle. Montoya and team owner Chip Ganassi did not. "Everyone is asking and everyone is interested in the political side of things," Ganassi said. "And I'm not. This [Indy 500] is still the biggest race in the world and this is the biggest win in the world. And it will get bigger as time passes."

Montoya wasn't interested in making a political statement, only in winning the race. "We're here just like any other Indy Racing League team, believe me," Montoya said. "We're not here with any CART flags or anything like that. Right now, in my position, Chip decided to have an IRL team for the 500 and that's the way we took it. I took myself and I look at myself like any other driver out there."

The Indianapolis 500 crowd cheered Montoya like it would any other winner of the world's most famous race. "What makes this place special is the people," Montoya said. "It's a huge race track. I saw a lot of people standing. And it's just great. It's great to win here. It means a lot to me, to Target, to Budweiser, to everyone involved in this project. It's just over the roof."

2000 INDY 500 PERFORMANCE PROFILE

Starting Position:	2
Qualifying Average:	223.372 mph
Qualifying Speed Rank:	2
Best Practice Speed:	223.246 mph (5/20)
Total Practice Laps:	236
Finishing Position:	1
Laps Completed:	200
Highest Position 2000 Race:	1
Fastest Race Lap:	199 (217.69 mph)
2000 Prize Money:	$1,235,690
Indy 500 Career Earnings:	$1,235,690
Career Indy 500 Starts:	1
Career Best Finish:	1st 2000

2

BUDDY LAZIER

DALLARA/OLDSMOBILE/FIRESTONE

**#91 Delta Faucet/Coors
Light/Tae-Bo
Entrant: Hemelgarn Racing
Crew Chief: Dennis LaCava**

S tarting from the 16th position, Buddy Lazier fashioned a stirring charge up to second place and challenged Juan Montoya for the lead. The Indy Racing veteran wasn't able to overtake the rookie from Colombia and had to settle for a bittersweet runner-up finish.

"This is my second second," Lazier said. "I wanted my second win. It's great to finish second and it's a lot of prize money, but it's not a win." Lazier has been a model of high-level consistency at the 500 since 1996, when he won. He was fourth in 1997, second in 1998, and seventh in 1999. In the past five 500s, all with Hemelgarn Racing, Lazier has completed 998 of 1,000 possible laps.

"This year was like a sprint race," Lazier said. "It was flat out the whole race. We had a car with the performance capable of winning, but circumstances didn't fall our way. I got stuck, hammered, boxed in traffic a couple of times. If you get held up, it takes a lot of time to get the momentum back. This was one of the hardest races in my eight years here."

Lazier steadily moved up from the outset, expertly working traffic and passing on the inside going into Turns 1 and 3. He was in 13th by Lap 10, 7th by Lap 40, 4th by Lap 67, and 2nd by Lap 75. After pitting out of sequence on Lap 82, Lazier dropped back to eighth. Using traffic, he was back in second on Lap 114 after going three abreast on the front straight to overtake Jeff Ward on the inside. Lazier lost a position to Ward during a pit stop and regained it on a Lap 151 restart with a spectacular outside pass going into Turn 1.

Lazier's best chance to pass Montoya came following a restart with 39 laps remaining. With his Dallara's nose almost touching Montoya's G Force on the front straight for three laps, Lazier tried to overtake the leader on the inside in Turn 1, but he wasn't successful and three laps later, Lazier caught a slower car in the short chute between Turns 1 and 2 and fell back. Lazier lost positions to Eliseo Salazar and Ward on his final pit stop and fought his way back into second by Lap 186. By then, Montoya had built up an insurmountable lead.

Lazier started the 2000 season with a Riley & Scott chassis. He finished second in the opener at Walt Disney World Speedway and took the R&S to its first Indy Racing victory at Phoenix. But in testing at Indianapolis prior to the official opening of the track, the Hemelgarn team could not find the necessary speed to be competitive with the Riley & Scott team. Owner Ron Hemelgarn purchased a new Dallara and the Lee Kunzman-managed team put it together in a week in time for the opening of practice.

Lazier had the Dallara up to 221.250 miles per hour by the third day of practice and hit a best of 222.363 in the Pole Day morning practice. But in qualifying, Lazier averaged 220.482 for the 16th spot on the grid. "We're elated, because it's a hard race to make," Lazier said. "We've only had this car for seven days and other teams have had [theirs] for seven months.

Lazier was third fastest on Coors Carburetion Day at 217.728. Lazier said, "They gave me a great car and I'm happy about that."

Lazier had the fastest lap of the race at 218.494 miles per hour on Lap 198.

2000 INDY 500 PERFORMANCE PROFILE

Starting Position:	16
Qualifying Average:	220.482 mph
Qualifying Speed Rank:	19
Best Practice Speed:	222.363 mph (5/20)
Total Practice Laps:	324
Finishing Position:	2
Laps Completed:	200
Highest Position 2000 Race:	2
Fastest Race Lap:	198 (218.494 mph)
2000 Prize Money:	$574,600
Indy 500 Career Earnings:	$3,455,376
Career Indy 500 Starts:	8
Career Best Finish:	1st 1996

ELISEO SALAZAR

#11 Rio AJ Foyt Racing
Entrant: AJ Foyt Enterprises
Crew Chief: Bill Spencer

A s the surprising selection by owner A.J. Foyt in January to drive his Rio Hotel and Casino-sponsored car, Eliseo Salazar proved that faith in his ability was justified with a tremendous overall performance at Indianapolis.

The 44-year-old Chilean missed the pole by a fraction of a second, .171 slower than Greg Ray after 10 miles of qualifying, but showed his ability to charge ahead by finishing third in the race.

Foyt chose Salazar in part because of his previous record at Indianapolis. Salazar finished fourth in 1995 with Dick Simon Racing and sixth in 1996 with Team Scandia. However, he'd struggled in the races since then, for reasons that ranged from uncompetitive cars to being in the wrong place at the wrong time, and even failed to qualify in 1998.

Four-time Indy 500 champion Foyt supplied solid equipment and over 40 years of experience at Indy. There was only one rule for Salazar to follow: Listen to the boss.

"A.J. Foyt made a perfect plan," Salazar said. "A.J. said to run 95 percent. [Juan Montoya and Buddy Lazier] were a little faster, but we were adjusting the car. We were behind a lapped car at the end that held us up and hurt our chances of winning. We're satisfied with third, but we really wanted to have a go with Montoya and didn't get to."

Foyt kept to his game-plan of running limited miles early in the week of practice. On Friday, he turned Salazar loose for 48 laps and he hit 222.921 miles per hour. In the morning practice on Pole Day, Salazar streaked to 223.964—the fastest of the month. Then, he put together three laps above 223 and one above 222 for a 223.231 average. Salazar was on the pole for an hour and 12 minutes before Montoya replaced him and eventually ended up on the outside of the front row.

Salazar, who also started third in 1996, said he had a car to win the pole. "I made a slight mistake on the last lap and it cost us," Salazar said. "I went too deep into Turn 1, went too far inside and touched the rumble strip. It would have been great to get the pole, but I'm happy to settle for the front row."

Prior to moving into Indy Cars at age 39 in 1995, Salazar had an extensive and diverse career. He was the Chilean saloon—a type of stock car—champion in 1974, drove in British Formula 3 and Aurora championships, and spent parts of three campaigns (1981-1983) in Formula 1. In 1984 and 1985 he was the Chilean rally hill climb champion.

Resuming his international career, Salazar switched to sports car racing, driving at Le Mans from 1988 to 1990. In 1994, he won three IMSA World Sports Car races in the Momo Ferrari. Salazar overcame serious injuries in the 1996, 1997, and 1998 seasons to return to racing. Salazar solidified his comeback in 1997 with an Indy Racing triumph for Team Scandia at Las Vegas Motor Speedway.

2000 INDY 500 PERFORMANCE PROFILE

Starting Position:	3
Qualifying Average:	223.231 mph
Qualifying Speed Rank:	3
Best Practice Speed:	223.964 mph (5/20)
Total Practice Laps:	188
Finishing Position:	3
Laps Completed:	200
Highest Position 2000 Race:	3
Fastest Race Lap:	172 (217.057 mph)
2000 Prize Money:	$474,900
Indy 500 Career Earnings:	$1,302,970
Career Indy 500 Starts:	5
Career Best Finish:	3rd 2000

4

JEFF WARD

#14 Harrah's AJ Foyt Racing
Entrant: AJ Foyt Enterprises
Crew Chief: David Milby

For the third time in four Indy 500 starts, Jeff Ward was a contender to win. He ran steadily in the top six and brought A.J. Foyt's famous No. 14 car to the checkered flag in fourth place. "We had a good car," Ward said. "I like this track. You know where you are [on speed] pretty quickly. I was in the middle of a lot of restarts. Every time you'd pull out to pass, it was like hitting a wall. It was frustrating. It was hard to get by people. But all in all, it was a good race. There weren't many crashes. I'm pretty happy with fourth."

After starting sixth, Ward ran as high as second and was never out of the top five in the final 250 miles. He was running fourth with four laps remaining when third-placed Jimmy Vasser (who didn't pit under the previous caution) suddenly braked hard and turned left into the pits, forcing Ward to get on the binders to avoid him. Eliseo Salazar took advantage to get past his teammate.

The 38-year-old Ward ran sparingly early in the week of practice, but completed 78 laps on Thursday and Friday with a best of 222.949 miles per hour. Ward qualified at 222.639 for sixth; his best at Indianapolis. "The run was simple; pretty easy," Ward said. "We probably ran too short a gear. The car was perfect. I told Eliseo and he went up a gear on his run. I was happy to help him. There's a lot of grip in the track and no wind. It's a perfect day for qualifying. It's always good to start up front, especially here with three wide."

Born in Scotland but raised in southern California, Ward spent 15 seasons in professional motocross before moving to cars. He was the first rider to win the American Motorcyclist Association's four major motocross championships: the 125cc, 250cc, and 500cc Nationals, and the 250cc Supercross. He won seven championships in all and also represented the United States in seven International Motocross des Nations competitions.

Retiring from two-wheeled racing in 1992, Ward moved into Indy Lights in 1993 and spent four seasons there. Ward passed Indy's Rookie Orientation Program in 1995 and practiced at 226.074 in a year-old car, but failed to qualify for the 500 that year.

Ward joined the Indy Racing League in 1997, making his debut at Walt Disney World Speedway with Galles Racing. He drove the entire 1998 Indy Racing League season with ISM Racing, taking sixth in the championship with second-place finishes at Disney and Charlotte.

Ward started the 1999 season with ISM, but after finishing second at Disney, he switched to Pagan Racing. Ward finished 2nd at Phoenix and Indianapolis, but the underfunded effort ran out of steam and he slid to 11th in the points. Still, he had impressed Foyt, who signed him to the car vacated by 1999 Indy 500 and 1998 Indy Racing League champion Kenny Brack.

2000 INDY 500 PERFORMANCE PROFILE

Starting Position:	6
Qualifying Average:	222.639 mph
Qualifying Speed Rank:	6
Best Practice Speed:	222.949 mph (5/19)
Total Practice Laps:	208
Finishing Position:	4
Laps Completed:	200
Highest Position 2000 Race:	2
Fastest Race Lap:	192 (216.414 mph)
2000 Prize Money:	$361,000
Indy 500 Career Earnings:	$1,594,450
Career Indy 500 Starts:	4
Career Best Finish:	2nd 1999

5

DALLARA/INFINITI/FIRESTONE

EDDIE CHEEVER JR.

#51 Excite@Home Indy Race Car
Entrant: Team Cheever
Crew Chief: Owen Snyder

Eddie Cheever Jr. drove Nissan's Infiniti to its highest Indy 500 finish, completing all 200 laps to take fifth. The 1998 Indy champion reached a high point of second in the 84th-annual race and was in the top five over the final 400 miles. Cheever was happy with the Infiniti's performance, but wasn't pleased with the final result.

"The Infiniti engine was superb," he said. "We tried hard to break it. I ran it as fast as I could and it did very, very well. The Infiniti is here. I'm very proud of how it did and I want to thank everyone at Infiniti for plugging away at it. It won't be too long before everybody is going to want to be running an Infiniti." Cheever was one of two Infiniti-powered cars in the race. He could take special pride in its competitiveness. Team Cheever became the program's developmental partner in 1999.

"We could have won if we had not had a few little moments," Cheever said. "I lost half a lap [on Lap 131] when I changed gears from fifth to sixth and all I had was a bunch of neutral. I thought the race was over, but I put it in gear, it vibrated a little bit and something inside decided to fix itself.

"I got stuck in traffic a lot and didn't come off the corners as well as I should have. We also had a lot of problems in the pits waiting for fuel to go in, but the whole team did an awesome job. I'm just sorry that I couldn't do better."

Cheever's fifth was his third-best Indy result in 11 starts. He was also steady in practice and qualifying. Cheever had a lap of 220.881 miles per hour on the second day of practice and a fast lap of 223.892 for the week. He qualified 10th at 221.270.

"We made a choice on our aerodynamics in qualifying that was conservative," Cheever said. "There's nothing worse than a loose car. I was driving the whole four laps with a smile on my face. That's all we had."

Born in Phoenix but raised in Italy, Cheever drove in Formula One for parts of 11 seasons from 1978 to 1989. He made 132 F1 starts; the most by any American.

Cheever made the transition to Indy Cars in 1990 and was the Indy 500 rookie of the year after finishing eighth with Ganassi Racing. He continued to compete in CART and the Indy 500, driving for several teams, before becoming a charter member of the Indy Racing League in 1996. That summer he formed Team Cheever. He captured the opening race of the 1997 Indy Racing League season at Walt Disney World Speedway. Cheever climbed from 17th on the grid to win at Indy in 1998 and started the 1999 campaign off with a victory at Disney, his third Indy Racing triumph. Cheever took his fourth Indy Racing triumph—and the first for Infiniti—in 2000 at Pikes Peak International Raceway.

2000 INDY 500 PERFORMANCE PROFILE

Starting Position:	10
Qualifying Average:	221.270 mph
Qualifying Speed Rank:	11
Best Practice Speed:	223.892 mph (5/20)
Total Practice Laps:	372
Finishing Position:	5
Laps Completed:	200
Highest Position 2000 Race:	2
Fastest Race Lap:	199 (218.134 mph)
2000 Prize Money:	$364,500
Indy 500 Career Earnings:	$3,558,452
Career Indy 500 Starts:	11
Career Best Finish:	1st 1998

6

ROBBY GORDON

#32 Turtle Wax/Burger King/Moen/Johns Manville/Menards
Entrant: Team Menard
Crew Chief: Chris Sumner

With 50 laps remaining, Robby Gordon's plan to win the Indianapolis 500 was right on the money. He'd raced hard early and established his position in the lead group of cars, then took a conservative approach to set up a final assault. Gordon found, however, that he couldn't muster the speed at the end and was forced to settle for sixth place.

"We had a good car, just not a great car," Gordon said. "The unfortunate thing is the race went the way we wanted it. We didn't have any problems, our pit stops were very fast, and we were in the hunt and on the lead lap with 50 to go.

"That's what we talked about and that's where we were. We just didn't have the power to handle Montoya and the guys ahead. On the second to last [pit] stop, we pulled the wicker [removing downforce and drag] and decided this was it, we needed to find straightaway speed or we were never going to catch Juan [Montoya]. But pulling the wicker didn't really help."

Gordon qualified fourth in Team Menard's Dallara/Oldsmobile and took the lead at the start in Turn 1 with a bold move to the inside of teammate and pole-sitter Greg Ray. "I tried to take the lead on the start and Greg and I almost got into each other," Gordon said. "I thought if the lane was there and I could grab it, I'd do it, but Greg tried to shut the door. We almost touched and I thought maybe we ought to take it easy early. I had a feeling Juan would run out and be the rabbit. Sometimes, though, that's not the best strategy. This is a tough race. You have to take care of your car, save fuel, and keep out of trouble. Juan basically ran away and everything in our car held up."

Gordon did take the lead for three turns, but Ray and Montoya both passed him before the initial lap was over. Gordon ran as high as second through the opening stages and was in that position when he pitted out of sequence under caution on Lap 75. It cost him track position that was never regained and he ran steadily in the top eight to the checkered flag. Gordon, who spent the 2000 season in NASCAR's Winston Cup, waved off two attempts on Pole Day before completing the third at 222.885 miles per hour. "The run wasn't difficult," he said. "We were flat the whole way around from the warmup lap on. I just needed a little bit of speed to get the pole."

Although he hadn't been in an open wheel car in six months, Gordon was on the pace immediately in practice. He had a lap of 223.120 miles per hour on the third day.

This was Gordon's sixth 500. He finished fourth in 1999, when a gamble on fuel fell two gallons short of victory, and was fifth in both 1994 and 1995. During his career the 31-year-old Californian has won races in off-road, sports cars, and CART's.

2000 INDY 500 PERFORMANCE PROFILE

Starting Position:	4
Qualifying Average:	222.885 mph
Qualifying Speed Rank:	4
Best Practice Speed:	223.515 mph (5/20)
Total Practice Laps:	164
Finishing Position:	6
Laps Completed:	200
Highest Position 2000 Race:	2
Fastest Race Lap:	199 (217.865 mph)
2000 Prize Money:	$216,355
Indy 500 Career Earnings:	$1,238,058
Career Indy 500 Starts:	6
Career Best Finish:	4th 1999

JIMMY VASSER

#10 Target
Entrant: Target/Chip
Ganassi Racing
Crew Chief: Ricky Davis

Jimmy Vasser and his side of the Target/Chip Ganassi Racing operation tried to parlay strategy and nature into victory. While running seventh and the final car on the lead lap with 25 laps remaining, Vasser and Managing Director Tom Anderson decided to stay out as the top six cars pitted under caution. It was a calculated risk. Vasser hadn't been able to make progress toward the front for the previous 100 laps, so when a few drops of rain fell onto the front straight around Lap 170, Vasser and Anderson hoped that, after taking the lead, the skies would open and the final laps would be washed away. The rain did arrive, but it was 30 minutes too late for Vasser.

Teammate Juan Montoya emerged from the pit stop in second. He passed Vasser going into Turn 3 on Lap 180. Buddy Lazier took second from Vasser on Lap 193. With four laps left, Vasser was forced to pit for fuel and went a lap down.

In reality, Vasser's gambit didn't cost him anything. He still finished seventh. "We tried to stretch the fuel as far as we could," Vasser said. "It just didn't work out. We didn't get our car right in the second half of the race. It was pretty good, but not fast enough. We were hoping that things would fall our way and they didn't. I'm really happy for Juan. It's great. The best team won."

Vasser had been stretching his fuel throughout the race. He didn't make his first pit stop until Lap 30 and led that time around. Vasser was in second, but trailed Montoya by 30 seconds, before making his second pit stop on Lap 64. Vasser began losing spots just past the 100-lap mark and by Lap 140, was down to fifth. With the exception of his gamble on fuel, Vasser never moved above fifth the rest of the way.

After missing the opening two days of practice because he was competing at a CART race in Japan, Vasser was on the pace immediately. He practiced at 220.146 miles per hour in only nine laps on Monday's third day and reached 223.447 in the Pole Day morning practice.

Vasser fell off that pace in qualifying, however, and his average of 221.976 placed him seventh. "I'm not happy, but we'll take it," Vasser said. "I had half a notion to turn in after the 222 [.107 first lap], but Tom Anderson said, 'Get in the race, this place can turn on you, let's get it in the race.'

"We went out to work on our qualifying setup on Friday and smoke started coming out of the dash. We didn't get to run as much as we wanted. We tried to hurry the process up and made some mistakes."

Vasser progressed smoothly through the training ground open-wheel formulas before moving into Indy Cars in 1992. He qualified 28th for the 500 as a rookie. He raced at Indy for the next three years, with a best finish of fourth in 1994.

2000 INDY 500 PERFORMANCE PROFILE

Starting Position:	7
Qualifying Average:	221.976 mph
Qualifying Speed Rank:	8
Best Practice Speed:	223.447 mph (5/20)
Total Practice Laps:	254
Finishing Position:	7
Laps Completed:	199
Highest Position 2000 Race:	1
Fastest Race Lap:	191 (215.337 mph)
2000 Prize Money:	$207,505
Indy 500 Career Earnings:	$1,023,527
Career Indy 500 Starts:	5
Career Best Finish:	4th 1994

G FORCE/OLDSMOBILE/FIRESTONE

STEPHAN GREGOIRE

#7 Mexmil/Tokheim/ Viking
Air Tools/Dick Simon Racing
Entrant: Dick Simon Racing
Crew Chief: Rich Simon

Stephan Gregoire's fifth 500 was his most successful. The Frenchman started 20th and persistently passed cars, up to 8th place at the checkered flag. He went a lap down in the opening 50 laps, but stayed on the same lap as the leader the rest of the way. The 199 laps completed were the most completed by Gregoire at Indianapolis.

"I am very pleased for my team," he said. "My car was really good for the whole race. But we had too much downforce for the heavy air after the rain this morning and I could not go fast enough. Overall, I am delighted with my top-10 finish. My car was handling well all the race and easy to drive in traffic. We had good pit stops. They were fast."

Gregoire had a problem selecting first and second gears in the later stages of the race, forcing his Dick Simon Racing crew to push him to leave the pit box. "It was hard to select the lower gears," he explained. "So, I left the pits in third gear for my last two pit stops with my crew pushing hard. Aside from my gear selection troubles, it was an easy race for me."

Gregoire did not gain his positions through attrition. There were 22 cars running at the end of the race. He moved up consistently to 14th at the midway point and finally cracked the top 10 on Lap 125. Gregoire was up to eighth by Lap 130.

This was a comeback campaign at Indy for Gregoire and the Simon team. They failed to qualify in 1999, the first time for either the driver or the team. It took Gregoire four days in practice to get above 220, and when he finally hit 221.397 miles per hour, he never went above that for the rest of the week. He waved off two attempts on Pole Day (both abbreviated runs were in the 219s), and averaged 219.970 in his third attempt.

"We've been struggling to get some speed," Gregoire said. "We ran 221.3 this morning in practice with no draft and 20 gallons of fuel in the car. I'm not sure the engine was pulling as good as it was this morning. We were loose in Turn 1 and lost some speed. I hope that's enough to make the race. I'd be very happy tomorrow [Bump Day] if we make it."

Gregoire's first time driving an Indy Car was at Indianapolis in 1993. A former French karting champion and race winner in the French Formula 3 championship, Gregoire qualified 15th in a Lola-Buick for Simon and finished 19th in his rookie year. He practiced but did not make a qualification attempt in 1994 and missed 1995 entirely.

With the start of the Indy Racing League, Gregoire put together a deal with Hemelgarn Racing in 1996. He qualified 13th, but dropped out early with a mechanical problem. Gregoire qualified at Indy for Chastain Motorsports in 1997, but was taken out in a crash approaching the race start. In 1998, he qualified for a second time with Chastain and finished 17th.

2000 INDY 500 PERFORMANCE PROFILE

Starting Position:	20
Qualifying Average:	219.970 mph
Qualifying Speed Rank:	24
Best Practice Speed:	221.397 mph (5/16)
Total Practice Laps:	263
Finishing Position:	8
Laps Completed:	199
Highest Position 2000 Race:	8
Fastest Race Lap:	171 (215.636 mph)
2000 Prize Money:	$306,900
Indy 500 Career Earnings:	$1,025,906
Career Indy 500 Starts:	5
Career Best Finish:	8th 2000

DALLARA/OLDSMOBILE/FIRESTONE

SCOTT GOODYEAR

#4 Pennzoil Panther Dallara
Entrant: Panther Racing
Crew Chief: Kevin Blanch

Scott Goodyear had an uneventful Indy 500. For a driver that has been in position to win the race on three occasions, a steady run to ninth place was a big disappointment to him and the Panther Racing.

Goodyear started 13th and finished a lap down. He and the team were never able to develop a setup in race trim that allowed Goodyear to make one of his trademark late runs at the checkered flag. "It was difficult to work through traffic and it was certainly a competitive field out there," Goodyear said. "We came here to win, so we're not happy with ninth. We had strong pit stops all day and I'm very proud of my guys [who serviced him quickly on the pit stops]."

Goodyear fell to 19th in the early going and went a lap down by Lap 50. Goodyear and the team made his Dallara/Oldsmobile slightly faster with changes through the opening two pit stops, and he moved up to ninth position by Lap 60. Goodyear was never able to return to the lead lap and ran between 9th and 12th for the remainder of the race.

Goodyear ran a whopping 480 laps—1,200 miles—in practice; the most of any driver. But the speed came painstakingly slow. Through four days, Goodyear's fastest lap was 219.384 miles per hour. He didn't crack 220 until Friday's seventh day and jumped up to 222.017 in the morning practice on Pole Day.

The 40-year-old Canadian qualified at 220.629 in his first attempt. His starting position of 13th was his lowest since 1994. Goodyear had not been concerned that he wasn't starting farther toward the front. He knew, from the 1992 race when he started 33rd and finished second by .043 of a second to Al Unser Jr., that it was possible to contend from anywhere on the grid.

"The [qualifying] time was a reasonable time," he said. "The first lap [219.769] was not as strong as I wanted, but at least we're in the show and we're ready to go racing. Being in the top 12 or 15 should be OK. We worked hard on getting through Turn 1 this week. We didn't start trimming the car until Friday. After all, we weren't running for the pole. We just wanted to make sure we were there for race day."

This was Goodyear's 10th 500, his third in the yellow Pennzoil livery with Panther. He'd been a contender just past the halfway point in 1999 when an engine failure took him out. Goodyear has finished second twice at Indy. In addition to the thrilling 1992 finish, Goodyear lost a duel with Treadway Racing teammate Arie Luyendyk in 1997 by .57 of a second. Goodyear was the leader with 11 laps remaining in 1995, but passed the pace car on the restart. He was black flagged. Told to ignore it by his Tasman team, Goodyear kept racing to the checkered flag. Race officials quit counting Goodyear's laps with five remaining and he finished 14th.

2000 INDY 500 PERFORMANCE PROFILE

Starting Position:	13
Qualifying Average:	220.629 mph
Qualifying Speed Rank:	16
Best Practice Speed:	222.017 mph (5/20)
Total Practice Laps:	480
Finishing Position:	9
Laps Completed:	199
Highest Position 2000 Race:	9
Fastest Race Lap:	26 (213.833 mph)
2000 Prize Money:	$348,800
Indy 500 Career Earnings:	$2,856,665
Career Indy 500 Starts:	10
Career Best Finish:	2nd, 1992, 1997

10

SCOTT SHARP

**#8 Delphi Automotive
Systems/MCI WorldCom
Entrant: Kelley Racing
Crew Chief: Robert Perez**

Scott Sharp went into the 500-mile race optimistic that the work the Kelley Racing had done in practice would provide a strong platform. "We have a fabulous car for next Sunday," he said after qualifying fifth. "It's easily the best car we've ever had."

Sharp's high hopes for the race weren't realized, however. His Dallara/Oldsmobile was slightly off the pace of the fastest cars and the Kelley team never found the proper adjustments to make it more competitive. They tried to take away downforce and free it up aerodynamically, but it didn't respond. "There was a lot of downforce," Sharp explained. "The car was good in traffic, but it was puzzling. The more wing we took out, we lost speed. We just couldn't figure it out."

Sharp stayed on the lead lap until his second pit stop on Lap 62. The team had lost several positions on Sharp's first pit stop on Lap 29 because of a faulty fueling connection, and also had the same problem on the second stop. "We had a fuel nozzle problem in our first and second pit stops that caused us to go a lap down," he said.

Sharp ran steadily around 10th position for 70 laps in the middle stage of the race, then moved up to 8th at the 180-lap mark. But a loss of power dropped Sharp back to 10th at the checkered flag. "Late in the race, we had an engine header break that probably cost us a position or two. Overall, we had a positive race that was compromised by our fuel nozzle problem."

It was the first time Sharp had been running at the finish of the 500 since 1994, his rookie year, and his 10th-place finish equaled his previous best 500 finish from 1996.

Sharp was impressive in practice and qualifying. He had a lap of 223.936 miles per hour on the fourth day of practice. It was the second fastest of the 500 in practice. Sharp qualified fifth at 222.810 on his first attempt. It included a lap of 223.447. "We're pleased, particularly with the 223 for one lap," Sharp said. "The car was flawless. We ran flat for four laps. I didn't have a dash because the battery died. I held the pedal down and hoped the car turned."

The 32-year-old has been one of the most successful drivers in the Indy Racing League, with victories in four straight seasons. He also was the co-champion of the inaugural, three-race season in 1996.

Sharp won three straight Sports Car Club of America national championships from 1986 to 1988. He moved into the SCCA's Trans-Am series and captured the crown in 1991 and 1993. He also won the Daytona 24-Hour, co-driving with Wayne Taylor and Jim Pace, in 1996.

Sharp made his debut in CART competition in 1993 and drove the entire season with PacWest Racing in 1994. He joined A.J. Foyt's team at Indianapolis in 1995 and stayed with Foyt through an injury-shortened 1996–1997 campaign. He signed with Kelley Racing in 1998 and solidified his status as a frontrunner over the next three seasons.

2000 INDY 500 PERFORMANCE PROFILE

Starting Position:	5
Qualifying Average:	222.810 mph
Qualifying Speed Rank:	5
Best Practice Speed:	223.936 mph (5/16)
Total Practice Laps:	438
Finishing Position:	10
Laps Completed:	198
Highest Position 2000 Race:	4
Fastest Race Lap:	86 (215.193 mph)
2000 Prize Money:	$313,000
Indy 500 Career Earnings:	$1,290,019
Career Indy 500 Starts:	6
Career Best Finish:	10th 1996, 2000

11

DALLARA/OLDSMOBILE/FIRESTONE

MARK DISMORE

#28 On Star/GM BuyPower/Bryant Heating & Cooling
Entrant: Kelley Racing
Crew Chief: Glenn Scott

For the first time in five Indy 500s, Mark Dismore reached the checkered flag. "We brought the car home and finished. That was one of our main goals," he said. But he fell short of the team's other mission. "I'm disappointed we couldn't get a top-five finish," Dismore said.

En route to his 11th-place finish, Dismore hung onto the lead lap through his initial two pit stops and went a lap down by the 70-lap mark. He didn't lose another lap until making a late pit stop from eighth position with four laps remaining. Dismore had pitted out of sequence under caution on Lap 159 in an effort to gain positions if he could go the distance. It moved him from 11th—where he'd been since Lap 130—but he was forced to make a final stop four laps from the finish and fell back to 11th. "Overall, we had a car that was mechanically sound and flawless," Dismore said. "We just had a few problems in traffic that slowed us down a bit."

Dismore concentrated on developing a race setup in practice until Friday's seventh day, when the Kelley team switched to low downforce for qualifying. Dismore turned a 222.117-mile per hour lap and then the team installed a fresh Oldsmobile built specifically by Comptech for qualifying.

Heading out for a couple of laps with only a few minutes remaining, Dismore hit the inside retaining wall exiting the pits. His Dallara was heavily damaged and it forced him into the backup car for qualifying.

Dismore qualified in 11th position at 220.970 miles per hour. "With the qualifying motor we had yesterday, we had a shot at the front row," Dismore said. "We had the bull by the horns and I made a mistake. I was absolutely convinced we could run 223-something. Going out of the pit lane [Friday] on cold tires, I gassed it and it got away. We had to qualify with a motor that had 400 miles on it."

After a long career in karting, the 43-year-old native Hoosier didn't start racing professionally until he was 26, but he progressed rapidly. Dismore's first major victory was in the SCCA Corvette Challenge in 1988. In 1989 and 1990, Dismore dominated the Formula Atlantic Pacific Division, winning 11 races including a record six in a row.

Driving at Indianapolis for the first time in 1991, Dismore was seriously injured in a crash in practice. He suffered fractures to his neck, both feet, right wrist, and right kneecap. He recovered from his injuries in time for the 1992 season and won three more Formula Atlantic races. In 1993, co-driving with P.J. Jones and Rocky Moran for Dan Gurney's All American Racers, Dismore won the 24 Hours of Daytona in a Toyota GTP.

Five years after his devastating crash, Dismore qualified for his first Indy 500 with Team Menard. He started 14th and fell out with an engine failure, finishing 19th. Dismore joined Kelley Racing in 1997 and captured his first Indy Racing triumph at Texas in 1999.

2000 INDY 500 PERFORMANCE PROFILE

Starting Position:	11
Qualifying Average	220.970
Qualifying Speed Rank:	12
Best Practice Speed:	222.117 mph (5/19)
Total Practice Laps:	337
Finishing Position:	11
Laps Completed:	198
Highest Position 2000 Race:	4
Fastest Race Lap:	197 (215.244 mph)
2000 Prize Money:	$294,500
Indy 500 Career Earnings:	$1,058,353
Career Indy 500 Starts:	5
Career Best Finish:	11th 2000

12

DALLARA/OLDSMOBILE/FIRESTONE

DONNIE BEECHLER

#98 Cahill Racing
Entrant: Cahill Racing
Crew Chief: Rob Long

Veteran open-wheel short-track driver Donnie Beechler had his best Indy showing, with career-high results in both qualifying (15th) and finishing (12th). "Indy was very satisfying for me and our team," Beechler said.

It was the third 500 for Beechler, a 39-year-old from Springfield, Illinois, and the first 500 he finished. (He dropped out of the 1998 and 1999 races with engine failures.) "In 1998, Indy was our first adventure in an Indy Car," Beechler said. "We were a completely rookie team. We came from Sprint Cars and put a deal together. We made the race, but had an engine failure, then another one last year. After two engine failures, we wanted to run all day. We saw the checkered flag, and it was a milestone for my career and great for the team.

"We ran a conservative setup. It [the setup] was pretty pinned down. We stalled on the first pit stop and lost six or seven seconds, but everything else went smoothly."

The team switched to Comptech-built Oldsmobile engines for the 2000 season and owner Larry Cahill hired veteran engineer Darrell Soppe. Beechler and the unsponsored team built momentum for Indianapolis by finishing sixth in the opener at Walt Disney World Speedway and third at Phoenix.

Beechler was eighth fastest at 220.702 miles per hour in Monday's third day of practice. "We're getting up to speed," he said. "Yesterday we had some problems with some bodywork on the car, which held us back. We got that fixed, so we're back in the hunt. We'll mileage-out the engine we have in the car. Then, on Wednesday, we'll put a new bullet in the car and start trimming the car out for qualifying."

But that plan went awry Tuesday when Beechler hit the outside retaining wall in Turns 1 and 2, sustaining heavy left-side damage. Beechler wasn't hurt. "We were just fine-tuning the car," he said. "I was going into the turn and [the car] just turned around. Just a little adjustment here makes a big difference."

The team spent the following day building up a new car. Beechler struggled to regain the speed during the next two days, topping out at 219.832. "I think we've struggled all day and all week with the crash and we lost a motor today," he said Friday. But he practiced at 220.318 on Pole Day morning and qualified at 220.482 miles per hour. "We're just glad to be in," Beechler said.

Beechler began racing Sprint Cars in 1982 and moved into USAC national competition in 1988. He has USAC national event victories in the Silver Bullet and Midget divisions. Larry Cahill is a longtime owner and former Sprint Car driver who had competed against Beechler and hired him to drive for his Indy Racing League team in 1998.

2000 INDY 500 PERFORMANCE PROFILE

Starting Position:	15
Qualifying Average:	220.482 mph
Qualifying Speed Rank:	18
Best Practice Speed:	220.702 mph (5/15)
Total Practice Laps:	253
Finishing Position:	12
Laps Completed:	198
Highest Position 2000 Race:	10
Fastest Race Lap:	158 (213.245 mph)
2000 Prize Money:	$283,000
Indy 500 Career Earnings:	$558,300
Career Indy 500 Starts:	3
Career Best Finish:	12th 2000

13

JAQUES LAZIER

**#33 Miles of Hope/Truscelli
Team Racing
Entrant: Truscelli Team Racing
Crew Chief: Bill Winkelblech**

Jaques Lazier enjoyed a strong run during his rookie year at Indianapolis. From 26th on the grid, Lazier marched up to 13th at the checkered flag. He was the second highest finishing rookie behind winner Juan Montoya.

"I'm proud of this team," Lazier said. "The car was awesome. It was extremely consistent the entire race. The race was exciting. It was everything I expected and more so I'm thrilled to death for this team. We're very excited to finish."

Lazier went two laps down through two rounds of pit stops but didn't lose another over the final 140 laps. He was in 20th position at the 100-lap mark before making a steady advance to 13th. "Our car stayed under us, and we were able to start passing cars that didn't stay as consistent," Lazier said. "We just went after them one at a time. Our major focus was getting to the end."

Lazier, the 29-year-old brother of 1996 Indy 500 champion Buddy, began practice with a 1999 G Force chassis. He managed to practice at 217.928 miles per hour by the fourth day of practice on Tuesday. It was the fastest lap of any of the non-2000 cars, but when it became clear that a 1999 chassis would not be capable of getting into the race, owner Joe Truscelli leased a 2000 G Force from TeamXtreme Racing.

The team spent two days building the out-of-the-box G Force and Lazier finally got back on the track on Friday. He did 217.236 miles per hour in 47 laps. Lazier missed the Pole Day morning practice because the team was making changes to the car. He waved off a three-lap qualifying run late in the day that averaged 218.8 miles per hour. Lazier practiced at 219.260 on Bump Day morning before qualifying at 220.675 miles per hour. His four-lap run included three of his four fastest laps of the month, topped off by a 221.762.

"The crew deserves all the credit," Lazier said. "All we came with was the 1999 car and they've busted their butts to get the 2000 ready. I thought realistically we could do a 220 flat, then I came by and saw the 221. The car started getting loose and at the end I was hanging on for dear life. I had to back off a bit in Turn 3 and adjust the weight jacker a bit. That's why we had a little slower lap at the end.

"The thing to do now is . . . have one heck of a party and then let the crew get some rest. Three days ago this car was a bare tub. We had a collaborative effort with TeamXtreme. They were kind enough to provide us with one of their tubs."

Lazier made his Indy Racing League debut in 1999, driving impressively in seven races. He had a best finish of seventh place on three occasions, but he had to deal with the disappointment of failing to qualify for the 1999 Indy 500. Driving for a small team put together by his father Bob at Indianapolis, Lazier qualified at 219.165 on Pole Day, but was knocked out of the field on Bump Day. He joined Truscelli for the remainder of the season.

2000 INDY 500 PERFORMANCE PROFILE

Starting Position:	26
Qualifying Average:	220.675 mph
Qualifying Speed Rank:	14
Best Practice Speed:	219.260 mph (5/21)
Total Practice Laps:	149
Finishing Position:	13
Laps Completed:	198
Highest Position 2000 Race:	13
Fastest Race Lap:	128 (213.787 mph)
2000 Prize Money:	$290,250
Indy 500 Career Earnings:	$290,250
Career Indy 500 Starts:	1
Career Best Finish:	13th 2000

14

JERET SCHROEDER

#6 Kroger/Tri Star Motorsports Inc.
Entrant: Tri Star Motorsports
Crew Chief: Derrick Stephan

Jeret Schroeder felt like a survivor at the end of the Indy 500. He fought a underperforming engine, balky traffic, and near misses with the competition to climb from 29th on the grid to finish 14th. "I had a million close calls," Schroeder said. "I'm glad we finished. That was our goal."

Although he managed to clear some of the traffic ahead, Schroeder was battling understeer and an engine that bogged down in the mid-rpm range, and went a lap down by Lap 25. Schroeder was up to 22nd by Lap 40 and 17th by Lap 60, two laps before his second pit stop.

The 30-year-old from Vineland, New Jersey, was forced to make an unscheduled third pit stop six laps later for new tires because Greg Ray crashed in front of him, forcing Schroeder to run over debris that cut the left-front tire on his Dallara. The misfortune cost Schroeder valuable track position and he dropped to 23rd, two laps down.

Schroeder did not lose another lap over the final 130, but making progress through the field was slowed by his engine problem. "It just didn't get going until it reached about 10,400 rpms [10,700 are allowed]," Schroeder explained. "I had to downshift every single lap a minimum of two times and I should have been able to go flat out. Even when I was in a draft the motor didn't pick up [rpms]. The car would push on the exit of the turns and then I had to pedal out of the throttle, which compounded the problem. We just didn't have enough power."

Schroeder was nearly caught up in Ray's second crash, on Lap 144, but his Dallara escaped unharmed. He was up to 15th by Lap 150. Schroeder was still in that position when Sam Hornish Jr. crashed in front of him in Turn 2 on Lap 158.

Schroeder gained one more spot with six laps remaining. "Our pit stops were great," Schroeder said. "We made some stops that I wish we didn't have to make, like when we had a left-front tire go down when I ran over some debris. That was early, when Greg Ray had his first problem. I was close to his other problem, too, and I had a close call when Sam Hornish crashed, too. Really there were a million close calls. A lot of people were brake-checking out there and some were blocking. One time on a restart, one guy brake-checked in front of me in Turn 4, and four or five other guys blew by us both. I got back by most of them pretty quickly, but little things like that take you out of the picture here."

Schroeder had problems finding speed during practice and qualifying. Through six days of practice, his best lap was 217.402 miles per hour. But on Friday's seventh day, Schroeder broke new ground with a 219.634. During the Pole Day morning practice he improved to 220.488, but doing one fast lap in practice and putting four together during qualifying are entirely different propositions.

The Tri Star Motorsports team, led by veteran team manager Larry Curry, waved off Schroeder's first attempt after two laps that averaged 217.5. Later during Pole Day, Schroeder did two laps at 219-flat before aborting the attempt. Schroeder was left with only one more attempt on the only 2000 Dallara he had. On Bump Day, Schroeder's qualifying motor blew up. The team changed engines and with eight minutes remaining, Schroeder bumped his way into the field at 219.322.

2000 INDY 500 PERFORMANCE PROFILE

Starting position:	29
Qualifying Average:	219.322 mph
Qualifying Speed Rank:	29
Best Practice Speed:	220.488 mph (5/20)
Total Practice Laps:	297
Finishing Position:	14
Laps Completed:	198
Highest Position 2000 Race:	14
Fastest Race Lap:	170 (212.445 mph)
2000 Prize Money:	$279,000
Indy 500 Career Earnings:	$454,250
Career Indy 500 Starts:	2
Career Best Finish:	14th 2000

15

BILLY BOAT

#41 Harrah's AJ Foyt Racing
Entrant: A.J. Foyt/Kenny Brack
Motorsports
Crew Chief: Craig Baranouski

Billy Boat gained more positions from start (31st) to finish (15th) than any other driver in this year's 500. It was the type of performance that owner A.J. Foyt had been confident Boat could produce when he put him in the car late on MBNA Bump Day.

Boat had driven at Indy for Foyt in the three previous races and had finished third in 1999, but Foyt believed a change for both his team and Boat was necessary following the 1999 season and didn't re-sign him. Still, they remained friends.

Joining Team Pelfrey, Boat labored to develop a competitive car during practice. He hit 220.283 miles per hour in Team Pelfrey's Dallara/Oldsmobile on Friday's seventh day, but slid to 219.233 in the Pole Day morning practice. Boat made one qualification attempt on Pole Day, but it was waved off after three laps in the 218s.

Boat practiced at 220.227 during Bump Day's morning practice, but when he went out early to qualify, his car spun on the second lap and made contact with the outside wall in Turn 1. He wasn't hurt, but the Dallara—Team Pelfrey's only 2000 car—couldn't be repaired in time for another attempt. Boat set out searching for something else to drive.

Foyt had hired Roberto Guerrero to drive his No. 41 entry, but Guerrero failed to make the field in two qualification attempts on Pole Day. When Guerrero couldn't find the speed in practice on Bump Day, Foyt decided to let Boat have a shot with it.

Boat's attempt with less than an hour remaining was spoiled by a failed ignition. He took a four-lap average of 192.105 that the team knew would not hold up. Foyt sent his team running for Gasoline Alley to roll out Eliseo Salazar's backup car (entered as 11T), which had never turned a lap. "I normally keep all my cars identical," Foyt said. "So, I knew it had a very close setup. I told Billy if he liked the way 41 felt, he'd be fine."

Boat, going out less than a minute before the gun sounded ending qualifications, qualified at 218.872, fast enough to make the show. "If you want to make the show, sometimes you have to stand up in the seat," Boat said. "I didn't have any radio communication, so I didn't know what speed I was running, but it felt pretty good."

Foyt had a choice of several drivers to put in his third entry, but thought Boat was the only one capable in that situation. "I've got a lot of respect for Billy and he's a good racer," Foyt said. "But I know that or otherwise I'd have never had him as a driver. He's done a hell of a job and I'm real proud of him."

Boat made consistent upward progress in the race, breaking into the top 20 by Lap 80. He briefly was up to seventh on Lap 30 by stretching his fuel, but went a lap down following his first pit stop.

"My car was pretty good in the race when I was by myself, but I had a very bad push when I was behind another car," Boat said. "This made it very difficult to pass. When you start 31st, not being able to pass is not good. We were also hurt by how long the race went green. We needed a yellow earlier in the race to stay on the lead lap.

"The car was capable of a top 10 speed-wise, but we didn't get the breaks in order to stay on the lead lap."

2000 INDY 500 PERFORMANCE PROFILE

Starting Position:	31
Qualifying Average:	218.872 mph
Qualifying Speed Rank:	31
Best Practice Speed:	220.283 mph (5/19) (with Team Pelfrey)
Total Practice Laps:	335
Finishing Position:	15
Laps Completed:	198
Highest Position 2000 Race:	7
Fastest Race Lap:	155 (213.569 mph)
2000 Prize Money:	$211,000
Indy 500 Career Earnings:	$1,269,100
Career Indy 500 Starts:	4
Career Best Finish:	3rd 1999

G FORCE/OLDSMOBILE/FIRESTONE

RAUL BOESEL

#55 EPSON
Entrant: Treadway-Vertex
Cunningham Racing
Crew Chief: Steve Fried

Raul Boesel had a late start at Indianapolis during 2000. He didn't have a regular ride in the Indy Racing Northern Light Series and didn't finalize his agreement to drive the Treadway-Vertex Cunningham Racing entry until practice had started.

Boesel had driven in 11 previous 500s and he showed his experience at the Brickyard by getting up to speed quickly. The Brazilian didn't start running until Thursday's sixth day of practice and was up to 219.791 miles per hour on Friday. The team ran into a brick wall, however, on Saturday, in both practice and qualifying. Boesel ran 219.755 in practice, and then during his first qualification attempt, the team waved off after Boesel completed three laps with a 218.2 average.

"We couldn't get a good straight-line speed," Boesel said. The team installed one of teammate Robby McGehee's backup Oldsmobile engines in Boesel's G Force and made no other changes. Boesel practiced at 221.760 in only seven laps in the morning on MBNA Bump Day. He was ready for his second qualification attempt.

"I went out this morning and said, 'Park it. Let's put it in line and go'," Boesel said. It was the day's fastest run, four laps that averaged 222.113. If he had done it on Pole Day, Boesel would have started 7th, but as a Bump Day qualifier, he was relegated to 24th.

"The balance is really good," Boesel said. "We had a new, fresh engine and we had four good laps. That's what made the difference. It means a lot to qualify. I have been close to winning this race several times. It is history to me. I can tell my kids this is my 12th Indy 500."

Boesel stretched his fuel early, hoping for a caution that would allow him to stay on the lead lap. His good fuel economy allowed him to cycle up to fifth on Lap 30, but when he pitted one lap later, he went a lap down. He stayed only one lap down for 130 laps and was running 12th with 30 laps to go, but he started having an engine problem and fell to 16th and was three laps down at the checkered flag, finishing 16th.

"My engine began to misfire," Boesel said. "There was just nothing we could do. It's definitely not something we expected and no matter how hard we pushed, the car just didn't have the horsepower to be really competitive. We worked so hard to put this deal together at the last minute. It is too bad that we had to end up this way."

Although Boesel's effort was put together late, he worked with a very capable group led by engineer Dave Conti and crew chief Steve Fried. Conti had helped McGehee finish fifth and win Bank One Rookie of the Year honors at Indy in 1999. Fried was McGehee's crew chief and had been critically injured in an accident in the pits early in the race.

The 42-year-old Boesel finished third at Indy in 1989 and fourth in 1993. He was the World Sports Car champion in 1987 and also spent two seasons in Formula One.

2000 INDY 500 PERFORMANCE PROFILE

Starting Position:	24
Qualifying Average:	222.113 mph
Qualifying Speed Rank:	7
Best Practice Speed:	221.760 mph (5/21)
Total Practice Laps:	179
Finishing Position:	16
Laps Completed:	197
Highest Position 2000 Race:	5
Fastest Race Lap:	64 (215.069 mph)
2000 Prize Money:	$213,000
Career Indy 500 Earnings:	$2,272,634
Career Indy 500 Starts:	12
Career Best Finish:	3rd 1989

G FORCE/OLDSMOBILE/FIRESTONE

JASON LEFFLER

#50 UnitedAuto Group Special
Entrant: Treadway Racing
Crew Chief: Jamie Nanny

Rookie Jason Leffler completed 492.5 miles of the 2000 Indy 500, all of them advancing his learning curve and whetting his appetite for more miles at the Speedway. Leffler's drive paid off with a worthwhile 17th at the checkered flag.

"I was real excited," Leffler said. "I haven't had much training in an Indy Car. My crew did an awesome job and I was able to gain a lot of experience. The car just got faster and faster and I realized how inexperienced I was. I thought if I did this once, I might think about doing it again, but now I definitely want to come back."

Leffler, a 24-year-old from Long Beach, California, was competing in his third Indy Racing League event. He was Treadway's test driver for six months starting in July 1998 and made his Indy Racing League debut at Walt Disney World Speedway in January 1999. Roger Penske scheduled Leffler to test for his CART team two months later, but another driver testing for Penske crashed the previous day and Leffler lost the opportunity.

After signing with NASCAR team owner Joe Gibbs, Leffler (a national champion in USAC's Silver Bullet and Midget Divisions) began competing in the Busch Grand National Series. Leffler, who continued to race in the Busch series for Gibbs in 2000, landed his ride in the 500 through a cooperative effort between Penske and Treadway. Penske provided sponsorship through the UnitedAuto Group. Treadway supplied the G Force chassis, Comptech-built Oldsmobile, crew and other equipment, and a warmup race for Leffler at Las Vegas Motor Speedway in April.

It was also a way for Roger Penske, whose 10 Indy victories are the most for a car owner, to evaluate the competition and equipment for a possible return as a car owner in the future. He sent in Penske Racing President Tim Cindric to oversee the operation and direct Leffler's race from the pits, Ian Reed to engineer, and consultant Rick Mears, who served as Leffler's spotter in the race.

Leffler had an incident-free 500. He ran 220.448 miles per hour in his second day at the track on Monday. "I feel, with Treadway Racing and with the help of Roger Penske, that I could win this race," he said after that practice. "I'm not saying that we will win the race, but we have everything it takes to do so."

Leffler was up to 221.613 on Friday and qualified 17th at 220.4217 in his first attempt on Pole Day. "We had a real solid effort," Leffler said. "The car has been real solid all week long. We haven't been super fast, but we've never been bad, either."

Leffler slipped back to 21st after 50 laps in the race and went two laps down by Lap 64. But he picked up the pace and remained only two laps down and climbed, with some help through an out-of-sequence pit strategy, up to 12th by Lap 176. Leffler needed some yellow-flag laps in his final fuel load to go the distance and didn't get them. He was forced to pit in the closing laps under green, lost another lap, and fell to 17th.

2000 INDY 500 PERFORMANCE PROFILE

Starting Position:	17
Qualifying Average:	220.417 mph
Qualifying Speed Rank:	20
Best Practice Speed:	221.613 mph (5/19)
Total Practice Laps:	341
Finishing Position:	17
Laps Completed:	197
Highest Position 2000 Race:	12
Fastest Race Lap:	183 (215.791 mph)
2000 Prize Money:	$179,905
Indy 500 Career Earnings:	$179,905
Career Indy 500 Starts:	1
Career Best Finish:	17th 2000

18

DALLARA/OLDSMOBILE/FIRESTONE

BUZZ CALKINS

**#12 Bradley
Motorsports/Team CAN
Entrant: Bradley Motorsports
Crew Chief: Todd Tapply**

Buzz Calkins and Bradley Motorsports qualified for their fifth consecutive 500 and were running at the finish for the third straight year. Both are noteworthy accomplishments, but Calkins and the team were disappointed with their performances in qualifying (22nd) and the race (18th). "We had much higher expectations," Calkins said.

The 29-year-old Calkins ran 219.807 miles per hour during his second day of practice on Monday and, while concentrating on race setups, ran consistently in that range the rest of the week. He was first out on Pole Day and posted his fastest lap of the event (220.124) on the first timed lap, but fell off to 214.459 on his second lap forcing the Bradley Motorsports team to wave off the attempt. "We had a fuel pressure problem," Calkins said. "It started sputtering and then shut off. We had to take the engine out and replace the fuel system."

Calkins returned 4-1/2 hours later to qualify with a four-lap average of 219.862, which included his two fastest laps, 220.178 and 220.140. "On our first qualifying attempt, we hit the rev limiter [at the maximum of 10,700 rpms] at start/finish and were in fifth gear," Calkins said. "We decided to use sixth gear on the second attempt. It was a little sluggish off the corners, and it probably cost us a little time. We're frustrated because we didn't show the speed we were capable of, but it was a good decision to take the speed and get into the race.

"There's an old adage that you should take a speed you know will get in the race, and we were confident that it would. There was a lot of time for qualifying left, both on Saturday and all day Sunday, but our speed held up very well. We didn't have a car that could go for the pole and if you don't have that [then] the idea is to get in the race. We accomplished that."

After losing several positions early in the race (eventually dropping to 29th), Calkins started a consistent ascent. He was up to 20th by Lap 140 and 18th by Lap 180. "We couldn't run in traffic," Calkins said. "When I got behind another car, our car would lift up. We didn't have any downforce and couldn't do anything about it when we tried to adjust on the pit stops. When I was by myself, it would be all right for awhile, but then we'd be back in traffic and the car was junk. We're disappointed. We had better potential than that."

The Bradley team was sponsored by the non-profit foundation Cure Autism Now at Indianapolis. "We were really pleased to be associated with a group that was trying to use the Indy 500 to help raise awareness and financial support to find a cure for autism," Calkins said.

Calkins won the first Indy Racing League race ever in 1996, outdueling Tony Stewart at Walt Disney World Speedway. He also set an Indy Racing record by finishing 13 straight races in the 1999 and 2000 seasons.

2000 INDY 500 PERFORMANCE PROFILE

Starting Position:	22
Qualifying Average:	219.862 mph
Qualifying Speed Rank:	27
Best Practice Speed:	219.807 mph (5/15)
Total Practice Laps:	274
Finishing Position:	18
Laps Completed:	194
Highest Position 2000 Race:	18
Fastest Race Lap:	85 (210.250 mph)
2000 Prize Money:	$169,000
Indy 500 Career Earnings:	$1,020,053
Career Indy 500 Starts:	5
Career Best Finish:	10th 1998

19

STEVE KNAPP

**#23 Team Purex Dreyer &
Reinbold Racing
Entrant: Dreyer & Reinbold Racing
Crew Chief: Mitch Davis**

Steve Knapp had to get up to speed in a hurry to qualify for this year's 500, but the 1998 Indianapolis 500 Bank One Rookie of the Year was up to the task. He had only 27 laps of practice prior to averaging 220.290 miles per hour on MBNA Bump Day to qualify for the 27th starting position.

Knapp had not driven an Indy Car in 10 months. He had suffered a broken neck at Atlanta Motor Speedway and pondered retirement. "I'd had a few crashes and thought if I was doing that, I really shouldn't be out there, " he said.

Mitch Davis played a pivotal role in Knapp's decision to continue driving and helped him land the opportunity at Indy. Davis had been team manager for Knapp's 1998 effort at ISM Racing and was currently working in the same capacity for Dreyer & Reinbold Racing. The team's priority was getting regular driver Robbie Buhl in the race on Pole Day, but once that was completed, Davis wanted to run Knapp in Buhl's backup car.

Davis convinced Knapp that the crash at Atlanta wasn't driver error. "Mitch had bought the actual car I had crashed," Knapp said. "When he took it apart, he found the right real wheel bearing had failed. All along, I thought the crash was my fault."

Knapp was also influenced to return by the death of friend and amateur racer Bruce May, who had passed away from a heart attack in early May. He believed that May wanted him to resume his career. Knapp called Davis and said he wanted to drive a few days before Pole Day. Knapp put together an associate sponsor deal and went to Indianapolis. Buhl qualified solidly in the field on Pole Day and the team began preparing Knapp's G Force-Infiniti.

Buhl drove the first 14 laps the car had ever run in the Bump Day morning practice, topping out at 214.774. Knapp went out in the mid-afternoon practice, ran 27 laps with a best of 219.853, and got in line to qualify. The plan was to make a trial attempt, wave off, adjust the car, and get back into line. "About six cars pulled into the line behind us and we decided we had to take it, because we didn't know if we could get back out again," Knapp said.

Knapp found the car perfectly balanced. "I just ran flat out for four laps," he said. He had made it into the field with 37 minutes to spare. His lack of time to prepare a race setup during practice caused the team to use a conservative setup for the race. Knapp also stalled the car on the first pit stop, causing him to lose two laps. He stretched his fuel mileage prior to that initial stop to run as high as 11th, but fell back to 32nd following it.

"I think our overall package had too much downforce," Knapp said. "We went in knowing that, but hoped the race would come to us."

Knapp helped Infiniti reach a milestone. It was the first time the engine had two running at the end of the 500. "The motor was flawless," Knapp said. "It never missed a beat."

2000 INDY 500 PERFORMANCE PROFILE

Starting Position:	27
Qualifying Average:	220.290 mph
Qualifying Speed Rank:	22
Best Practice Speed:	219.853 mph (5/21)
Total Practice Laps:	45
Finishing Position:	19
Laps Completed:	193
Highest Position 2000 Race:	11
Fastest Race Lap:	148 (211.919 mph)
2000 Prize Money:	$167,000
Indy 500 Career Earnings:	$720,750
Career Indy 500 Starts:	3
Career Best Finish:	3rd 1998

G FORCE/OLDSMOBILE/FIRESTONE

DAVEY HAMILTON

**#16 FreeInternet.com/
TeamXtreme/G Force
Entrant: TeamXtreme Racing
Crew Chief: John King**

D avey Hamilton spent part of his fifth 500 stalled on the track and later spent time in the pits while his crew made repairs. Even when it was healthy, Hamilton's G Force/Oldsmobile wasn't capable of running up front. It made for a long day for Hamilton, whose finish of 20th was the worst of his Indy 500 career. "It was a rough day," Hamilton said. "We lost an alternator, and it was tough to drive without the dash and all of that. It was no one's fault. It was just one of those days."

Hamilton's car wasn't trimmed out enough aerodynamically. "The car handled really well, maybe too well," he said. "I was flat out all the way around, except in Turn 1."

Starting from 28th position, Hamilton went a lap down by the first round of pit stops. He was two laps down and running 22nd by the 60-lap mark. During a caution period, Hamilton coasted to a halt on the back straight. After being towed in, the team was able to restart the car and Hamilton resumed five laps down.

Hamilton's wounded, down-on-power G Force continued to circulate. Finally, Hamilton was forced to come in on Lap 128 to repair the electrical system and returned 10 laps down. Hamilton went the rest of the distance and was 12 laps down at the checkered flag.

Although the team was persistent in practice, Hamilton had problems cracking the 220-mile-per-hour barrier in the week leading up to Time Trials. His fastest lap through seven days of practice was 219.593 miles per hour, achieved in Tuesday's fourth session. "We lost it toward the end of the week," Hamilton said. "We worked on race setups all week. That's all we did. We thought we could come out [on Pole Day] and qualify. We thought we could trim it out and go fast enough and we couldn't."

The team decided against making a Pole Day qualifying attempt after running 219.307 in the morning practice. In the Bump Day morning practice, Hamilton found the speed he'd been wanting, with a lap at 220.627 miles per hour. Hamilton took the green for a first attempt early in the session, but didn't complete the lap at speed. After the team changed motors, he went back out nearly three hours later and qualified at 219.878.

"It's been a long week," Hamilton said. "We're happy to be in. We were flat out all four laps. We have always run good at Indy, and we've struggled this year. We struggled today. I held [the throttle] down and it's hard when you qualify. The car was a little loose; the tail end was out there. We thought it would go out and get free [aerodynamically]. It was as free as it gets."

By qualifying at Indy, Hamilton remained the only driver to compete in every Indy Racing League race. Hamilton had qualified no worse than 11th and finished no worse than 12th in the previous four 500s. He finished sixth in 1997 with A.J. Foyt's team and seventh in 1998 with Nienhouse Motorsports.

2000 INDY 500 PERFORMANCE PROFILE

Starting Position:	28
Qualifying Average:	219.878 mph
Qualifying Speed Rank:	26
Best Practice Speed:	220.627 mph (5/21)
Total Practice Laps:	463
Finishing Position:	20
Laps Completed:	188
Highest Position 2000 Race:	19
Fastest Race Lap:	21 (210.462 mph)
2000 Prize Money:	$166,500
Indy 500 Career Earnings:	$1,135,653
Career Indy 500 Starts:	5
Career Best Finish:	4th 1998

21

ROBBY McGEHEE

#5 Meijer/Energizer
Advanced Formula/Mall.com
Entrant: Treadway Racing
Crew Chief: Rick Hurford

Robby McGehee emerged as a bona fide contender to win the 500 in the opening 100 laps before an engine problem caused him to fade to a 21st-place finish. "It was just awesome at the start," McGehee said. "We were trying to catch [Juan] Montoya and we definitely had the car to do it."

McGehee gained ground steadily from 12th on the grid. Stretching his fuel beyond the other front runners, McGehee took the lead for Laps 31 and 32. After pitting, McGehee dropped to 10th. McGehee stayed out longer than the competition and moved up to second on Lap 67. He pitted under caution and came out in eighth.

McGehee's strategy continued to pay dividends. He moved into second on Lap 92. After pitting under caution on Lap 100, McGehee was fifth. But on the ensuing restart, McGehee's G Force/Oldsmobile was sluggish. "Something in the motor was amiss," he said. "We lost several laps in the pits trying to fix it, but ended up just cruising around on seven cylinders for the remainder of the race. It was a big letdown, especially when we determined that we had been slowed by a broken spark plug. I think we easily had a top-three car. I guess they always talk about the sophomore jinx and it happened to us."

This was McGehee's second 500. In 1999, he finished fifth and was Indy's Bank One Rookie of the Year. Moving from Conti Racing to the larger Treadway Racing operation, McGehee had gone into Indy with high hopes. He practiced at 220.383 miles per hour on Monday's third day, took two days off as the team prepared teammate Raul Boesel's car, and reached 220.964 on Thursday.

McGehee nearly crashed in the Pole Day morning practice while doing a three-quarter spin in Turn 3. "It was very cold," he said. "I had a big wake-up call. Coming out of the pits going into Turn 3 on cold tires, the car stepped out so far, I started bracing myself for impact. But again the racing gods were looking down on me and I saved it."

The incident had an affect on McGehee's first qualifying attempt, which he aborted prior to taking the green flag. "That took a little confidence away, especially when during the first attempt, the car stepped out big in Turn 1," McGehee explained.

He practiced in the mid-afternoon, then qualified with four straight laps above 220 and averaged 220.661. "That run, we were pretty happy with," McGehee said. "I've never been so excited to qualify in my life. We actually had a really great week until we put in our qualifying motor yesterday. We broke two gearboxes with it. It certainly feels good after what's transpired with the Meijer car this week. We've just been through a little more than I would have liked to have."

"I wasn't happy those couple of hours after we waved off. Last year, we were 27th and we sat and waited to see if we'd get bumped. You don't want to have to qualify on the second day."

2000 INDY 500 PERFORMANCE PROFILE

Starting Position:	12
Qualifying Average:	220.661 mph
Qualifying Speed Rank:	15
Best Practice Speed:	220.964 mph (5/18)
Total Practice Laps:	354
Finishing Position:	21
Laps Completed:	187
Highest Position 2000 Race:	1
Fastest Race Lap:	93 (214.777 mph)
2000 Prize Money:	$281,400
Indy 500 Career Earnings:	$528,150
Career Indy 500 Starts:	2
Career Best Finish:	5th 1999

22

JOHNNY UNSER

**#22 Delco-Remy/Microdigicom/
Homier Tools/G Force/Olds
Entrant: Indy Regency Racing
Crew Chief: Mark Killgo**

There were three Unsers entered at Indianapolis this year and Johnny posted the top finish, 22nd, for the legendary family. Unser, whose father Jerry was the first family member to drive in the 500 in 1958, would have liked to been higher in the order, but he was happy to have reached the checkered flag for the first time in five 500s.

Unser started losing power shortly after the start and was forced to make a pit stop on Lap 8. The team changed the spark box, and Unser returned nine laps down. "That really dictated the rest of the race," Unser said. "We weren't trouble-free, but we certainly would have had a better finish if we hadn't had that long stop. After that pit stop, I had to be very careful racing the leaders. I certainly didn't want to mess them up."

Unser's Indy Regency Racing team, co-owned and run by Indy 500 veteran Sal Incandella, was competing in an Indy Racing League event for the first time. The team did not do any pre-event testing. "Next year, I want to come here early and test and be race ready," Unser said. "It was great, though, to finish the 500. Now I want a much higher placing."

Unser, who had only one chassis for Indy, didn't get on the track until Sunday's second day of practice, when he managed only six shakedown laps. The 41-year-old from Hailey, Idaho, slowly built up to speed, peaking at 219.625 miles per hour in Friday's practice. Unser made his first qualifying attempt early on Pole Day, but waved off after laps of 217.003 and 217.229.

Unser practiced at 218.957 in the Bump Day morning practice. He attempted to qualify early, but aborted the run on the first time. Unser was down to his third and final chance. Unser went out four hours later and averaged 219.066 to qualify for 30th position. The effort included his fastest lap of the event, 219.904, on the second lap. Considering the team's budget and inexperience with the equipment, Unser did well to qualify for the race.

"The 500 means so much to me because of my family history," Unser said. "It is more than you can imagine. My dad was the first Unser to race here and was killed [in practice] here the next year. My uncles [Al and Bobby] and my cousin [Al Jr.] are winners. I get very emotional about this place. I remember coming here as a boy and always watching the race."

Unser spoke about his qualifying run, saying "I can't take too many more days like this when I qualify on my last attempt. Our first two laps were the best. The car then began to tighten. This is a new team and we didn't even run the first two days. We found our real speed during qualifying—a great time to peak."

The Unser family members who entered this year's race were all first cousins. Al Jr. qualified 18th and finished 29th. Robby, Bobby Unser's son, tried to put the uncompetitive Riley & Scott chassis into the field, but was bumped.

2000 INDY 500 PERFORMANCE PROFILE

Starting Position:	30
Qualifying Average:	219.066 mph
Qualifying Speed Rank:	30
Best Practice Speed:	219.625 mph (5/19)
Total Practice Laps:	225
Finishing Position:	22
Laps Completed:	186
Highest Position 2000 Race:	22
Fastest Race Lap:	121 (210.251 mph)
2000 Prize Money:	$161,000
Indy 500 Career Earnings:	$760,253
Career Indy 500 Starts:	5
Career Best Finish:	18th 1997

23

DALLARA/OLDSMOBILE/FIRESTONE

STAN WATTLES

#92 Hemelgarn/Metro Racing
Entrant: Hemelgarn Racing
Crew Chief: John West

Stan Wattles showed some impressive speed this year at Indianapolis. He qualified at 221.508 miles per hour, an effort that rewarded him the eighth starting position. Wattles had the second (218.187) and third (218.145) fastest laps of the race, but an early problem pushed him down the running order and an engine failure with 26 laps remaining relegated him to a 23rd-place finish.

Wattles was two laps down when his car stopped, costing him a potential top-10 finish. "It's too bad the motor didn't last," Wattles said. "We had such a great car."

Wattles was running ninth when he came in for his first pit stop, under green, on Lap 25. The team had problems with the fueling mechanism and Wattles went a lap down, falling to 25th. By the 65th lap, he worked his way back up to 14th and was still one lap down following his second pit stop when he brushed the wall exiting Turn 1. He was forced to make an unscheduled stop to check for damage. The team didn't find any and, because a caution came out at the same time, he didn't lose another lap. Wattles lost three positions, resuming the race in 17th.

"The car actually ran better after my little mishap," Wattles said. His lack of track time in practice—the effort didn't come together until late April—caught up with him in traffic. He went another lap down by Lap 90. "We just needed a little more practice time to get the car handling in traffic," Wattles said. "No one could touch me when I was by myself, but unfortunately it's not qualifying."

Wattles moved up to 13th by Lap 130 and was running 15th when he fell out from the engine failure on Lap 176. Of the 50 fastest laps in the race, Wattles had 12. The 38-year-old from Sewall's Point, Florida, had raced in the previous two 500s. He had stopped racing Indy Racing League cars following the 1999 Indy 500 and decided, at the urging of his Metro Racing Team Manager and cousin Greg Wattles, to return in April. The Stan Wattles-owned team had missed the entry deadline and worked out a deal with Ron Hemelgarn to use one of his.

Originally, the plan was for Wattles to drive a Riley & Scott chassis. But when Hemelgarn's Buddy Lazier couldn't get it up to speed and switched the Dallara, Wattles took the same path. He purchased an unfinished Dallara from Kelley Racing and put it together in a week.

Wattles missed the opening three days of practice and got out for only eight shakedown laps on the fourth day. He was up to 220.728 by Friday's seventh day and, in the Pole Day morning practice, Wattles had a lap of 221.251.

Wattles, on his first qualifying attempt, had four laps above 221, topped by a 221.888. "I knew the speed was there," Wattles said. Needing more laps, Wattles practiced on Bump Day and hit the wall in Turn 1. The car was repaired allowing Wattles to retain his starting spot in the middle of the third row.

2000 INDY 500 PERFORMANCE PROFILE

Starting Position:	8
Qualifying Average:	221.508 mph
Qualifying Speed Rank:	9
Best Practice Speed:	221.251 mph (5/20)
Total Practice Laps:	188
Finishing Position:	23
Laps Completed:	172
Highest Position 2000 Race:	9
Fastest Race Lap:	110 (218.187 mph)
2000 Prize Money:	$159,000
Indy 500 Career Earnings:	$455,550
Career Indy 500 Starts:	3
Career Best Finish:	17th 1999

24

DALLARA/OLDSMOBILE/FIRESTONE

SAM HORNISH JR.

#18 Uniden/Hornish Bros. Trucking/
Advantage Powder Coating
Entrant: PDM Racing
Crew Chief: Paul Murphy

With Juan Montoya and Sarah Fisher taking most of the headlines, it was easy to overlook Sam Hornish Jr. as a member of Indy's outstanding rookie class of 2000. Hornish's race ended prematurely when he spun and made contact with an outside wall, but he turned in an overall performance worth noting.

Hornish, only 20 years of age and driving for a team that was one of the lowest funded at Indy, started from the 14th position and was a solid Pole Day qualifier. He was the 11th-ranked driver in the fastest-lap-of-the-race category at 215.326 miles per hour. Hornish drove for PDM Racing, owned by Chuck Bucknam and Paul Diatlovich. They're very good at what they do, but raising money has been a problem for PDM since they started the operation to join the Indy Racing League in 1996. "We have a great team with a small budget," Hornish said. "They're great mechanics. The guys definitely put together a good car."

Hornish qualified at 220.496 miles per hour. He had an impressive week of practice heading into Pole Day. He did tap the wall on Monday's third day when an oil line broke and spun him into the Turn 4 wall. The damage to his Dallara/ Oldsmobile was moderate. The team had him back on the track by Wednesday for six shakedown laps, and by Friday he was over 220 miles per hour. In the Pole Day morning practice, Hornish was up to 221.534 miles per hour. He qualified in his first attempt.

"I'm real happy," Hornish said. "I'm happy for the guys at PDM Racing. It's great to be here. First of all, we just wanted to get qualified. We were pretty happy with that. We were actually looking for a little bit more. We went faster this morning in practice in a mock-up qualifying run. We've had a great month so far. I love this track. I'm not saying it's easy. It's very difficult to go fast here and I'm still working on going fast here."

Hornish maintained his starting position through the opening 21 laps before pitting. The car had a fuel pickup problem that caused Hornish to stall and have a longer than normal stop. He went two laps down and slid to 31st.

Hornish had some handling problems, but had climbed to 19th before he spun 180 degrees in the short chute between Turns 1 and 2 and made contact with the outside wall. "The car went real loose all of a sudden," Hornish said. "It had a bit of a push before, but turned loose pretty fast."

Hornish, from Defiance, Ohio, had an outstanding karting career, winning the World Karting Association U.S. Grand National Championship in 1995. He moved into the U.S. F2000 championship in 1996 and into CART's Toyota Atlantic championship in 1999. Hornish won at Chicago Motor Speedway and was seventh in the points, the top rookie finisher in the Atlantic series. He moved into Indy Racing in 2000 and originally signed with PDM Racing for one race. After he finished 20th in the season opener at Walt Disney World Speedway, they decided to continue together. At Las Vegas, his third Indy Racing League race, Hornish finished third.

2000 INDY 500 PERFORMANCE PROFILE

Starting Position:	14
Qualifying Average:	220.496 mph
Qualifying Speed Rank:	17
Best Practice Speed:	221.534 mph (5/20)
Total Practice Laps:	287
Finishing Position:	24
Laps Completed:	153
Highest Position 2000 Race:	13
Fastest Race Lap:	35 (215.326 mph)
2000 Prize Money:	$268,250
Indy 500 Career Earnings:	$268,250
Career Indy 500 Starts:	1
Career Best Finish:	24th 2000

25

AIRTON DARÉ

G FORCE/OLDSMOBILE/FIRESTONE

#88 TeamXtreme/USA Credit.com/
FreeInternet.com/G Force
Entrant: Team Extreme Racing
Crew Chief: Mark Lubin

Rookie Airton Daré's promising effort in the 500 was cut short by engine failure. Through a combination of competitiveness and pit-stop savvy, Daré reached third in the running order just past the halfway point. The 22-year-old was in fourth on Lap 126 when a long trail of smoke on the front straight signaled the engine's demise. He finished 25th.

"I was going into Turn 4 and it began to vibrate a lot," Daré said. "And then it just went. It's too bad. I was really comfortable in the car. I had a little bit of understeer, but things were going well."

Daré consistently moved up from his 21st starting position. Although he had gone a lap down, Daré was 15th by Lap 40. His TeamXtreme Dallara was stronger following his first pit stop on Lap 28. With his quicker pace, Daré was able to take advantage of circumstances to return to the lead lap. He had completed his second pit stop on Lap 56 and was fully back up to speed when the race's first caution came out on Lap 66. Leader Juan Montoya pitted on Lap 63 and was just getting back up to speed when the yellow came out, allowing Daré to squeeze past.

Daré, the ninth and final car on the lead lap at that point, was called in for an out-of-sequence pit stop on Lap 67. Daré was up to fifth by Lap 79 and third by Lap 98. He made his fourth pit stop, getting back on sequence, on Lap 100 and emerged in third. Daré then remained in the top five until falling out.

The week of practice leading up to qualifying went smoothly. With the team concentrating on race setups, Daré ran 82 laps on Sunday's second day, and 87 laps, with a best of 219.518 miles per hour, on Monday. Daré switched to his second G Force on Tuesday and ran it exclusively for three straight days. On Thursday, Daré did 117 laps, with a best of 217.187. It was time to work on a qualifying setup and Daré went back to the car he used earlier in the week for the morning practice on Pole Day. He ran 220.627 in 29 laps.

Daré completed three laps on his first attempt in qualifications, all in the 219.4 range, before waving off. Three and a half hours later, Daré started off with a lap of 220.135, did three laps of 219.834 or better, and qualified at 219.970. It put him 21st on the grid. "I've watched Indy since I was six years old and this is a dream come true," Daré said. "It [his qualifying attempt] wasn't as good as we expected. We'd run 220.8 for four laps [average] 10 minutes before, come into the pits and put fuel and a set of [new] tires on, and didn't run the same in qualifying. We had a little push on the exit and scrubbed off some speed."

Prior to entering the Indy Racing Northern Light Series, Daré spent two seasons in the Indy Lights Series. He had a victory in each of the 1998 and 1999 campaigns.

2000 INDY 500 PERFORMANCE PROFILE

Starting Position:	21
Qualifying Average:	219.970 mph
Qualifying Speed Rank:	24
Best Practice Speed:	220.867 (5/20)
Total Practice Laps:	487
Finishing Position:	25
Laps Completed:	126
Highest Position 2000 Race:	3
Fastest Race Lap:	93 (213.934 mph)
2000 Prize Money:	$262,250
Career Indy 500 Starts:	1
Career Best Finish:	25th 2000

26

ROBBIE BUHL

G FORCE/OLDSMOBILE/FIRESTONE

**#24 Team Purex Dreyer
& Reinbold Racing
Entrant: Dreyer & Reinbold Racing
Crew Chief: John O'Gara**

Robbie Buhl's initial foray into Indianapolis with the dual role of owner/driver was both successful and disappointing. Buhl qualified ninth at 221.357 miles per hour and ran solidly in the race until a broken engine knocked him out at the halfway point. "When we came in for a pit stop," Buhl said, "something broke. Something engine related, I think. I don't know why or what. It's frustrating. You all know how hard everyone works to prepare for this race. And to have something break, just like that, it stinks."

Buhl joined with partners Dennis Reinbold and Eric DeBord to form the team in late December. They signed Purex as primary sponsor and hired veteran Team Manager/Engineer Mitch Davis and Crew Chief John O'Gara. Impressively, the team won the first race it competed in, the Indy Racing Northern Light Series opener at Walt Disney World Speedway in January.

Buhl had a smooth week of practice, concentrating on race setups and sneaking up on speed. Buhl went 220.536 miles per hour in Friday's seventh day and had his fastest lap of the week, 221.656, in the Pole Day morning practice.

The 36-year-old Detroit native put it in the show in his first attempt, averaging 221.357. "It really has been a pretty good week," Buhl said. "We've done a lot of full tank stuff and started to trim it out [reducing downforce for the running-alone conditions of qualifying] yesterday. The car is good and consistent. It's just what we wanted."

He added, "Being a car owner hasn't been a distraction. Its been an advantage because I know what I want from the car and have some control of how we get there. We have a very strong team."

In the race, Buhl stayed in the top 10 through the first pit stop. He moved up to third by getting excellent fuel mileage before pitting on Lap 31. Unable to keep pace with the leaders, Buhl went a lap down and slipped to 17th by Lap 50. Buhl was 13th and still one lap down when the track went yellow for debris. With his engine smoking, Buhl pitted on the 99th lap and retired.

This was Buhl's fifth 500. He finished ninth in his rookie season of 1996 with Beck Motorsports. He competed for Team Menard in 1997 and 1998. He had a strong race in 1997, leading 16 laps and finishing eighth despite some bad luck on catching yellows right after making pit stops. Buhl had a remarkable run in 1999 driving for A.J. Foyt, climbing from 32nd on the grid to 6th at the checkered flag.

Buhl's triumph in January was the second of his Indy Racing career. He also won in 1997 at New Hampshire. Buhl has shown the ability to win races and championships throughout his career. He was the 1989 Barber Saab Pro Series champion in 1989, when he had six consecutive and seven total victories. He moved up to Indy Lights and won the championship in 1992. Buhl has also won races in IMSA's Firestone Firehawk showroom stock and GTS races.

2000 INDY 500 PERFORMANCE PROFILE

Starting Position:	9
Qualifying Average:	221.357 mph
Qualifying Speed Rank:	10
Best Practice Speed:	221.656 mph (5/20)
Total Practice Laps:	286
Finishing Position:	26
Laps Completed:	99
Highest Position 2000 Race:	3
Fastest Race Lap:	87 (212.822 mph)
2000 Prize Money:	$258,500
Indy 500 Career Earnings:	$1,168,903
Career Indy 500 Starts:	5
Career Best Finish:	6th 1999

DALLARA/OLDSMOBILE/FIRESTONE

RICHIE HEARN

#75 Pagan Racing
Indy Racing League Special
Entrant: Pagan Racing
Crew Chief: Tim Broyles

Richie Hearn was thrilled to be back at Indianapolis in 2000. Hearn finished third as a rookie in 1996 and then had to wait through three 500s for his second chance. He was a Pole Day qualifier and had a competitive car in the race until an engine problem eliminated him after completing 97 laps. The final results showed Hearn in 27th position. "It was incredible to be there again and I don't want to miss it again," the 29-year-old Hearn said. "I'll be back next year no matter what else I'm driving."

Indy was Hearn's debut with Pagan Racing, which made the 500 its sole event in 2000. Hearn and the team had difficulty finding a base setup in the opening days of practice. His fastest lap during the initial five days of practice was an uncompetitive 213.935 miles per hour. "We were doing 210 and I was holding my breath all the way around," Hearn said. "It was the toughest thing I'd come across in racing. We were pulling our hair out for a couple of days. Allan [Pagan, team co-owner] knew we were in trouble Tuesday and went out and hired Derrick Walker's CART team. He knew we needed some help."

With the help of engineer Al Bodey and crew chief Tim Broyles, Hearn practiced at 218.657 on Friday's seventh day. Hearn reached 221.141 in the morning practice on Pole Day. The team waved off Hearn's first attempt after he completed two laps that averaged 218. Hearn came back late in the afternoon to average 219.816 and secure the 23rd starting spot. "Basically, we started on Friday," Hearn said. "I wish we'd had Walker's guys on Tuesday. Our [qualifying] run was okay. I wish it were a little faster, but it was flat out. That was all the car had. I tried different lines on the run to find more speed, but it didn't really help. I'm disappointed we didn't qualify higher."

Hearn was in 20th when he made his first pit stop on Lap 30. "I went a little slow at first," he said. "I'd never raced with those guys or in those cars and I was taking my time. The car was really good and I was gaining confidence. I came in for our first pit stop. I was running with [Walker Racing's Sarah] Fisher and we came in at the same time.

"Because we were using Walker's CART crew, my crew had the same kind of uniforms as hers. Before the race, they told me the left front guy on my crew would have a fluorescent arm band. I went to pull into the pit stall and it was her guy, not my guy. I was past my pit. I had to go all the way around and lost a lap."

Because of lost power, Hearn was two laps down when he pitted on Lap 93. "The car was really good, really strong until the engine quit running right," Hearn said. "We went down to seven cylinders. We thought it might be electronics. We changed some things and went back out, but it wouldn't pull and we stopped. I think a valve spring broke."

2000 INDY 500 PERFORMANCE PROFILE

Starting Position:	23
Qualifying Average:	219.816 mph
Qualifying Speed Rank:	28
Best Practice Speed:	221.141 mph (5/20)
Total Practice Laps:	255
Finishing Position:	27
Laps Completed:	97
Highest Position 2000 Race:	20
Fastest Race Lap:	26 (214.572 mph)
2000 Prize Money:	$155,000
Indy 500 Career Earnings:	$530,203
Career Indy 500 Starts:	2
Career Best Finish:	3rd 1996

DALLARA/OLDSMOBILE/FIRESTONE

ANDY HILLENBURG

**#48 The Sumar Special By Irwindale Speedway
Entrant: Fast Track Racing Enterprises
Crew Chief: Tim Bumps**

When Andy Hillenburg climbed out of the car after qualifying for the 500, it was clearly an emotional moment. "This is a day I'll remember for the rest of my life," he said, his voice cracking and tears trickling down his face. "This is the greatest thing I've ever done."

Born and raised in Indianapolis, Hillenburg had set his sights upon racing in the 500 in 1969 at the age of six. "I've worked on this forever," Hillenburg said. "Every book report I ever did, even in grade school; everything has always been about being here. This is something I've wanted ever since I can remember. I told my dad the first time he ever brought me here [in 1969] that someday I would be here driving."

Hillenburg's career had started in Midget and Sprint Cars, but he switched from open wheel to stock cars in the mid-1990s. His resumé featured nine races in NASCAR's Winston Cup, including a 29th-place finish in the 1998 Daytona 500. Despite these early accomplishments, Indy was still of paramount importance to Hillenburg. With the help of Preston Root and Usona Purcell, Hillenburg began making plans to run at Indy. "Every time they'd bring it up, we'd say, `Yeah, we need to do that. It would be great.' And we just decided to do it. We asked Bill Simpson [of safety equipment fame] if he'd like to join us, and he stepped up to the plate in a big way."

The team hired 500 veteran crew chief Tim Bumps to run the operation and entered a 1999 Dallara. Hillenburg spent three days and ran 72 laps of practice, with a best lap of 216.747 miles per hour. The team realized it needed a 2000 chassis to be competitive, and Simpson purchased a new Dallara. Hillenburg missed three days of practice while the car was prepared.

Hillenburg returned on Friday's seventh day of practice and had a best lap of 219.261. During the morning practice on Pole Day, Hillenburg improved to 219.933. Four minutes before the end of the session, Hillenburg lost control exiting the warm-up lane in Turn Two. He hit the outside wall. Hillenburg wasn't injured, and the Dallara was repairable. He missed the rest of Pole Day, but was ready for the morning practice on MBNA Bump Day. Hillenburg did 10 laps, with a best of 215.638.

The team decided to wait until later in the day to attempt to qualify. With four-time Indy winner Rick Mears in the team's pit making set-up suggestions, Hillenburg finally found a comfort level in the car during the midafternoon practice. Hillenburg, with an hour remaining, qualified with a four-lap average of 218.285 miles per hour. An hour later, when Bump Day was over, he was in the 33rd starting position. "Earlier in the week, I had [retired 500 veteran] Pancho Carter helping me find my line," Hillenburg said. "Rick [Mears] helped bridge the gap between Tim [Bumps] and myself to interpret what I was feeling about the car and what it was doing."

Hillenburg drove steadily in the race. He was up to 26th position by lap 90, but dropped out with a wheel bearing failure a lap later. Hillenburg finished 28th. "It was really heartbreaking," Hillenburg said, "but I learned a lot."

2000 INDY 500 PERFORMANCE PROFILE

Starting Position:	33
Qualifying Average:	218.285 mph
Qualifying Speed Rank:	33
Best Practice Speed:	219.933 mph (5/20)
Total Practice Laps:	206
Finishing Position:	28
Laps Completed:	91
Highest Position 2000 Race:	26
Fastest Race Lap:	36 (210.138 mph)
2000 Prize Money:	$154,250
Career Indy 500 Starts:	1
Career Best Finish:	28th 2000

G FORCE/OLDSMOBILE/FIRESTONE

AL UNSER JR.

#3 Galles ECR Racing Tickets.com
Starz Encore Superpak
Entrant: Galles ECR Racing
Crew Chief: Darren Russell

Al Unser Jr.'s dramatic return to Indianapolis had an anticlimactic conclusion. The two-time 500 champion, who hadn't qualified for the race since 1994, was executing his game plan to perfection before running into misfortune on lap 66. Unser had advanced from his 18th starting position to 9th when his G Force ran over debris from Greg Ray's crash. "Ray hit the wall in [Turn] Two and I got debris in the radiator and lost all the water," Unser said.

Unser's Galles ECR Racing crew took the car to Gasoline Alley and repaired it. Hoping to pick up some positions and points in the Indy Racing Northern Light Series, Unser re-emerged and ran 23 more laps before deciding to park it. He was credited with a 29th-place finish. "I wasn't racing anybody," Unser said. "The car just wasn't working. This isn't NASCAR. It's 220 miles per hour Indy Cars and I didn't want to be a danger. I just didn't have anybody to race. I ran like this when I was 25, but I know better now."

Unser enjoyed the time he had in the race. "It was great," Unser said. "To go around those pace laps and see those cheering fans and be back at the Greatest Spectacle in Racing, it was incredible. I had a great car. The team did a great job. We had a little too much downforce in it, but we were dialing it out. It's too bad the day ended by something getting stuck in the radiator. We'll be back with a vengeance. It's just too bad we have to wait 364 days for it."

Unser had last entered Indy in 1995, the year after his second triumph. He had failed to qualify; a disappointment that lingered for five years. Unser had spent that period with Penske Racing and when his contract ran out, he decided to rejoin the team owned by fellow Albuquerque, New Mexico, resident Rick Galles. Galles had first taken Unser to Indy in 1983 and they won the 1992 500 together.

On the opening day of practice, Unser posted the fastest speed at 217.223 miles per hour. He was welcomed back by a cheering throng of spectators. On Sunday's second day of practice, Unser improved to 220.686; second fastest behind Eddie Cheever, Jr. And on the third practice day, Unser was second again at 221.861.

Unser was over 221 on two other days during the rest of the week. He was the first car to qualify on Pole Day with a four-lap average of 220.293, and was secure in the field in 18th position. "It's great," he said. "I can officially say we're back." Unser's first lap was 218.187 and he went faster on each of the succeeding three, up to 221.440. "I was watching everybody spin on cold tires [in the Pole Day morning practice]," Unser explained. "I wanted to get in so bad, I was being cautious. You can win this race from anywhere in the field. My dad [four-time Indy winner Al Unser Sr.] has proven that. I was too careful because I wanted to make sure everything was warm.

"Was I worried about making the race? The answer is definitely yes. In 1995, I was going fast enough [in a qualifying run] and blew that engine up and didn't make it. My main concern this year was putting it in the show."

2000 INDY 500 PERFORMANCE PROFILE

Starting Position:	18
Qualifying Average:	220.293 mph
Qualifying Speed Rank:	21
Best Practice Speed:	221.861 (5/15)
Total Practice Laps:	341
Finishing Position:	29
Laps Completed:	89
Highest Position 2000 Race:	9
Fastest Race Lap:	18 (215.008 mph)
2000 Prize Money:	$256,000
Indy 500 Career Earnings:	$4,520,710
Career Indy 500 Starts:	13
Career Best Finish:	1st 1992, 1994

30

JIMMY KITE

G FORCE/OLDSMOBILE/FIRESTONE

**#27 Big Daddy's BBQ/Founders
Bank/ZMAX/Blueprint Racing Special
Entrant: Blueprint Racing Enterprises
Crew Chief: Randy Ruyle**

Jimmy Kite's race was a like a roller coaster ride. In Friday's practice, he posted a 222.700 mile per hour lap and was in position to challenge for a spot up front in qualifying. During Pole Day, on his first attempt, Kite crashed on a warm-up lap. His G Force was beyond immediate repair and it was the only chassis in the Blueprint Racing garage. The team spent the rest of Pole Day searching for a replacement. That evening, the team announced it had purchased a G Force for $300,000 from Target/Chip Ganassi Racing. The car had been run by Jimmy Vasser in practice, with a best lap of 221.773.

Kite practiced at 219.796 in the Bump Day morning practice. He qualified at 220.718 a couple hours later. Kite's speed was 13th fastest at the end of Time Trials, but he would have to start from 25th position.

The 24-year-old from Stockbridge, Georgia, ran as high as 21st in the race, but an engine failure after completing 74 laps left him with a 30th-place finish. "We were making changes on every pit stop," Kite said. "The car was getting better and better. If I was running 120 laps from now, then I'd be happy."

Kite ran impressively from the opening of practice. He had a lap of 221.217, seventh fastest for the session, on Monday's third day of practice. The Blueprint team took the next two days off before Kite resumed. On Friday, he had his best lap and eighth fastest in practice for the event at 222.700. "We just put together three laps of 222 right there," Kite said. "If I hadn't been such a wuss on the first lap, it would have been four in a row, but I lifted a little. I think that should put us in the top two rows. I feel good that we can go out and run in Time Trials tomorrow what we ran in practice today."

The crash on Pole Day scuttled those high hopes. "I don't think it was a flaw in the car," Kite explained. "I think it was cold tires. It was such a blow. This wasn't supposed to happen to me. This was our week. After we tore up our car, I knew that was the only chance with one of our cars because our backup was a '99. When I came in and asked the guys, 'What are we going to do?' They said, 'We have a line on a couple of cars.' When Ganassi was mentioned, I said, 'Really?'"

Kite rebounded on Bump Day with laps of 219.777, 221.806, 221.478, and 220.324 to qualify for his third 500. "I've got to thank Chip Ganassi and everybody at Ganassi Racing for giving us the opportunity that they didn't have to give us, especially with them coming in here from CART. It shows what a class act they are."

Kite admitted he took it a little easy on his qualifying run. "We didn't have much time in the car," he said. "I was a little cautious, especially coming into Turn One, even though this car was so good. I was just so happy to see the green flag."

2000 INDY 500 PERFORMANCE PROFILE

Starting Position:	25
Qualifying Average:	220.718 mph
Qualifying Speed Rank:	13
Best Practice Speed:	222.700 mph (5/19)
Total Practice Laps:	261
Finishing Position:	30
Laps Completed:	74
Highest Position 2000 Race:	21
Fastest Race Lap:	13 (212.364 mph)
2000 Prize Money:	$164,000
Indy 500 Career Earnings:	$679,300
Career Indy 500 Starts:	3
Career Best Finish:	11th 1998

31

SARAH FISHER

#15 Walker Racing
Cummins Special
Entrant: Walker Racing
Crew Chief: Ron Catt

At the age of 19, Sarah Fisher drove splendidly in her rookie campaign at Indianapolis. Fisher became the youngest driver to start the race since Josele Garza in 1981. Fisher also was the third woman to qualify for the 500, joining Janet Guthrie and Lyn St. James in that category.

Fisher was a Pole Day qualifier at 220.237 miles per hour and started 19th. She was eliminated from the race on the 74th lap after wheel-to-wheel contact with St. James sent her into the outside wall between turns one and two. Entering Turn One, Fisher had committed to trying to overtake St. James. At the same time, Jaques Lazier attempted to pass Fisher to the inside. It didn't leave enough room for all three cars to come out on the other side.

"I was in Turn One trying to pass Lyn [St. James] on the inside," Fisher said. "Things do not happen very nicely when you try to go three abreast. I was stuck in the middle. I was a sitting duck in this case. It's not anyone's fault. It's a very narrow line. We are very disappointed."

Fisher was running 24th, two laps down, before the crash. She lost one lap on speed and the second when her Dallara/Oldsmobile stalled in the pits. Fisher finished 31st.

Fisher's age and gender had made her a focus of media and fans at Indianapolis and her speed in the race car showed she belonged. "It's been wonderful," Fisher said. "I've had a great time. We love all the attention we have been getting. I've learned a lot of things here. You can't learn unless you do it. I've got more experience for next year."

Fisher ran long and hard in the early days of practice. After skipping Saturday's opening day, Fisher logged 55 laps with a best of 216.993 on the second day. On the third day, Fisher ran 89 laps with a best of 219.882, and on the fourth, she did 92 laps with a best of 220.881. "It was great that we broke the 220 barrier," Fisher said. "That's good for a rookie to do. It gives us more momentum. Now, we just need to keep running that consistently. We did the same thing with the 218 and 219 speeds—ran those consistently and in two steps. I'm getting a lot more comfortable with running at the Indianapolis Motor Speedway. I'm comfortable in three out of the four turns now and we're working on breaking that last corner into segments so we can master that one, as well."

Fisher practiced at 221.219 on Friday's seventh day and went 221.203 in the Pole Day morning practice. She qualified with four laps above 220 on her first attempt. "So far, this has been a tremendous thrill," Fisher said. "It's really cool to run around this track. It's so unique. It's not stamped out and takes a different technique."

Fisher graduated from high school, in Commercial Point, Ohio, in May 1999. She'd competed in Sprint and Midget Cars for several years, but hadn't anticipated being at Indianapolis by 2000. "Absolutely not," she said. "I thought it would be another couple of years in a Midget. It's an honor being here. There's nothing bigger than the Indy 500."

2000 INDY 500 PERFORMANCE PROFILE

Starting Position:	19
Qualifying Average:	220.237 mph
Qualifying Speed Rank:	23
Best Practice Speed:	221.219 mph (5/19)
Total Practice Laps:	430
Finishing Position:	31
Laps Completed:	71
Highest Position 2000 Race:	20
Fastest Race Lap:	36 (213.569 mph)
2000 Prize Money:	$165,750
Indy 500 Career Earnings:	$165,750
Career Indy 500 Starts:	1
Career Best Finish:	31st 2000

LYN ST. JAMES

#90 Yellow Freight System
Entrant: Dick Simon Racing
Crew Chief: John Martin

Lyn St. James bounced back from a Pole Day crash to qualify MBNA Bump Day for her first 500 since 1997. The race, her seventh at Indianapolis, proved to be full of trials and tribulations. St. James struggled mightily with the handling of her G Force. It went from bad to worse when St. James and Sarah Fisher clipped wheels on the 74th lap, sending St. James into the Turn One outside wall.

"My car wasn't handling well," St. James said. "I was driving with my mirrors a lot. We did a lot of work on it on that last yellow-flag stop. I saw a car [Fisher's] coming behind me into Turn One. I took a defensive line, but wanted to stay out of the loose stuff [on the outside]. Whoever it was, I was surprised they would try to force a pass at that point. I'm extremely disappointed it happened, but I'm even more disappointed it happened under these circumstances."

St. James' 32nd-place finish equaled the poorest of her Indy 500 career. She was 11th and Bank One Rookie of the Year in 1992, 13th in 1997, and 14th in 1996. St. James had qualifying runs and failed to make the race in 1998 and 1999. She returned to Dick Simon Racing, who she had raced for in the 1992 through 1995 Indy 500s, when an opportunity opened up a few days prior to the beginning of practice. Simon had put together an effort for Wim Eyckmans, but his sponsorship failed to materialize.

St. James and Simon put together a deal with Yellow Freight System and announced it on the morning of the opening practice. St. James ran only 32 laps in the initial three days of practice. She'd run over some debris and damaged the tub on the second day, and had electronic and mechanical problems on the third. But with everything working, St. James ran 37 laps on Tuesday's fourth day, with a best of 219.518 miles per hour.

In the Pole Day morning practice, St. James had her fastest lap at 221.539. She waved off her first qualifying attempt after laps of 217.649 and 218.383. Several hours later, St. James was on a warm-up lap for her second attempt when a spin between Turns One and Two sent her into the inside wall. The G Force ricocheted across the track and hit the outside wall in Turn Two.

"Something in the rear on the car broke," St. James said. St. James wasn't seriously hurt, but the car was damaged beyond immediate repair. Simon had leased Stephan Gregoire's backup G Force to Jonathan Byrd/McCormack Motorsports with the provision that it could be reclaimed if the Simon team needed it. The G Force was returned to Simon, whose crew worked non-stop to refit it for St. James.

St. James bumped her way into the field with 26 minutes remaining, averaging 218.826 mph. She would start in 32nd position. "It was a good first lap [219.464]," St. James said. "The car was wonderful. That helped gain my confidence back. The second lap, the car picked up a big push and I made all the adjustments. There was a broken piece in the back. That is why the speeds went down.

2000 INDY 500 PERFORMANCE PROFILE

Starting Position:	32
Qualifying Average:	218.826 mph
Qualifying Speed Rank:	32
Best Practice Speed:	221.539 mph (5/20)
Total Practice Laps:	169
Finishing Position:	32
Laps Completed:	69
Highest Position 2000 Race:	28
Fastest Race Lap:	30 (206.171 mph)
2000 Prize Money:	$152,000
Indy 500 Career Earnings:	$1,175,974
Career Indy 500 Starts:	7
Career Best Finish:	11th 1992

33

DALLARA/OLDSMOBILE/FIRESTONE

GREG RAY

#1 Team Conseco/Quaker State/Moen/Menards
Entrant: Team Menard
Crew Chief: Chris Sumner

Greg Ray achieved a significant milestone in his career by winning the pole for the 84th 500, but the race was a heartbreaker. Ray led the opening 26 laps, then started dropping in the running order. Trying to find more speed for race conditions, the team adjusted the car during two pit stops. Ray was in sixth when he hit the outside wall in Turn Two on Lap 66.

"We took downforce out because we selected the wrong gears," Ray said. "We got caught by the wind. With the gust coming down out of Turn Two, what can you do?"

Ray said the team could have made better decisions for the car's setup before and during the race. "There were certain things we could have done leading up to and in the race," he said. "I'm frustrated by that. You take the risk. It's a live by the sword, die by the sword attitude. It's very clear to me what happened. At the end of the day, I drive the car, my hands are on the steering wheel, and I crashed. Things are not as simple as they seem. Indy happens once a year. I want to get up the next morning and do it again. But nothing ventured, nothing gained. We ventured the wrong way."

Ray returned to the race later, after the Team Menard crew made repairs to the suspension, but crashed on his second lap out. That sealed his fate as the fourth driver to start on the pole and finish last in 33rd.

The 33-year-old Texan turned in a string of powerful performances in practice and qualifying. He had a lap of 221.735 miles per hour on the third day of practice. On Friday's seventh day, Ray had the second fastest lap of the month at 223.948 miles per hour.

The week of preparation leading up to Pole Day had not gone as well as Ray would have liked. The team had expanded to a two-car effort and added Robby Gordon a few days prior to the opening of practice. "We are running two drivers out of one stable which has limited us on track time and it's been a bit of an issue," Ray said. "The setups that we've been running are hybrid setups that [team manager/engineer] Tom [Knapp] and I have had since '98. Between the weather [rain] and some of the timing, we haven't had much on-track time."

Ray's 223.948 had been a confidence booster. "It's going to make me sleep a hell of a lot better than I would have if we would have quit two sessions before that," he said.

The reigning Indy Racing League champ's first qualifying attempt was waved off on its opening lap. "The car was a little more reluctant to turn in Turn One at 233 miles per hour and I had to back off and there was no reason to continue," Ray explained.

Ray averaged 223.471 on his second attempt to take the PPG Pole. "The car was definitely on the edge," Ray said. "I was flat all four laps and grazing the wall. The four laps of qualifying here are the ultimate speed event. You've got to drive it for all it's worth. You do everything you can to go fast. It [winning the pole] is a very neat experience. I'd be lying to you if I said it wasn't a big, big focus. It's very rewarding for our team. It's very rewarding for me."

2000 INDY 500 PERFORMANCE PROFILE

Starting Position:	1
Qualifying Average:	223.471 mph
Qualifying Speed Rank:	1
Best Practice Speed:	223.948 mph (5/19)
Total Practice Laps:	233
Finishing Position:	33
Laps Completed:	67
Highest Position 2000 Race:	1
Fastest Race Lap:	20 (214.741 mph)
2000 Prize Money:	$388,700
Indy 500 Career Earnings:	$940,250
Career Indy 500 Starts:	4
Career Best Finish:	18th 1998

Always there at the finish.

The goal of every driver. The checkered flag. And the milk.

got milk?

An Iron Will to Win

BUDDY LAZIER CAPTURES THE NORTHERN LIGHT CUP

Buddy Lazier opened the season well with a solid second place at Walt Disney World Speedway, but he was in a tough spot lining up for the next race at Phoenix International Raceway. Lazier and Hemelgarn Racing had been dreadfully slow during practice and qualifying for the MCI WorldCom Indy 200. They decided something was fundamentally wrong with their primary Riley & Scott chassis and substituted the backup R&S for the race. That meant that Lazier had to start 26th in a 26-car field. In a remarkable display of speed and aggressive driving, Lazier transformed a potential disaster into a stunning success. He charged to a victory that catapulted him forward in his run to the championship of the Indy Racing Northern Light Series.

By Tim Tuttle

Lazier had a second triumph at Kentucky and added two second places, at Indianapolis and Atlanta, for a total of five top-two finishes in the nine-event campaign. Needing to finish only 14th or better to clinch the title in the season-closing second race at Texas, Lazier tempered his aggression slightly and brought the Delta Faucet/Coors Light/Tae-Bo-sponsored machine home fourth.

There were only two races in which Lazier was not a contender. He was taken out by a broken fuel pump at Las Vegas, finishing 22nd, and a first-lap engine failure at Pikes Peak relegated him to 26th. Lazier was able to overcome those two poor

results to win the championship over Pennzoil Panther Racing's Scott Goodyear, 290 to 272. Owner/driver Eddie Cheever was third with 257 points.

Lazier's margin of victory was created from his victories at Phoenix and Kentucky. Goodyear finished second in both races. Phoenix was pivotal. Lazier and the Hemelgarn team had not won since Charlotte in 1997 and it supplied spark and a spike of confidence. "Phoenix was the beginning of the roll for us," Lazier said. "Second place at Disney was, too, but Phoenix was a huge turnaround."

The Hemelgarn team continued with the R&S chassis through the third round at Las Vegas. When the team struggled mightily with the car in pre-event testing at Indianapolis, owner Ron Hemelgarn purchased a Dallara. Lazier drove it the remainder of the season.

Lazier and Hemelgarn were one of two driver/team combinations that had been together since the formation of the IRNLS in 1996. They won the Indy 500 that year, but their highest finish in the championship through four seasons had been fifth in 1998. Team manager Lee Kunzman, engineer Ronnie Dawes, and chief mechanic Dennis LaCava had been with Lazier from the outset, and Hemelgarn continued to use Oldsmobile Auroras built by Speedway Engines.

Lazier says the jump in performance came from a refined driving style and the switch to Firestone tires. The team had used Firestones in 1996 and 1997, but moved to Goodyear in 1998 and 1999. Goodyear withdrew from Indy Racing at the end of the 1999 season, leaving Firestone as the sole supplier and further balancing the playing field.

"I made an off season effort to try to find improvement in my driving," Lazier explained. "I reviewed how I had been driving and adjusted my style.

I think I found a hole in my swing last winter. I worked on new lines. And even though we'd been together for a long time, we kept jelling more in each race. Our racing together had taken on a new light.

"We were back on Firestone tires and they suited my style better. You can be aggressive and it rewards you."

Lazier and Hemelgarn have won Indy Racing's crown jewels—the Indy 500—and now the Northern Light Cup. "Winning the Indy 500 and the championship are so similar," Lazier said. "They're both huge. The championship has stepped up our team to another level and I've never won a championship close to this significance. We had a super strong season. It's been an awesome season. It's an awesome race team. We were first or second five times."

Goodyear's trademark consistency kept him in title contention. He informed the Panther team in June that he would not be returning, but the lame-duck status did not undermine the effort. It was evidence of real professionalism by both driver and crew.

Goodyear put pressure on Lazier by winning the final race, his third series victory. The Canadian had become the chief threat to Lazier's lead by finishing second at Kentucky. In addition to his second at Phoenix, Goodyear was fourth at Disney, and fifth at the first Texas race. His worst finish was 16th, at Pikes Peak, and Goodyear led the series with 1,806 of 1,832 laps completed. He was running at the finish in eight of the nine races. Goodyear's triumph in the second race at Texas Motor Speedway was his highlight of a demanding season. "I am obviously very pleased," he said following his victory over Cheever by .140 of a second.

Cheever drove Nissan Infiniti to its first Indy Racing victory at Pikes Peak. He was third at Disney in R&S, but switched to Dallara in the eight races that followed. Cheever was fourth at Kentucky, and fifth at Indianapolis. "We did a superb job all year long," Cheever said. "Our goal was to finish well in the championship and win a race, and we accomplished that."

Eliseo Salazar, driving A.J. Foyt's Rio G Force-Oldsmobile Aurora, had his finest season by taking fourth in the championship. Driving for unsponsored and underbudgeted Cahill Racing, veteran short-track star Donnie Beechler was a surprising sixth.

TeamXtreme's Airton Dare was the RaceSearch.com Rookie of the Year. The 22-year-old was second at Pikes Peak. He was 16th in the points. Sarah Fisher, Sam Hornish Jr., Shigeaki Hattori, and Jeret Schroeder also had promising rookie seasons. Fisher, only 19, became the third woman to qualify for the Indianapolis 500. Driving for Walker Racing, Fisher finished third at Kentucky, where she led nine laps. Hornish, driving for low-budget PDM Racing, was third at Las Vegas, qualified solidly at Indianapolis, and led 38 laps at Kentucky. Hattori had four top-nine finishes in five starts for Treadway Racing. Schroeder, competing for Tri Star Motorsports, was runner-up for rookie honors. His top finish was fourth at Las Vegas.

Two-time Indianapolis 500 winner Al Unser Jr. won in his third Indy Racing League race at Las Vegas and was third at the first Texas race and Atlanta. He led in four races, for 220 laps, in Galles ECR Racing's G Force/Oldsmobile.

The fifth series race produced its typical tight competition. At Texas in June, 12 cars ran wheel-to-wheel in rows of two for virtually the entire race. Kelley Racing's Scott Sharp held off Treadway Racing's Robby McGehee by .059 of a second, the closest in Indy Racing League history. Target/Chip Ganassi Racing's Juan Montoya won at Indianapolis and Dreyer & Reinbold Racing's Robbie Buhl won at Disney.

The series founded by Indianapolis Motor Speedway President Tony George made significant off-track progress, too. Northern Light signed a five-year contract worth $50 million to be the title sponsor and several teams added primary sponsors. Attendance in the series' fifth year showed a good increase overall. The series will expand to 13 events in 2001, its most ever and strong evidence of its vitality.

Greg Ray and Team Menard won the 1999 Indy Racing Series, but they finished 13th in 2000. Ray won the fourth race of his Indy Racing League career at Atlanta, but crashed out of three races and was either slowed or knocked out of four more by mechanical problems. Ray earned five poles, bringing his career total to a series-leading nine, and led the series in laps led with 299.

Buddy Lazier's intensity and commitment to winning the 2000 championship never wavered during the season. When Lazier started last at Phoenix because of a chassis switch, he didn't throw in the towel. He put in an electrifying drive and sliced through the field to take the win. In the last race of the year, he only needed to finish 13th to take the championship. Rather than play it safe, Lazier raced hard, took fourth, and put his stamp on the championship. *Jim Haines*

BUHL BOLTS PAST RIVALS

Well-timed pit stops, quick driving, and capitalizing on other's misfortunes during the last two action-packed laps of the Delphi Indy 200 allowed Robbie Buhl to charge from the 22nd starting position to victory. The Indy Racing League also scored a victory by securing a five-year, $50 million title sponsorship program with internet search engine Northern Light Technology.

The win was Buhl's second Indy Racing League career victory, and the first win for his newly formed team. "I don't feel like it was handed to us at all," Buhl said. "We were in position, and we capitalized on it. We all had good cars, and what was going to shake things up was traffic. That's the way it is on the 1-mile ovals." Buhl crossed the finish line 3.165 seconds in front of Buddy Lazier. Eddie Cheever and Scott Goodyear trailed across the line close behind them. Eliseo Salazar, driving for the AJ Foyt team, rounded out the top five, only 6.990 seconds behind. Donnie Beechler, who started in the 15th position, fought his way into 6th when the checkered flag fell.

While Buhl's win was certainly opportunistic, it was well earned. He led the most laps (49) and made the greatest climb to victory in league history. He credited an early pit stop on a yellow, which was called by team manager Mitch Davis, for getting him in sync with the other contenders.

"We had a car capable of winning and put ourselves in a good position," said Buhl, who averaged 102.292 miles per hour in a race that had eight leaders and the same number of caution flags. "We don't think we had anything handed to us today. Obviously, we all want to win [the] Indy [500]. But I just remembered when Buzz Calkins won this first race down here [in 1996]; all the attention he got. So I said, 'Yeah, that's something else I want to win.' So it's good."

Al Unser Jr. made an impressive IRL debut, moving from the 24th starting position up to 9th place. Unser turned laps comparable to the leaders before an engine failure took him out of the running on Lap 64. "It was going well," said Unser. "I was trying to get up and join the leaders and stay on the lead lap. I was taking quite a few chances to get up there, and then I'd settle down. The competition is strong. Fierce."

Buhl's stunning performance was especially spectacular considering how quickly the team and the car came together. Buhl began assembling the Dreyer & Reinbold Racing team at the end of the last season. Dennis Reinbold and Eric DeBord joined him in partnership, and the team announcement was made 11 weeks before the race. The new car was assembled only three weeks prior to the race. Team manager Mitch Davis' and crew chief John O'Gara's experience and racing acumen were key to the success at Disney. O'Gara was chief on Greg Ray's 1999 championship Menard team, winning the Pennzoil Chief Mechanic of the Year Award, but had worked with Buhl the year before.

Buhl started his climb up the leaderboard early in the race. He took advantage of Davey Hamilton's accident on Lap 24 to pit out of sequence. The incident helped move him to 17th position. When the next yellow came out on Lap 44 for debris, reigning IRL Champion Greg Ray, piloting a Dallara/Oldsmobile, and the rest of the leaders pitted. That moved Team Pelfrey's Billy Boat into the lead, and Buhl jumped to second. Buhl bolted past Boat on the Lap 49 restart and led for 47 laps. Hemelgarn Racing's Buddy Lazier, driving the new Riley & Scott chassis, was closing in on Buhl and passed Ray for second place on Lap 75. Buhl needed a yellow to make the early pit stop strategy work, and he got it on Lap 95.

Lazier worked his way into the lead after 11 of the 12 cars on the lead lap pitted on Lap 122. What eventually developed was some of the most thrilling racing in series history, but it also proved to be extremely frustrating for two veteran drivers. Lazier

A dramatic Lap-199 pass around leaders Buddy Lazier and Eddie Cheever Jr. gave Robbie Buhl (24) the lead and the victory in the Delphi Indy 200 at Walt Disney World Speedway. *Walt Kuhn*

Eddie Cheever Jr. took on fuel en route to a third-place finish in the season opener. As Cheever and Buddy Lazier fought for the lead, slower traffic held them up and Robbie Buhl flew by to win. *Jim Haines*

DELPHI INDY 200 • WALT DISNEY WORLD SPEEDWAY

passed Kelley Racing's Mark Dismore with a daring move on the outside, but he was being stalked by the Riley & Scott/Infiniti of Eddie Cheever. When Lazier tried to lap rookie Sam Hornish in Turn 1 on Lap 192, Hornish slowed dramatically, forcing Lazier off line to the outside and allowing Cheever to squeeze by on the inside to take the lead. A hard-charging Buhl slipped by Lazier as well.

Once again, traffic played a decisive role in the outcome of the race. Buhl was following in Cheever's wheel tracks entering Turn 1 on the penultimate lap when Cheever darted low to go under Doug Didero. However, Didero also went low. To counter the move Cheever tried to pass on the outside, but was forced out of the racing groove. The door was left wide open for Buhl, and he swept into the lead. He never looked back as he sprinted to the checkered flag. What looked to be the Infiniti powerplant's first series race win had evaporated. But Cheever's troubles weren't over. Lazier was re-mounting a challenge and sliced past Cheever on the inside of Turn 1 on the final lap.

After the race, Lazier said, "With 10 laps to go, we had it. We need to win badly. Second place isn't bad and I don't mean to be a poor sport, but we were in a position to win and somebody [Hornish] who shouldn't have gotten in the way did. It ruined our chances for the win."

"I so badly wanted to give [Infiniti] that first win," Cheever said about his engine manufacturer. As for the problem he encountered with the slower car, he said: "It's really annoying. I'm very angry at the back markers who got in my way, but I am even madder at myself. I don't know exactly what happened, but back

Buddy Lazier led 47 laps at Walt Disney World Speedway, but not the final one. When he veered from the racing line on Lap 199, he lost his momentum and the race. *Jerry Lawrence*

markers should know better than to get in the way of people who are faster."

This was Buhl's first Indy Racing victory since 1997 when he won at New Hampshire. His victim in that race was also Cheever, who was leading with two laps to go when his gearbox failed.

complete results listed on page 92

Chilean Eliseo Salazar got the season and his new partnership with car owner A.J. Foyt off to a great start as he finished fifth in the season opener. *Roger Bedwell*

77

LAZIER CHARGES FROM LAST TO FIRST

When a miserable-handling primary car forced Hemelgarn Racing to run Buddy Lazier's new Riley & Scott backup car, a strong race result seemed quite unlikely. But the big gamble paid off for Lazier at Phoenix International Raceway. Through aggressive driving and well-timed pit stops, Lazier grabbed one of the most improbable victories in Indy Racing Northern Light Series history, and the series points lead. Although Lazier had struggled with his primary vehicle, the backup performed superbly, and in turn, Lazier gave the Riley & Scott its first IRL race victory. The win also helped make up for the bitter disappointment at the previous race in Walt Disney World Speedway, where lapped traffic thwarted a potential victory.

Lazier climbed from the 26th—and last—starting position to the victory on the 1-mile oval, to beat Scott Goodyear to the line by 4.191 seconds for his first Indy Racing victory since July 1997. Cahill Racing's Donnie Beechler finished a career-best third. In his second race for team owner A.J. Foyt, Eliseo Salazar, driving a G Force/Oldsmobile, came home fourth, and Scott Sharp in the Kelley Racing Delphi Dallara/Oldsmobile rounded out the top five.

Lazier averaged 111.957 miles per hour in a race slowed by seven cautions for 56 laps. It was the first time in series history that a driver has started from the last position and won. After Lazier and his poor-handling primary car produced a 24th position qualifying effort, the team was forced to switch to the team's backup Delta Faucet/Coors Light/Tae-Bo/Hemelgarn Racing Riley & Scott-Oldsmobile. According to series rules, any driver who switches to a backup car after qualifying must start from the rear of the field, but because he had qualified in the 24th position, Lazier lost only two positions when bumped down to 26th.

"There was something vicious in that [primary] car," team owner Ron Hemelgarn said. "My gut feeling is a motor mount loosened up. It was something we couldn't find unless we tore the entire car apart. We tried running it soft [setup] and hard and nothing changed. You can't do all those changes and not have it change. There was real trouble somewhere."

"We couldn't do anything with the primary car," Lazier said. "I have to tell you I was frightened in the car, and I don't normally frighten easily. My guys did a great job. Ron [Hemelgarn] made the decision to roll out the backup car, and the guys worked through the night. We started last. I can't believe we can come through the field like that from last to first."

When the green flag dropped, Lazier went on a tear. By Lap 24, he had passed 13 cars and was running in 12th position. "Buddy Lazier went by me like I was parked on the second or third lap," said Al Unser Jr., who had started 20th. Lazier took the lead on Lap 151 when Unser was forced to come in for fuel. On Lap 155, Lazier pitted and surrendered the lead to Robbie Buhl. Lazier took the lead for good when Buhl pitted on Lap 162. Lazier gradually pulled away from Goodyear after the restart on Lap 167, navigating lapped traffic for the improbable victory despite suffering from a stomach virus. Lazier stayed comfortably in front until the checkered flag dropped.

Buddy Lazier (91) led Tyce Carlson (20) and the field into a turn at Phoenix. Lazier started last because he switched to his backup car after qualifying, yet he went on to win. *Walt Kuhn*

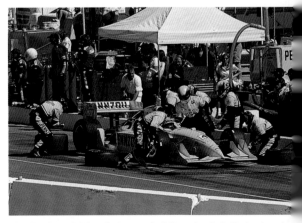

Canadian Scott Goodyear's team rushed through a fast pit stop to get him back into the race at the Phoenix International Raceway, where he finished second to race-winner Buddy Lazier. *Walt Kuhn*

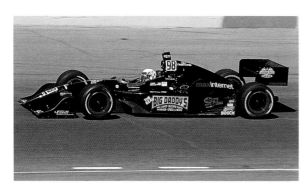

Springfield, Illinois racer Donnie Beechler (98) achieved his best Indy Racing League finish to date with a strong third-place finish at Phoenix in the Big Daddy's Specialty Foods/Race Car Café-Las Vegas entry. *Jim Haines*

"This was just a tough week," Lazier said. "I had a nasty stomach bug. I couldn't eat or drink, and each day while we were here, I would go back to the hotel and try to recover." But it was an impressive performance for the 1996 Indy 500 winner as the drivers prepared themselves for the 500.

Unser came within a couple of laps of being in a prime position to win in the Galles ECR Racing's G Force/Oldsmobile. Unser had pitted with the leaders under caution on Lap 33 and came out 15th. Then he pitted on half tanks on Lap 77 under caution and emerged 13th. He steadily marched his way up the field.

Kelley Racing's Scott Sharp held the lead from Lap 46 to 101, when he made his second pit stop under caution. Unser moved into the lead on Lap 129 by passing Dick Simon Racing's Stephan Gregoire into Turn 3. A short time later Donnie Beechler moved into third. When Gregoire pitted for fuel on a green flag stop on Lap 140, Lazier moved up to second. Unser had built-up a 6.5-second lead before pitting on Lap 151, but when Sam Hornish crashed as he re-entered the track, his victory chances were squashed.

"I was just sad. When I saw those yellows, I just could not believe it." Unser said. "It's nothing if you don't [lead] on the last lap. I'm very happy that we finished. What this proves is we can go to Indianapolis and run with anybody. We learned we could run with these guys." Unser's misfortune promoted Lazier into the lead, and on the restart Lazier had no equal.

Once again, Scott Goodyear methodically worked his way up through the field. He started seventh and stayed within reach of the lead cars during the course of the race. He tweaked his setup through his pit stops with the intention of charging for the lead in the waning stages of the race.

Goodyear said, "We were strong all day. We changed the car on pit stops—the tire pressures, the sway bars—and just about got it right. After the last fuel stop, you see who is in front of you and who is behind, and that's who you are going to race."

By Lap 167, Goodyear had worked his way up to second position behind Lazier, but in the end he didn't have enough. "We tried

Scott Sharp of Carmel, Indiana, piloted the Delphi Automotive Systems/MCI WorldCom Dallara/Oldsmobile/Firestone on the inside racing line at the tight oval at Phoenix.

to get Buddy on the restart, but we didn't get it," said Goodyear, who challenged strongly on the inside of Turn 1. "He was strong. Overall through the whole lap, Buddy's car was better. I was sliding a little in Turns 3 and 4. I was pretty disappointed going around the last few laps, but we'll take the second-place points."

For Donnie Beechler, he was experiencing the fruits of a revitalized crew and a third-place finish. "You've got to have the same equipment those guys have out there," Beechler said. "And now we have everything we need to be competitive. We have the car, the engine, and now we've got the engineer."

complete results listed on page 93

Billy Boat of Phoenix, Arizona, hoped a little home cooking would earn him a victory in front of the hometown fans, but he had to settle for a sixth-place finish in the Team Pelfrey entry. *Walt Kuhn*

UNSER STRIKES GOLD IN LAS VEGAS

When Al Unser Jr. left Team Penske at the end of the 1999 season and rejoined Galles Racing in the Indy Racing Northern Light Series for 2000, many pundits predicted that it wouldn't take him long to get into the winning groove. After all, Unser won the 1992 Indy 500 and a multitude of other races with Galles Racing before moving on to Team Penske. Although Unser hadn't won a race in five years, he had established himself as a one of the savviest and quickest drivers racing in the United States. At the Vegas Indy 300 held at the Las Vegas Motor Speedway, he proved he still has what it takes to win by methodically working his way up from the 21st starting position to seize victory.

The two-time Indianapolis 500 champion drove smart and consistently throughout the race, staying clear of several wrecks and eventually reeling in Mark Dismore, who led for the most laps. Scott Goodyear was at the front during the closing laps, but was black flagged with mechanical problems, transforming Unser's strong command of second place into an easy victory.

From the drop of the green flag, pole-sitter Dismore in his Dallara/Oldsmobile leapt to the front of the pack. A. J. Foyt Racing driver Eliseo Salazar slotted into second place, with fellow teammate Jeff Ward third, Menard's Greg Ray fourth, and Eddie Cheever, running the only Infiniti-powered car in the field, rounding out the top five by Lap 3.

By the 10th lap, Dismore had established the pace at the head of the field. He would hold the lead for much of the race. Salazar, Ward, Ray, and Cheever filled the top five. Gregoire was the first driver to bring out the caution flag by crashing in Turn 4 on Lap 5. When the green flag waved on Lap 15, the lead group circulated in a tight pack with Salazar trailing Dismore by a mere 0.2 of a second. But Kelley Racing's Dismore, who scored his maiden IRL win at Texas Motor Speedway in 1999, had found a fast setup. In five laps,

Mark Dismore won the Vegas Indy 300 pole but couldn't run with race winner Al Unser Jr. Dismore finished second in the On Star/GM BuyPower/Bryant Heating & Cooling Dallara/Oldsmobile/Firestone.
Ron McQueeney

Al Unser Jr. (3) passed Ronnie Johncox (30) at Las Vegas en route to his first win in the Indy Racing Northern Light Series. It was the two-time Indy 500 winner's first win in five seasons. *Roger Bedwell*

he steadily pulled ahead and was 1 second up on Salazar. Cheever was on the charge and moved up to third.

Donnie Beechler brought out the race's third yellow flag during the next lap when he spun into the Turn 4 wall. The leaders, except for Ray and Billy Boat, took advantage of the caution to make their first pit stop. Unser's G Force/Oldsmobile took on four tires and fuel. Staying on the track moved Ray and Boat up to the first and second positions, but Dismore was in the zone and moved up through the field quickly. He grabbed fourth place going into the 40th lap. On the backstretch he sliced past Robbie Buhl to take third. Ray held off all his pursuers through Lap 50, but three laps later Dismore came knocking after getting past Cheever.

By Lap 62, Ray, Dismore, and Cheever were running nose-to-tail in the first three positions, but Ray was forced to pit. Once Ray pitted, Dismore started to ease away from Cheever, but Cheever reeled in the Kelley Racing driver again and looked for a way past. However, Cheever's day would come to a premature end when a few laps later he pitted with an electrical problem but returned to the race. Dismore was having problems with his car's handling. He radioed his crew the car had developed a strong push, and he wasn't able to hold off rivals.

On Lap 78 Robby McGehee in Treadway Racing's G Force-Oldsmobile stormed past Dismore for the lead and then Airton Dare swept by later on the same lap. Dismore waited for a yellow flag, so he could pit to adjust the push out of his car without losing a lap. Ward gave him the yellow flag he was waiting for, making light contact with the wall on Lap 87. Out came the yellow, and into the pit went the leaders.

At the halfway point, Lap 104, Salazar led the race with a comfortable lead of 2-plus seconds over Dismore. Goodyear was

now pushing the leaders in third, with Sarah Fisher holding fourth, and Jason Leffler in fifth. Unser had crept quietly into ninth place. The top five runners remained the same until Lap 118. Six laps later, all of the leaders pitted except for Dismore, Fisher, and McGehee, putting Dismore back out front. Salazar and Fisher ran into trouble on Lap 127. The two drivers made contact in Turn 4 and both cars went into the wall. Although neither was injured, they were done for the day.

Dismore seemed to take the space Salazar and Fisher's disappearance created and put it between himself and the field. He led Goodyear by 3.7 seconds on Lap 139, by almost 8.5 seconds on Lap 147, and by 9.6 seconds in Lap 149. He continued to stretch this lead to nearly 11 seconds before pitting on Lap 155. Dare shot by Goodyear three laps later, taking his turn at the front.

Exiting Turn 2 on Lap 168, Leffler hit the wall, bringing the yellow flag out once again. Three laps later, Dare lost his gearbox and his shot at victory. "I went for first, and the gearbox broke," said Dare. "I don't know. I didn't have any gears." Goodyear and Ray pitted on the same lap, and Unser on the following lap. All took four tires and fuel for the dash to the finish line.

Misfortune had shaken up the race leaders and created opportunities for those behind them. This fit Unser's plan just fine. By Lap 174, with just 34 laps remaining, the legendary son of Al Unser was sitting comfortably in second place behind Goodyear. Dismore, holding third position, was about 20 seconds behind Unser. In pursuit of Unser, he set the fastest lap of the race on Lap 180 at 204.623 miles per hour.

Goodyear held the front until Lap 186, when race control reported smoke coming from his car. Three laps later they showed Goodyear

the black flag. At that moment, Unser knew victory was within his grasp. Dismore, so strong in the first half of the race, was 20 seconds back. Third-place driver, Sam Hornish, Jr., was a lap behind.

Dismore pushed hard to close the gap during the final laps, but Unser had established an insurmountable lead. He eased the pace so his car would last and to avoid making any significant mistakes in the run to the checkered flag. Dismore was able to take more than seven seconds off Unser's lead, but he was never in a position to threaten him. In celebration of ending a long, five year victory drought, Unser punched the air with his fist as he crossed the finish line. Dismore took second, Hornish third, Jeret Schroeder fourth, and Buhl fifth.

"We actually came out here to just try and stay in the top 10," said Hornish. "It was a great day. I never expected any of this."

The crowd gave Unser a standing ovation. Unser averaged 136.691 miles per hour to take his first victory in only three starts in the Indy Racing Northern Light Series. He added his first Indy Racing League win to the 31 victories he racked up on the CART series. Interestingly, it was the third consecutive Northern Light Series victory for a driver with a starting position of 21st or higher, and it further proved a driver could win from anywhere in the field.

"My crew had everything to do with it," said a tearful Unser in victory lane. "We never gave up. We fought really hard and got our lap back. I had my head down all the way to the checkered flag. When Roger [Penske] made the announcement in Detroit about his two drivers, Rick Galles called me the next day. There are people in this world that never give up on you, and Rick Galles is one of those people."

complete results listed on page 94

Indy Racing Northern Lights Series rookie Jeret Schroeder, shown here taking on fuel during a quick pit stop, finished fourth at Las Vegas. *Roger Bedwell*

SHARP PREVAILS IN EPIC DUEL

With foreboding clouds looming overhead and determined contenders swarming around him, Scott Sharp dashed across the finish line just .059 of a second ahead of a charging Robby McGehee to claim his fifth Indy Racing Northern Light Series win in the Casino Magic 500. At the price of a few raindrops and a brief delay, spectators at Texas Motor Speedway were treated to what many have called the best race in series history. From the drop of the green flag to Sharp's hair's-breadth victory, no driver was able to assume a commanding lead. The pack shrank at times but never disappeared, and the leaders never let up, trading the front position a record 31 times. When the finish line finally came, it was Sharp in the lead—but add a car length to the race and it might have ended differently.

Taking off from pole position, Buddy Lazier was first to the front. Scott Goodyear set his sights on Lazier, and as they dueled for the lead, other drivers closed in behind them, forming a pack two and three cars wide that hurled over the track in unison like a load of buckshot. Almost everyone was locked in the draft, with the spacing so close it gave the front runners no chance to pull away.

Just 19 laps in, a light rain stopped the race but the delay lasted only 36 minutes, 48 seconds. The drivers then ran four laps under yellow before returning to green flag racing. This time it was Chilean Eliseo Salazar nipping at Lazier's heels lap after lap. The other drivers who would vie for the lead also moved up the pack, including Mark Dismore, Goodyear, and Sam Hornish, Jr., soon to be joined by Eddie Cheever, Jr., Al Unser, Jr., and McGehee.

It was Unser who broke up Salazar's fight with Lazier, slipping past both drivers on the outside and pulling Sharp along with him. Sharp had his first glimpse of the lead in a battle with Unser, before Lazier slipped past him again. Billy Roe broke up the action this time with an engine problem that dumped fluid onto the track.

Al Unser Jr. enjoyed another podium finish as he finished third at Texas. He was in position to fight for the win, but a late-race green flag pit stop cost him valuable track position. *Steve Snoddy*

After a pit stop under caution, Unser and Lazier resumed and escalated their bare-knuckle battle, fighting to hold the lead by inches for over 20 laps. Behind them, Salazar and Goodyear fought with equal zeal until Goodyear displaced him and pushed his way to the front of the pack. Unser pitted early with telemetry problems, and Cheever claimed the lead briefly until he made for the pits. Cheever waited too long, however, running out of fuel as he entered the pit. By the time his crew refired his car, the stop had cost Cheever over 30 seconds.

As he came back onto the track, Unser was unable to overtake Cheever, allowing the pack to close up again. Unser eventually passed Cheever with Salazar and Lazier following, soon to be joined by Goodyear, Dismore, and Sharp. This group kept the brawl going into the last round of pits.

With 48 laps to go, Unser came in first—still suffering telemetry problems—followed by Lazier and Goodyear. Like Cheever, Lazier had stretched his fuel load too far, requiring a restart in the pits and losing 18 seconds. Kelley team drivers Sharp and Dismore, who were getting great fuel mileage, held out and were rewarded. Jeff Ward suffered engine failure during Lap 171, allowing Sharp and Dismore to pit under caution. At the restart, they shared the front with Buzz Calkins and McGehee, nearly a lap in front of Unser, Salazar, and Goodyear.

The drivers got to battle in this formation for only a short time before bad luck hit the Foyt team with a second engine failure, this one taking Salazar out of the race on Lap 180. Since Goodyear and Unser had stayed within a lap of Sharp, they were able to restart at the back of the field, setting the stage for the final laps of the race.

Sharp took the lead over Calkins and pushed it to two seconds. McGehee overcame Dismore then got by Calkins, as well as Greg Ray, who was a lap back. Only Sharp stood between McGehee

Race winner Scott Sharp (8) took an inside line to pass teammate Mark Dismore (28) in the Casino Magic 500 at Texas. This type of side-by-side racing was typical in the most exciting Indy Racing League race ever. *Ron McQueeney*

Robby McGehee (5) made a furious charge to the front but he was held off by eventual race winner Scott Sharp in one of the greatest duels ever staged on a race track. *Steve Snoddy*

and victory, and McGehee appeared to have a winning car. Driving the Mall.com G Force/Oldsmobile, McGehee pulled up on Sharp's gearbox, but Sharp protected the inside line. Taking the outside line on the corners, McGehee couldn't get past, though he nosed into the lead on the straight in Lap 202. Closing on the final lap, their cars passed within inches of one another again and again, with McGehee slipping back into the draft as the white flag dropped.

On the final lap, they raced side-by-side out of Turn 2 and McGehee, the 1999 Indianapolis 500 Bank One Rookie of the Year, actually edged ahead by half of a car length. But Sharp clung to the inside line. Rounding Turn 3 on the inside, Sharp kept McGehee off the faster inside line. As they came down the final straight full out, McGehee ran out of racetrack.

Sharp took the checkered flag a mere .059 of a second ahead, the slimmest margin of victory in league series history (topping the .064 of a second by Robbie Buhl over Vincenzo Sospiri at New Hampshire in 1997). He also set another record: the most series victories of any driver, surpassing Kenny Brack and Arie Luyendyk at four wins apiece. Unser fought back to third, Calkins took fourth, Goodyear claimed fifth, and Dismore sixth. Lazier, who drove such a great race early on, went home with seventh.

"I was all out . . . the whole [final] lap," said Sharp. "If [McGehee] had 2 or 3 more feet, he would have got by me. I got in the corner and drove it in deep and said, 'If you come down on me, we're both going to wreck.' But he raced me clean, and I raced him clean, and it was just a great race."

McGehee knew he'd get a great fight from Sharp. "When I passed Buzz [Calkins], I said I was going to get Sharp," McGehee said. "Getting him and passing him were two different things. I probably made a mistake. I should have done every-

thing I could to get the inside lane. It was the most exciting racing I've ever been involved in."

For winning the race, which was postponed to Sunday June 11 because of rain, Sharp earned $124,300 and the Foyt-Rutherford Trophy. He averaged 169.182 miles per hour in his Delphi Automotive Systems/MCI WorldCom Dallara/Oldsmobile/Firestone, another series record. His final lap speed was 208.527 miles per hour—slower than McGehee's speed of 208.552.

Sharp led the race for 38 laps, behind Lazier with 62 lead laps and Unser with 79. Lazier retained his lead in the quest for Northern Light Cup with 164 points, followed by Goodyear with 142 and Cheever with 126. Cheever turned the fastest lap, 24.584 seconds at 213.065 miles per hour, on Lap 61.

complete results listed on page 96

Buzz Calkins (12) was among the racers who dueled wheel-to-wheel for laps at a time in Texas. He finished fourth. There were 31 official lead changes and dozens more lead changes all around the track. *Steve Snoddy*

CHEEVER TAKES INFINITI TO VICTORY

In the experienced hands of Eddie Cheever Jr., the Nissan Infiniti engine program chalked up its first win as the 1998 Indianapolis 500 champion drove away from the field in the Radisson Indy 200 at Pikes Peak International Raceway. The victory ended a string of 35 winless outings for Infiniti, and moved Cheever into first place in the chase for the Northern Light Cup. Cheever avoided several mishaps and overcame handling problems that challenged the field at the Fountain, Colorado, racetrack.

In a glimpse of what lay ahead, Robbie Buhl put his Infiniti-powered car into the lead after the first turn of the race, passing pole-sitter Greg Ray. Points leader Buddy Lazier had far worse luck, suffering engine failure in the first lap. The breakdown was a serious setback in Lazier's quest for the title. Buhl held the lead early, with Scott Sharp, the winner of the previous week's Casino Magic 500, pressuring from second place.

During Lap 6, two more drivers ran into trouble when Sarah Fisher collided with Billy Boat in Turn 2. Boat spun into in the infield grass, while Fisher went into the wall. Although she walked away from the crash, her day was over. Boat pitted for new tires and rejoined the race, but engine trouble would take him out on Lap 158.

Buhl and Sharp maintained the first and second position after the restart, with Ray, Mark Dismore, and Cheever not far behind. The two leaders would hold position, while third through fifth positions swapped back and forth. On Lap 35, Cheever muscled past Dismore, who began to fade after experiencing handling problems. Eliseo Salazar moved up to claim fifth position, running behind Buhl, Sharp, Ray, and Cheever, by Lap 40. Ten laps later, the lead group of four remained in front, while Beechler edged out Salazar for fifth

Several seasons of determined effort finally paid off for the Nissan Infiniti engine program as Eddie Cheever Jr. (51) won the Radisson Indy 200 at Pikes Peak International Raceway. *Jim Haines*

Eddie Cheever Jr. persevered with the Infiniti engine and rode it to victory at Pikes Peak. His fourth career win in the IRL put him in the lead in the points race. *Jim Haines*

position. On Lap 54, a loose-handling car forced Cheever to surrender fourth to Beechler.

By Lap 61, Buhl stayed on point, giving Infiniti its most laps ever in the lead, but his day came to a premature end when his Infiniti let go. The leaders took advantage of Buhl's misfortune by pitting under caution.

At the first pit stop, Beechler took only tires and fuel, while Sharp, Cheever, Dismore, and Al Unser, Jr., also received wing adjustments. Sharp moved into first place on Lap 62, with Beechler, Cheever, Unser Jr., Salazar, Dismore, and Buzz Calkins behind.

In Lap 78, Shigeaki Hattori brought out the yellow flag when he spun exciting Turn 2. He also avoided the wall. Sharp stayed ahead after the restart, with Cheever and Unser Jr. trailing. By Lap 94, Sharp had a lead of over 1 second.

Ray spun on Lap 96 trying to pass Dismore on the inside of Turn 4. He lost control and slid into the wall, bringing out the fourth caution in the first half of the race. After the restart, Sharp still clung to first, with Cheever, Unser Jr., Beechler, Salazar, and Dismore breathing down his neck.

Cheever set his sights on Sharp while the others near the front traded positions. Beechler made it past Unser Jr. on Lap 107. Brazilian Airton Daré, who had fought his way into sixth place mid

Scott Sharp (8) led the Radisson Indy 200 at Pikes Peak for several laps, but couldn't hold off eventual winner Eddie Cheever, Jr. to earn his second-straight win. Sharp finished third. *Ron McQueeney*

With a heavy throttle foot and a sponsor's youthful inspiration on his car, Brazilian Airton Daré achieved his best finish to date in his rookie Indy Racing League season in the Uproar.com/TeamXtreme G Force. *Jim Haines*

way through the race, also tried to pass Unser Jr. on Lap 111. This time Unser Jr. held station. By Lap 130, Cheever was starting to reel in Sharp, whittling away his lead to under 1 second.

Four laps later, Cheever made his move. Sharp held him off coming into Turn 1, but Cheever kept the pressure on. Cheever got a better drive off Turn 2 and swept past Sharp down the back straight. In Lap 135, Sharp told his pit that his car had gone so loose he was having a hard time holding the wheel. Cheever held onto the lead until he pitted on Lap 144.

Although Cheever got out in 12.6 seconds, the lead traded hands several times as the front cars went into the pits. Beechler held the front until he pitted in Lap 147, at which point Sharp took back the lead. Teammate Dismore claimed it on 152, and passed it to Gregoire on Lap 155.

Yet Cheever was not to be denied. He ran down Gregoire and recaptured the lead on Lap 172. From there, he just kept pulling away. When Gregoire stopped for fuel on Lap 184—running dry as he entered the pit, Cheever was leading by over 11 seconds with Daré in second, Sharp third, and Beechler and Dismore in fourth and fifth.

With the end of the race just two laps away, bad luck reared its ugly head one more time. Heading into Turn 1 on Lap 198, Beechler tried to pass Unser on the outside. His right front wheel contacted Beechler's left rear, sending both cars into a spin. Sharp, who was below them in the turn, got past the trouble. Beechler hit the wall, rear end first, and injured his knee. Unser Jr. walked away unhurt. The yellow flag came out until the end of the race, ending the hopes of Cheever's challengers.

Daré finished second—his best showing in series competition—while Kelley teammates Sharp and Dismore claimed third and fourth.

Cheever's victory, his fourth in the Indy Racing League, was worth $124,400. The win moved him into first place in the $1 million Northern Light Cup, with 176 points. Lazier trailed with 168, followed

by Sharp with 159, Scott Goodyear with 156, and Dismore with 155.

At the wheel of the No. 51 Excite@Home Indy Race Car Dallara/Infiniti/Firestone, Cheever averaged 135.230 miles per hour. The race brought Cheever's lap total to 1,207, the most in the league.

Buzz Calkins, who went home in 12th place, turned the fastest lap of the race, at 167.131 miles per hour. During qualifying, pole-sitter Ray clocked the fastest lap time ever run at Pikes Peak, 179.874 miles per hour. Sharp led the most laps at 75, 15 more than Buhl, and more than twice as many as Cheever's 34. But it's the last lap that decides the winner, and this time it was Eddie Cheever—and the Infiniti engine program.

Cheever switched to an Infiniti engine prior to the 1999 Indy 500 and was the sole campaigner of that engine through most of last season and the first part of 2000. Buhl joined Cheever as driver of an Infiniti-powered car after this year's Indianapolis 500.

complete results listed on page 97

It was an Infiniti engine weekend at Pikes Peak. Eddie Cheever Jr. gave the Nissan engine its first Indy Racing League victory while Robbie Buhl (24) posted the second-best qualifying speed and led for several laps. *Jim Haines*

NO STOPPING RAY AT ATLANTA

By Dick Mittman

Imagine Mark McGwire going three-fourths of the baseball season without hitting a home run, Peyton Manning not completing an NFL pass, or Shaquille O'Neal not making his patented NBA slam dunk. That was the pickle Indy Racing Northern Light Series defending champion Greg Ray found himself in as he approached the Midas 500 Classic at Atlanta Motor Speedway, the seventh race of the nine-race season.

Not only had Ray not won a race, he hadn't even come close. He had led only five laps and his best finish was ninth and four laps down at Las Vegas. His other finishes had been 17th, 19th, 33rd (in the Indy 500, no less), 15th, and 20th.

It was time for the sun and the stars to shine on the talented Texan and the Menard team. Both shined in a race that started in bright daylight and finished under the lights and a beautiful Georgia moon. Finally, it was Ray's day . . . and night.

Ray had already put the other starters on guard by blasting around the 1-mile oval at 216.104 miles per hour in his Conseco/Quaker State/Menards Dallara-Oldsmobile-Firestone to capture the pole. His speed was nearly 3 miles per hour faster than his fellow front-row starter Eliseo Salazar, who clocked a fast lap of 213.194 in his Rio A. J. Foyt Racing G Force/Oldsmobile/Firestone.

The green flag waved shortly after 8 P.M., and Ray and Salazar blazed into the first turn facing a blazing sun shining across the Turn 1 wall. They continued their side-by-side duel down the backstretch, but Ray's machine edged away as they crossed the start-finish line to complete the first of 208 laps.

Scott Sharp, winner of the Casino Magic 500 at Texas Motor Speedway in June, slowed on the backstretch of the first lap and appeared to regain speed on the front stretch, but was lapped by Ray at the end of the third circuit. Sharp was forced to pit on Lap 4.

Donnie Beechler made an early charge in his Cahill Racing Dallara/Oldsmobile, passing Salazar to grab second place on Lap 5.

Greg Ray (1) was the fastest man in Atlanta in the sunshine at the start of the race and under the lights at the finish. He won the Midas 500 Classic in convincing fashion over Buddy Lazier.
Ron McQueeney

Robby McGehee (5) continued his strong sophomore season by finishing fourth at Atlanta in his Treadway Racing G Force/Oldsmobile.
Ron McQueeney

Ray, driving like he was on a mission, opened up a 2.595-second lead by Lap 8. Already, rookie J.J. Yeley had pulled out due to electrical problems, and on Lap 13 the car of another rookie, Brazilian Airton Dare, began smoking. His G Force/Oldsmobile abruptly spun, missing the wall and coming to rest in the infield grass. "The motor just let go with no warning," TeamXtreme team manager John Lopes said.

Sharp climbed out of his car as his Kelley Racing team replaced the gearbox. Ray pulled away from the pack once more when the green flag resumed the race on Lap 20. Making a move from the middle of the pack was Buddy Lazier, now fifth. Yeley returned after some lengthy repairs, Scott Harrington stopped for a battery replacement, and Jeret Schroeder slowed with a broken exhaust header as Ray continued to set a blistering pace. The sun finally settled behind the Turn 1 wall on Lap 34.

Harrington's car quit on the course and brought out a caution on Lap 40. All of the leaders dashed in for fuel and tires, with Beechler returning to the racing surface first. Sarah Fisher took off from her pit only to have the left rear wheel come loose. She had to be pushed back for reattachment.

Ray lost the lead because of a slow stop due to problems changing the right rear tire. That didn't deter the reigning IRL champion. The green waved on Lap 45 and eight laps later, he had exploded back into the lead, passing Mark Dismore. The tenacious Buddy Lazier, who had won from last place at Phoenix in March, now clung to second place.

Buzz Calkins' car was entering Turn 1 when suddenly it was engulfed with smoke as the engine exploded. He stopped in the middle of the track between Turns 1 and 2 as other drivers drove boldly through the smoke and swept by him on either side. "We were having a good race when the engine let go," Calkins said.

Dismore regained the lead during the second pit stop, but there was no holding off Ray. He established a 4.584-second advantage by Lap 97 when Eddie Cheever Jr. pulled his Infiniti-powered No 51 Excite@Home Indy Race Car machine through the pits into the

Al Unser Jr. (3) continued to pile up valuable Indy Racing Northern Light Series points as he finished in third place at Atlanta, barely losing a late-race duel with Buddy Lazier. *Roger Bedwell*

garage. Ray led Robby McGehee at the 100-lap segment and five laps later had runner-up Dismore covered by 12.083 seconds.

Ray visited the pits for the third time on Lap 123, yielding the lead once more to Dismore in his Kelley Racing On Star/GM BuyPower Dallara/Oldsmobile. Dismore pitted on the next circuit, and Ray regained control by a comfortable 12 seconds. Scott Goodyear also pitted and as he pulled into his stall, tire changer Scott Merryman was struck by the car's left front tire and knocked to the ground. "The car and myself were a bit too close to each other, and the left-front tire hit my upper legs," said Merryman, who had precautionary X-rays taken at the infield medical center.

As the race continued, a failed engine, which sent up a blue-white smoke screen in Turn 1 on Lap 147, doomed Dismore's hopes of a good finish. "All I can do now is wish the other fellas good luck," Dismore sighed.

During the yellow, Ray made his fourth stop for fuel and tires on Lap 157 and quickly stormed back to the front when the caution ended on Lap 165. Davey Hamilton, driving in his 41st consecutive Indy Racing League race, pulled off for long repairs during the next lap. Buddy Lazier and Al Unser Jr. trailed Ray as the race headed toward the home stretch. Only .24 of a second separated the two runners-up when Sarah Fisher spun in Turn 4 and hit the outside retaining wall. The car slid to a halt on the infield grass on the front straight and she climbed out unassisted.

On Lap 191, the field went green flag racing. With nine laps to go, nothing was going to keep Ray from receiving the checkered flag

in this race. He increased the gap between him and Lazier from 1.345 seconds to 1.688 seconds, then 2.356 seconds, and finally 3.054 seconds as he scored the fourth victory of his career. Ray averaged 153.403 miles per hour and picked up a winner's check totaling $143,400.

Lazier, Unser Jr. (his father Al was the race's grand marshal), and McGehee followed Ray across the finish line, all on the lead lap. Lazier's second place propelled him into the lead of the Northern Light Cup points race with 208 points.

"Team Menard has been working so hard all year long," said a happy Ray. "These guys deserve better results. We went back to details, working on the small things. We stopped worrying about the big things. The big things take care of themselves. The guys did a great job."

"The Menard car was a missile, and it was fun to drive."
complete results listed on page 98

Buddy Lazier (91) edged Al Unser Jr. at the finish line of the Midas 500 Classic to finish in second place and earn enough points to maintain his lead in the points race. *Ron McQueeney*

By Dick Mittman

The "kids" put on the show, but the veterans collected the dough. That was the story of The Belterra Resort Indy 300 at the new Kentucky Speedway on August 27, which was the penultimate round of the Indy Racing Northern Light Series. It was a race where the budding stars of the future—Sarah Fisher, Sam Hornish Jr., Jimmy Kite, and Jaques Lazier—shared the limelight with seasoned campaigners Buddy Lazier and Scott Goodyear, who showed their experience by running one-two at the checkered flag.

The Indy Racing drivers and teams were venturing into new territory when they came to this spiffy racing layout nestled in the rolling foothills of northern Kentucky, 30 miles southwest of Cincinnati and just a short distance south of the Ohio River. It was the latest of the new automobile race tracks popping up around the country. In 2001, the series will compete at freshly constructed venues at Joliet, Illinois; Kansas City, Kansas; and Nashville, Tennessee. Along with the Indy 500 and the Gateway International Raceway across the Mississippi River from St. Louis, the Kentucky Speedway helps centralize the league's racing in the Midwest where its fan base is strongest. This was obvious at Kentucky's inaugural race when an enthusiastic crowd of 61,214 packed the stands. They witnessed a tremendous show typical of the style the Indy Racing League has put on at all of its 1-mile ovals.

Most of the teams participated in several pre-race test sessions at the facility during the summer. Many drivers compared the track to the Las Vegas Motor Speedway, but yet it had its own eccentricities. Scott Goodyear, driving in his next-to-last race of a three-year stint with the Pennzoil Panther Racing team, was quickest to figure out the circuit and surprised even himself by capturing the pole with a blistering 219.191 mile-per-hour lap. It was the 40-year-old Canadian's first Indy Racing pole in 37 races.

Lazier ran well in practice, but could qualify no better than seventh in his Delta Faucet/Coors Light/Tae-Bo/Hemelgarn Racing Dallara-Oldsmobile. There is, however, no more dogged racer than Lazier. Two months after shattering his back in a crash at Phoenix, Lazier made a dramatic comeback and won the 1996 Indy 500. He also became the first winner of an open wheel race at then-Charlotte Motor Speedway later that summer. During the second race of the 2000 season he charged from last place to win at Phoenix, and at

the Indy 500 he was the only driver to stay in contention with winner Juan Montoya.

At Kentucky, he refused to allow early race difficulties to keep him down. He stayed out of trouble, plugged away, and eventually got the lead and held it to the finish by 1.879 seconds over Goodyear, averaging 164.601 miles per hour. It was a victory that put him in position to win the Northern Light Cup and $1 million check by finishing 13th or better in the season finale at Texas Motor Speedway.

Baseball's all-time hit leader Pete Rose, a former Cincinnati Reds' star, gave the command to start the cars as the race's grand marshal. Veteran Roberto Guerrero's engine wouldn't fire and had to be pushed aside as the other 26 cars pulled away. On the third warm-up lap, his car finally fired and he joined the field.

Sarah Fisher proved she can race with the best in the Indy Racing League. Aboard the Walker Racing Dallara/Oldsmobile , she qualified fourth fastest and ran near the front for most of the race. After the last round of pitstops, Fisher ran in the lead group and eventually finished behind Buddy Lazier and Scott Goodyear in third position. *Ron McQueeney*

The green waved and team Foyt driver Eliseo Salazar, starting on the outside of the front row, immediately challenged Goodyear for the lead and charged to the front in Turn 4. However, his stay there was short-lived. Rookie Jeret Schroeder powered to the front of the pack and by the start of the third lap was battling Salazar for the lead. The leading duo touched in Turn 1 sending Schroeder into the wall and the Chilean into the outside concrete in Turn 2. Two-time Indy 500 champion Al Unser Jr. smacked the wall trying to avoid the spinning cars, and Scott Sharp's Dallara/Oldsmobile was struck by flying debris.

"He just hit me from behind," Salazar said. "It's a shame because we just lost our chances at the championship."

Schroeder provided his prospective on the incident: "I figured he would stay high. I went down low, and he stuck me on the apron and I went around."

It took 15 laps to clean up the track. When the green flag flew, Goodyear had Greg Ray, defending series champion and winner of

Buddy Lazier came through with a big win when he needed to and closed in on his ultimate goal—the Northern Light Cup. Lazier and his Hemelgarn Racing Dallara-Oldsmobile took firm command of the race on Lap 171 and held it to the end. *Ron McQueeney*

the previous race, on his tail with Buddy Lazier up to fifth. However, it was young Georgian Kite who was on the move, passing Ray in Turn 1 for second on Lap 24. Another youngster, Hornish Jr., was hustling through the field. The 21-year-old rocketed up the order from fourth, third, second, and then blasted by Goodyear for the lead, all in five laps. Kite, 24, also slipped by Goodyear, making the combined age of the pair of pacesetters only five years more than the driver they had just passed.

But by Lap 38, Buddy Lazier was hounding Hornish Jr., following .878 of second behind. Then three laps later they were side-by-side and Lazier sliced past into the lead. Buddy wasn't the only Lazier making progress. Younger brother Jaques had moved up to third. The elder Lazier pitted with the pack on Lap 54 only to return two laps later. Buddy had missed the marks in his pit box on his first stop and the refueling hose couldn't reach the car. He slipped back into the field.

Meanwhile, Jaques was fighting tooth-and-nail with Hornish Jr. for the lead. From Lap 93 to Lap 100, they put on a tremendous duel that brought the crowd to its feet. Finally, on Lap 100 Jaques grabbed the lead as Hornish Jr.'s car began to slow. Hornish Jr. fell a lap down while the car was refueled and restarted and then he had to take a pit drive-through penalty for passing the pace car on his previous exit. He finished ninth.

Jaques' victory bid ended on Lap 123 as his engine expired. Kite, running in second, picked up the pieces and pulled out to a 3-second lead as Buddy Lazier, back in the hunt, passed Goodyear for second. Then Kite's car experienced the same fate as Hornish Jr.'s as he coasted into the pits with flames coming out of the engine compartment. That set the stage for 19-year-old Sarah Fisher, auto racing's female phenom, to soar into the lead as the crowd cheered wildly. It was the first time a woman had ever led an Indy Car race. Fisher held the spot for nine laps before pitting, and ceded the lead back to Buddy.

As one of the toughest drivers to pass, Buddy refused to yield

From a 15th starting position, Eddie Cheever, Jr. made steady progress all day climbing up the leaderboard. At the controls of the Dallara/Infiniti, he nailed down fourth position and was the last car on the lead lap. *Jim Haines*

to the pressure applied by Goodyear in his Dallara/Oldsmobile. Like in many races, lapped traffic played a decisive role in the outcome of the race. On Lap 195, Lazier easily moved around Jeff Ward's car, and Goodyear couldn't make the same maneuver and lost momentum. That break gave Lazier breathing room to run to the checkered flag without being challenged again. Fisher, who qualified fourth fastest, brought her Walker Racing Cummins Special Dallara/Oldsmobile home third only 7.749 seconds behind, with Eddie Cheever Jr., driving the Infiniti-powered No. 51 Excite@Home Indy Race Car, snaring fourth as the only other driver on the lead lap.

"It was a spectacular day for us," said Buddy Lazier, who had only Goodyear and Cheever Jr. remaining as title contenders heading into the last race. "It took everything we had."

And just how did the racing gods smile on him? His car broke fifth gear when he lifted off the throttle as he crossed under the checkered flag.

complete results listed on page 99

Jimmy Kite, driving the Aramis/Blueprint Racing Special, had one of his best showings of the year. Kite battled with Menard's Greg Ray, Panther's Scott Goodyear, and PDM Racing's Sam Hornish Jr. for second during the early going. He later led the race for 16 laps, but finished down in the 17th spot. Steve Snoddy

ROUND 9 — LAZIER CLINCHES CHAMPIONSHIP

By Dick Mittman

Buddy Lazier could have coasted through the Excite 500 at Texas Motor Speedway on October 15, 2000, and won the Indy Racing Northern Light Series season championship just by finishing 13th. Scott Goodyear could have coasted to a careful and safe finish and said farewell to the Pennzoil Panther Racing team. Eddie Cheever Jr. could have coasted and waited for the arrival of the updated Infiniti engine for the 2001 season.

Coast? The word isn't in their vocabularies.

Buddy Lazier didn't win the 1996 Indianapolis 500 two months after breaking his back in 40 places during a crash at Phoenix by

The No. 51 Dallara/Infiniti of Eddie Cheever, Jr. receives routine service from the Team Cheever crew. As amazing as Cheever's championship charge was, it was made more impressive by the fact that he developed the Infiniti engine over the entire season and was still in the championship hunt at the end of the season. *Roger Bedwell*

Boo! Billy Boat's pace in the No. 81 Pelfrey Dallara/ Oldsmobile was almost scary. Few expected Boat to run with the leaders, but Boat showed he still has what it takes to win. He led eventual winner Scott Goodyear in the No. 4 Pennzoil machine but took third at the end. *Walt Kuhn*

taking it easy. Cheever didn't win Indy two years later by being light on the throttle with Lazier in hot pursuit. Goodyear gave everything he had to finish second to Al Unser Jr. by the slightest of margins—.043 of a second—in the 1992 Indy 500, and by .570 of a second to Arie Luyendyk in 1997.

These were Indy Racing's version of the old Texas gunslingers, and with the Northern Light Cup and a $1 million bonus on the line, they were going to fire away until all of their bullets were gone. They never flinched during the 208-lap, 312-mile shootout at 210 miles per hour on the 1.5-mile oval.

And when the race reached its pulsating conclusion, Goodyear stood tall as the race winner by .140 of a second over Cheever, passing him three-fourths of the way around on the last lap. Sticking his nose into the mix just to make the finish that much more exciting was brazen Billy Boat, who was only .245 of a second behind Goodyear in third place at the checkered flag. Lazier roared across

the finish line only .701 of a second behind in fourth to claim the season title.

The race speed average of 175.276 miles per hour was the fastest in series history. It was a good thing, too, because thunder boomed over the track and lightning streaked across the sky as the racers charged across the finish line. By the time they had completed their slowdown lap, rain was pouring out of the dark clouds overhead. Still, that put no damper on the celebration by Lazier's Hemelgarn Racing team nor on Goodyear and his Panther Racing crew. They had produced a finely-honed car for their driver's last race.

Cheever, owner of his own team, wasn't totally let down by his narrow defeat. On Saturday, Cheever publicly invited Goodyear to drive for him next year, and Goodyear admitted he was considering the offer.

"We're just thrilled," said Lazier, who had to make a pit stop for a splash of fuel in his Delta Faucet/Coors Light/Tae-Bo/ Hemelgarn Racing Dallara/Oldsmobile/Firestone car with nine laps remaining and his car in the lead. "We had a great day today. This has been a long time coming. This team has been fighting hard for several years. This is the culmination of a lot of hard years of work." He added it was appropriate to clinch the championship in such a hair-raising fashion.

"I'm really happy and thankful to the sponsors, the crew, and the driver," said owner Ron Hemelgarn. "It was a total team effort."

Lazier entered the last race leading Goodyear by 38 points (258 to 220). Cheever, the other driver in mathematical contention for the championship, trailed by 41 points. He picked up 32 points for his fourth place and closed with a 28-point margin (290 to 272) over Goodyear, with Cheever ending in third with 257.

"The car was better as the tires wore," Goodyear said. "It was really close to the end and how we battled all year. I'm really happy for all the guys at Panther Racing. They worked hard, and it paid off."

Defending series champion Greg Ray of nearby Plano, Texas, ran away with the pole during qualifying with a speed of 215.352 miles per hour, beating Goodyear by nearly 1 mile per hour. But when the green flag dropped, his Conseco/Quaker State/Menards Dallara/Oldsmobile/Firestone went backward as Goodyear and Unser Jr. dueled for the lead. Ray was out after only 18 laps with an electrical problem. "It seems like the Team Menard ship has been sailing through the Bermuda Triangle all season," Ray said.

Unser Jr. nosed his black Galles ECR Racing Tickets.com Starz Encore Superpak G Force/Oldsmobile/Firestone by Goodyear on Lap 2 and maintained the front spot for 32 laps (he led the most laps, 99) before Goodyear throttled around him once more.

The first pit stops allowed Jaques Lazier and Sharp to set the pace briefly before they also had to make fuel and tire stops. Unser Jr. beat the crowd out of the pits and held off his pursuers until Lap 100 when a titanic duel developed between Unser Jr. and Goodyear. Both circulated side by side for five straight laps. Neither driver budged an inch, but Unser Jr. squeezed by and took the lead on Lap 104 and held it though Lap 121. The glory proved to be short lived as Unser Jr. dropped out after 155 laps with a failed clutch.

Brazilian newcomer Airton Dare added his name to the list of challengers as he shoved his way into second with 80 laps remaining. He would fall back later and finish 12th, but earned season rookie-of-the-year honors. Robbie Buhl then became part of the lead gaggle of cars and was the front-runner for two laps before it was Boat's turn for a single lap. Goodyear, Lazier, or Cheever led for the final 61 circuits.

Rookie Zak Morioka of Brazil hit the Turn 1 wall on Lap 193 to end a stretch of 401 consecutive laps spanning two races at Texas Motor Speedway without an accident. Lazier, running low on fuel, darted into the pits and dropped himself back from first to fourth.

That set the scene for the final duel between Cheever and Goodyear, with Boat trying to upstage them both and Lazier making a last-gasp banzai charge to catch up. The checkered flag waved over Goodyear's sunshine yellow machine an instant before the rain poured from above.

It was a racing day to remember.
complete results listed on page 100

Losing his Panther race seat to Sam Hornish Jr. didn't deter Scott Goodyear. He powered past Eddie Cheever Jr. out of Turn 3 on the last lap to take victory. It was the first win for Goodyear this season and it closed out his career with Panther Racing on a high note. *Roger Bedwell*

The culmination of five years of hard work for Team Hemelgarn and Buddy Lazier was the Indy Racing Northern Light Series championship. Here, Lazier celebrates a season well done with his fist in the air. *Jim Haines*

ROUND 1: DELPHI INDY 200

INDY RACING NORTHERN LIGHT SERIES
Walt Disney World Speedway, Saturday, January 29, 2000

FP	SP	Car		Driver	Car Name	C/E/T	Laps Comp.	Running/ Reason Out	IRL Pts.	Total IRL Pts.	IRL Standings	IRL Awards	Designated Awards	Total Awards
1	22	24		Robbie Buhl	Team Purex Dreyer & Reinbold Racing	G/O/F	200	Running	52	52	1	$89,200	$49,800	$139,000
2	5	91		Buddy Lazier	Delta Faucet/Coors Light/Tae-Bo/Hemelgarn Racing	R/O/F	200	Running	40	40	2	73,800	7,450	81,250
3	6	51		Eddie Cheever Jr.	Team Cheever/Firestone/Infiniti	R/I/F	200	Running	35	35	3	62,000	6,250	68,250
4	8	4		Scott Goodyear	Pennzoil Panther Dallara	D/O/F	200	Running	32	32	4	50,200	0	50,200
5	10	11		Eliseo Salazar	Rio A.J. Foyt Racing	G/O/F	200	Running	30	30	5	45,900	0	45,900
6	15	98		Donnie Beechler	Big Daddy's Sauces/Race Car Cafe Las Vegas	D/O/F	200	Running	28	28	6	40,600	10,000	50,600
7	2	14		Jeff Ward	Harrah's A.J. Foyt Racing	G/O/F	200	Running	26	26	7	39,500	0	39,500
8	11	12		Buzz Calkins	Bradley Food Marts/Sav-O-Mat	D/O/F	200	Running	24	24	8	38,400	0	38,400
9	9	81		Billy Boat	Team Pelfrey	D/O/F	200	Running	22	22	9	38,400	0	38,400
10	4	55		Robby McGehee	Energizer Advanced Formula/Energizer Motorsports	G/O/F	200	Running	20	20	10	37,400	0	37,400
11	25	88	R	Airton Daré	TeamXtreme Racing/G Force	G/O/F	199	Running	19	19	11	36,200	0	36,200
12	21	27	R	Niclas Jonsson	American Hotel Register/ZMAX	G/O/F	198	Running	18	18	12	35,200	0	35,200
13	23	20		Tyce Carlson	Hubbard-Immke Racing	D/O/F	197	Running	17	17	13	34,200	0	34,200
14	20	43	R	Doug Didero	Mid America Freight Systems/Western Star Trucks	D/O/F	195	Running	16	16	14	33,000	0	33,000
15	7	8		Scott Sharp	Delphi Automotive Systems/MCI WorldCom	D/O/F	186	Running	15	15	15	32,000	0	32,000
16	3	28		Mark Dismore	Bryant Heating & Cooling/On Star	D/O/F	183	Oil cooler	14	14	16	31,000	0	31,000
17	1	1		Greg Ray	Conseco/Menards	D/O/F	180	Running	13	13	17	29,800	0	29,800
18	13	7		Stephan Gregoire	Dick Simon Racing/Mexmil/Tokheim/Viking Air Tools	G/O/F	174	Running	12	12	18	29,800	0	29,800
19	16	6	R	Jeret Schroeder	Armour Swift Ekrich/Tristarmall.com	D/O/F	174	Running	11	11	19	28,800	0	28,800
20	19	18	R	Sam Hornish Jr.	Hornish Bros. Trucking/Advantage Powder Coating	G/O/F	172	Running	10	10	20	27,800	0	27,800
21	14	42		John Hollansworth Jr.	TeamXtreme/Lycos/G Force	G/O/F	136	Electrical	9	9	21	27,800	0	27,800
22	26	30	R	Jon Herb	Jonathan Byrd's Cafeteria	G/O/F	114	Handling	8	8	22	27,800	0	27,800
23	12	33		Jaques Lazier	Motorsportscity.com/Exodus Communications	G/O/F	110	Accident	7	7	23	27,800	0	27,800
24	18	9		Robby Unser	PetroMoly/Tristarmall.com	D/O/F	93	Accident	6	6	24	27,800	0	27,800
25	24	3		Al Unser Jr.	Galles ECR Racing Tickets.com Starz	G/O/F	64	Engine	5	5	25	27,800	0	27,800
26	17	44		Davey Hamilton	Ericsson/Spinal Conquest/SRS	D/O/F	22	Accident	4	4	26	27,800	0	27,800
				Brayton Engineering									600	600
				Speedway Engines									400	400
											TOTAL -	**$1,000,000**	**$74,500**	**$1,074,500**

Time of Race: 1:57:18.676   **Average Speed:** 102.292 mph   **Margin of Victory:** 3.165 sec.

Fastest Lap / Fastest Leading Lap: #28 Mark Dismore (Race lap 129, 162.126 mph, 22.205 sec.)

Firestone "First at 100" Award: #98 Donnie Beechler   **Coors Light "Pit Performance" Award:** #24 Robbie Buhl

"The Net Race Live Award" Lap Leader: #24 Robbie Buhl   **MCI WorldCom "Long Distance" Award:** #24 Robbie Buhl   **Lincoln Electric "Hard Charger" Award:** #24 Robbie Buhl

Legend: R=Indy Racing Northern Light Series Rookie   **Chassis Legend:** D=Dallara (12); G=G Force (12); Riley & Scott (2)

Engine Legend: O=Oldsmobile (25); I=Nissan Infiniti (1)   **Tire Legend:** F=Firestone (26)

Lap Leaders:

Laps	Car#	Driver	Laps	Car#	Driver
1-45	#1	Greg Ray	139	#51	Eddie Cheever Jr.
46-49	#81	Billy Boat	140-144	#55	Robby McGehee
50-96	#24	Robbie Buhl	145-191	#91	Buddy Lazier
97	#1	Greg Ray	192-198	#51	Eddie Cheever Jr.
98-99	#81	Billy Boat	199-200	#24	Robbie Buhl
100-108	#98	Donnie Beechler			
109-138	#28	Mark Dismore	**11 Lead changes among 8 drivers**		

Lap Leader Summary:

Driver	Times	Total
Robbie Buhl	2	49
Buddy Lazier	1	47
Greg Ray	2	46
Mark Dismore	1	30
Donnie Beechler	1	9
Eddie Cheever Jr.	2	8
Billy Boat	2	6
Robby McGehee	1	5

Caution Flags:

Laps	Reason/Incident
3-5	J. Lazier spun T2
24-34	Hamilton accident T1
44-48	Debris T1
67-74	Herb stopped on frontstraight
95-105	R. Unser accident T2
111-123	J. Lazier accident on frontstraight
136-143	Hornish spun T1
176-181	Didero spun backstraight
Total: 8 caution flags, 65 laps	

OFFICIAL BOX SCORE — ROUND 2: MCI WORLDCOM INDY 200

INDY RACING NORTHERN LIGHT SERIES
Phoenix International Raceway, Sunday, March 19, 2000

FP	SP	Car		Driver	Car Name	C/E/T	Laps Comp.	Running/ Reason Out	IRL Pts.	Total IRL Pts.	IRL Standings	IRL Awards	Designated Awards	Total Awards
1	26	91		Buddy Lazier	Delta Faucet/Coors Light/Tae-Bo/Hemelgarn Racing	R/O/F	200	Running	50	90	1	$94,600	$35,800	$130,400
2	7	4		Scott Goodyear	Pennzoil Panther Dallara	D/O/F	200	Running	40	72	3	79,000	2,050	81,050
3	11	98		Donnie Beechler	Big Daddy's Specialty Foods/Race Car Café-Las Vegas	D/O/F	200	Running	35	63	4	67,200	2,150	69,350
4	17	11		Eliseo Salazar	Rio A.J. Foyt Racing	G/O/F	200	Running	32	62	5	55,300	0	55,300
5	3	8		Scott Sharp	Delphi Automotive Systems/MCI WorldCom	D/O/F	200	Running	33	48	8	51,000	20,000	71,000
6	16	81		Billy Boat	Team Pelfrey	D/O/F	200	Running	28	50	7	45,700	10,000	55,700
7	9	24		Robbie Buhl	Team Purex Dreyer & Reinbold Racing	G/O/F	200	Running	26	78	2	44,500	500	45,000
8	12	7		Stephan Gregoire	Dick Simon Racing/Mexmil/Tokheim/Viking Air Tools	G/O/F	200	Running	24	36	10	43,500	0	43,500
9	20	3		Al Unser Jr.	Galles ECR Racing Tickets.com Starz Encore Superpak	G/O/F	200	Running	22	27	15	21,500	0	21,500
10	8	51		Eddie Cheever Jr.	#51 Excite@Home Indy Race Car	D/I/F	199	Running	20	55	6	42,500	5,000	47,500
11	13	14		Jeff Ward	Harrah's A.J. Foyt Racing	G/O/F	194	Running	19	45	9	41,300	0	41,300
12	5	6	R	Jeret Schroeder	Armour Swift-Eckrich	D/O/F	185	Running	18	29	14	40,300	0	40,300
13	21	15	R	Sarah Fisher	Walker Racing Cummins Special	R/O/F	183	Running	17	17	22	17,200	0	17,200
14	18	30		Ronnie Johncox	Jonathan Byrd's Cafeteria	G/O/F	181	Running	16	16	23	16,100	0	16,100
15	6	20		Tyce Carlson	Hubbard-Immke Racing	D/O/F	176	Running	15	32	11	37,100	0	37,100
16	2	28		Mark Dismore	On Star/GM BuyPower/Bryant Heating & Cooling	D/O/F	157	Running	16	30	13	36,000	0	36,000
17	19	18	R	Sam Hornish Jr.	Hornish Bros. Trucking/Advantage Powder Coating	G/O/F	151	Accident	13	23	20	34,900	0	34,900
18	10	16		Davey Hamilton	TeamXtreme/Lycos/USACredit.com/G Force	G/O/F	139	Handling	12	16	23	12,900	0	12,900
19	1	1		Greg Ray	Conseco/Menards	D/O/F	104	Accident	14	27	15	33,800	12,500	46,300
20	23	33	R	Bobby Regester	Miles of Hope	G/O/F	100	Accident	10	10	25	10,800	0	10,800
21	25	17	R	Niclas Jonsson	Nienhouse Motorsports Racing Special	G/O/F	84	Engine	9	27	15	10,800	0	10,800
22	24	88	R	Airton Daré	TeamXtreme/USACredit.com/G Force	G/O/F	74	Accident	8	27	15	32,800	0	32,800
23	15	12		Buzz Calkins	Bradley Food Marts/Sav-O-Mat	D/O/F	43	Accident	7	31	12	32,800	0	32,800
24	4	5		Robby McGehee	Energizer Advanced Formula/Energizer Motorsports	G/O/F	29	Accident	6	26	19	32,800	0	32,800
25	22	43	R	Doug Didero	Mid America Freight Systems/Western Star Trucks	D/O/F	24	Engine	5	21	21	32,800	0	32,800
26	14	27		Jimmy Kite	Founders Bank/ZMAX/Blueprint Racing Special	G/O/F	14	Engine	4	4	30	32,800	0	32,800
				Speedway Engines									600	600
				Comptech Engines									400	400
											TOTAL -	$1,000,000	$89,000	$1,089,000

Time of Race: 1:47:11.029   **Average Speed:** 111.957 mph   **Margin of Victory:** 4.191 sec.
Fastest Lap: #20 Tyce Carlson (Race lap 95, 164.782, 21.847 sec.) / **Fastest Leading Lap:** #8 Scott Sharp (Race lap 61, 164.632 mph, 21.867 sec.)
MBNA Pole Winner: #1 Greg Ray (176.566 mph, 20.389 sec.)
Firestone "First at 100" Award: #8 Scott Sharp   **Coors Light "Pit Performance" Award:** #81 Billy Boat
"The Net Race Live Award" Lap Leader: #8 Scott Sharp   **MCI WorldCom Long Distance Award:** #91 Buddy Lazier
Legend: R= Indy Racing Northern Light Series Rookie   **Chassis Legend:** D=Dallara (11); G=G Force (13); Riley & Scott (2)
Engine Legend: O=Oldsmobile (25); I=Nissan Infiniti (1)   **Tire Legend:** F=Firestone (26)

Lap Leaders:

Laps	Car#	Driver	Laps	Car#	Driver
1-18	#1	Greg Ray	151-155	#91	Buddy Lazier
19-29	#5	Robby McGehee	156-160	#24	Robbie Buhl
30-32	#8	Scott Sharp	161-200	#91	Buddy Lazier
33-45	#51	Eddie Cheever Jr.			
46-101	#8	Scott Sharp			
102-128	#7	Stephan Gregoire			
129-150	#3	Al Unser Jr.	**9 Lead changes among 8 drivers**		

Lap Leader Summary:

Driver	Times	Total
Scott Sharp	2	59
Buddy Lazier	2	45
Stephan Gregoire	1	27
Al Unser Jr.	1	22
Greg Ray	1	18
Eddie Cheever Jr.	1	13
Robby McGehee	1	11
Robbie Buhl	1	5

Caution Flags:

Laps	Reason/Incident
30-38	#5 McGehee accident T2
45-57	#12 Calkins accident T3
76-84	#88 Daré accident T3
98-103	tow in #20 Carlson
106-112	#1 Ray, #33 Regester accident T4
153-159	#18 Hornish accident T2
162-166	debris on track
Total: 7 caution flags, 56 laps	

INDY RACING NORTHERN LIGHT SERIES
Las Vegas Motor Speedway, Saturday, April 22, 2000

FP	SP	Car	Driver		Car Name	C/E/T	Laps Comp.	Running/ Reason Out	IRL Pts.	Total IRL Pts.	IRL Standings	IRL Awards	Designated Awards	Total Awards
1	21	3	Al Unser Jr.		Galles ECR Racing Tickets.com Starz Encore Superpak	G/O/F	208	Running	50	77	4	$94,400	$18,200	$112,600
2	1	28	Mark Dismore		On Star/GM BuyPower	D/O/F	208	Running	45	75	6	78,100	50,150	128,250
3	18	18	R	Sam Hornish Jr.	Hornish Bros. Trucking/Advantage Powder Coating	G/O/F	207	Running	35	58	11	66,300	2,650	68,950
4	8	6	R	Jeret Schroeder	Armour Swift-Eckrich/Tristarmall.com	D/O/F	207	Running	32	61	10	54,500	3,500	58,000
5	23	24		Robbie Buhl	Team Purex Dreyer & Reinbold Racing	G/O/F	207	Running	30	108	1	50,200	500	50,700
6	16	5		Robby McGehee	Mall.com/Energizer Advanced Formula	C/O/F	206	Running	28	54	13	44,900	0	44,900
7	5	81		Billy Boat	Team Pelfrey	D/O/F	206	Running	26	76	5	43,800	0	43,800
8	27	20		Tyce Carlson	Flamingo-Las Vegas/Hubbard-Immke/Dallara	D/O/F	205	Running	24	56	12	42,700	0	42,700
9	2	1		Greg Ray	Conseco/Menards	D/O/F	204	Running	24	51	16	42,700	0	42,700
10	22	33		Jaques Lazier	Miles of Hope/Exodus Communications/Team Truscelli	G/O/F	202	Running	20	27	23	19,700	0	19,700
11	7	51		Eddie Cheever Jr.	#51 Excite@Home Indy Race Car	D/I/F	201	Running	19	74	7	40,500	5,500	46,000
12	10	4		Scott Goodyear	Pennzoil Panther Dallara	D/O/F	192	Oil fitting	18	90	3	39,500	0	39,500
13	24	30		Ronnie Johncox	WorldBestBuy.com	G/O/F	188	Running	17	33	20	38,500	0	38,500
14	11	88	R	Airton Daré	TeamXtreme/USACredit.com/G Force	G/O/F	171	Gearbox	16	43	17	37,300	0	37,300
15	9	55	R	Jason Leffler	EPSON	G/O/F	167	Accident	15	15	27	14,300	0	14,300
16	17	27		Jimmy Kite	Founders Bank/Blueprint Racing Special	G/O/F	147	Running	14	18	26	13,300	0	13,300
17	12	15	R	Sarah Fisher	Walker Racing Cummins Special	R/O/F	126	Accident	13	30	22	12,100	0	12,100
18	4	11		Eliseo Salazar	Rio A.J. Foyt Racing	G/O/F	126	Accident	12	74	7	34,100	10,000	44,100
19	26	43	R	Doug Didero	Mid America Freight Systems/Western Star Trucks	D/O/F	115	Engine	11	32	21	11,100	0	11,100
20	28	16		Davey Hamilton	FreeInternet.com/TeamXtreme/G Force	G/O/F	89	Suspension	10	26	25	10,000	0	10,000
21	6	14		Jeff Ward	Harrah's A.J. Foyt Racing	G/O/F	87	Accident	9	54	13	32,000	0	32,000
22	20	91		Buddy Lazier	Delta Faucet/Coors Light/Tae-Bo/Hemelgarn Racing	R/O/F	65	Fuel pump	8	98	2	32,000	0	32,000
23	14	17		Scott Harrington	Nienhouse Motorsports Racing Special	D/O/F	65	Electrical	7	7	31	10,000	0	10,000
24	25	21		Jack Miller	Milk Chug/Century 21/Opalescence	D/O/F	54	Electrical	6	6	32	10,000	0	10,000
25	19	12		Buzz Calkins	Bradley Food Marts/Sav-O-Mat	D/O/F	45	Fuel pressure	5	36	19	32,000	0	32,000
26	13	98		Donnie Beechler	Cahill Racing/Race Car Café-Las Vegas	D/O/F	32	Accident	4	67	9	32,000	0	32,000
27	3	8		Scott Sharp	Delphi Automotive Systems/MCI WorldCom	D/O/F	22	Engine	4	52	15	32,000	0	32,000
28	15	7		Stephan Gregoire	Mexmil/Tokheim/Viking Air Tools/Dick Simon Racing	G/O/F	3	Accident	2	38	18	32,000	0	32,000
				Comptech Engines									600	600
				Speedway Engines									400	400
											TOTAL -	$1,000,000	$91,500	$1,091,500

Time of Race: 2:16:57.045 **Average Speed:** 136.691 mph **Margin of Victory:** 12.531 sec.

Fastest Lap: #28 Mark Dismore (Race lap 180, 204.623 mph, 26.390 sec.) **Fastest Leading Lap:** #28 Mark Dismore (Race lap 33, 203.459 mph, 26.541 sec.)

MBNA Pole Winner: #28 Mark Dismore (208.502 mph, 25.899 sec.)

Firestone "First at 100" Award: #11 Eliseo Salazar **Coors Light "Pit Performance" Award:** #28 Mark Dismore

"The Net Race Live Award" Lap Leader: #28 Mark Dismore **MCI WorldCom Long Distance Award:** #3 Al Unser Jr.

Legend: R= Indy Racing Northern Light Series Rookie **Chassis Legend:** D=Dallara (13); G=G Force (13); Riley & Scott (2)

Engine Legend: O=Oldsmobile (27); I=Nissan Infiniti (1) **Tire Legend:** F=Firestone (28)

Lap Leaders:

Laps	Car#	Driver	Laps	Car#	Driver
1-34	#28	Mark Dismore	124-155	#28	Mark Dismore
35	#11	Eliseo Salazar	156-158	#4	Scott Goodyear
36-62	#1	Greg Ray	159-171	#88	Airton Daré
63-78	#28	Mark Dismore	172-188	#4	Scott Goodyear
79-86	#5	Robby McGehee	189-208	#3	Al Unser Jr.
87-96	#28	Mark Dismore	**Total: 11 Lead changes among 7 drivers**		
97-123	#11	Eliseo Salazar			

Lap Leader Summary:

Driver	Times	Total
Mark Dismore	4	92
Eliseo Salazar	2	28
Greg Ray	1	27
Scott Goodyear	2	20
Al Unser Jr.	1	20
Airton Daré	1	13
Robby McGehee	1	8

Caution Flags:

Laps	Reason/Incident
5-14	#7 Gregoire accident T4
24-26	#21 Miller stopped on track
34-38	#98 Beechler accident T4
88-95	#14 Ward accident T2
122-125	#43 Didero car stopped T2 warmup lane
127-136	#15 Fisher, #11 Salazar accident T4
169-175	#55 Leffler accident T2

Total: 7 caution flags, 47 laps

INDY RACING NORTHERN LIGHT SERIES
Indianapolis Motor Speedway, Sunday, May 28, 2000

FP	SP	Car		Driver	Car Name	C/E/T	Laps Comp.	Running/ Reason Out	IRL Pts.	Total IRL Pts.	IRL Standings	IRL Awards	Designated Awards	Total Awards
1	2	9	R	Juan Montoya	Target	G/O/F	200	Running	54	54	18	$832,040	$403,650	$1,235,690
2	16	91	W	Buddy Lazier	Delta Faucet/Coors Light/Tae-Bo/Hemelgarn Racing	D/O/F	200	Running	40	138	1	500,655	73,945	574,600
3	3	11		Eliseo Salazar	Rio A.J. Foyt Racing	G/O/F	200	Running	36	110	4	382,655	92,245	474,900
4	6	14		Jeff Ward	Harrah's A.J. Foyt Racing	G/O/F	200	Running	32	86	8	304,655	56,345	361,000
5	10	51	W	Eddie Cheever Jr.	#51 Excite@Home Indy Race Car	D/I/F	200	Running	30	104	5	293,655	70,845	364,500
6	4	32		Robby Gordon	Turtle Wax/Burger King/Moen/Johns Manville/Menards	D/O/F	200	Running	28	28	26	186,655	29,700	216,355
7	7	10		Jimmy Vasser	Target	G/O/F	199	Running	26	26	29	178,655	28,850	207,505
8	20	7		Stephan Gregoire	Mexmil/Tokheim/Viking Air Tools/Dick Simon Racing	G/O/F	199	Running	24	62	15	272,655	34,245	306,900
9	13	4		Scott Goodyear	Pennzoil Panther Dallara	D/O/F	199	Running	22	112.	2	266,655	82,145	348,800
10	5	8		Scott Sharp	Delphi Automotive Systems/MCI WorldCom	D/O/F	198	Running	20	72	12	262,655	50,345	313,000
11	11	28		Mark Dismore	On Star/GM BuyPower/Bryant Heating & Cooling	D/O/F	198.00	Running	19.00	94.00	6.00	259,655	34,845	294,500
12	15	98		Donnie Beechler	Cahill Racing	D/O/F	198	Running	18	85.00	9.00	256,655	26,345	283,000
13	26	33	R	Jaques Lazier	Miles of Hope/Truscelli Team Racing	G/O/F	198.00	Running	17.00	44	21	259,655	30,595	290,250
14	29	6		Jeret Schroeder	Kroger/Tri Star Motorsports Inc.	D/O/F	198	Running	16	77	11	251,655	27,345	279,000
15	31	41		Billy Boat	Harrah's A.J. Foyt Racing	G/O/F	198	Running	15	91	7	148,655	62,345	211,000
16	24	55		Raul Boesel	EPSON	G/O/F	197	Running	14	14	31	171,655	41,345	213,000
17	17	50	R	Jason Leffler	UnitedAuto Group Special	G/O/F	197	Running	13	28.00	26.00	144,655	26,250	170,905
18	22	12		Buzz Calkins	Bradley Motorsports/Team CAN	D/O/F	194	Running	12	48	19.00	142,655	26,345	169,000
19	27	23		Steve Knapp	Team Purex Dreyer & Reinbold Racing	G/I/F	193	Running	11	11.00	32.00	140,655	26,345	167,000
20	28	16		Davey Hamilton	FreeInternet.com/TeamXtreme/G Force	G/O/F	188	Running	10	36.00	22.00	138,655	27,845	166,500
21	12	5		Robby McGehee	Meijer/Energizer Advanced Formula/Mall.com	G/O/F	187	Running	9	63	14	236,655	44,745	281,400
22	30	22		Johnny Unser	Delco-Remy/Microdigicom/Homier Tools/G Force/Olds	G/O/F	186	Running	8	8	35	135,655	25,345	161,000
23	8	92		Stan Wattles	Hemelgarn/Metro Racing	D/O/F	172	Engine	7	7.00	37.00	133,655	25,345	159,000
24	14	18	R	Sam Hornish Jr.	Hornish Bros. Trucking/Advantage Powder Coating	D/O/F	153	Accident	6	64.00	13.00	232,655	35,595	268,250
25	21	88	R	Airton Daré	TeamXtreme/USACredit.com/FreeInternet.com/G Force	G/O/F	126	Engine	5.00	48.00	19.00	231,655	30,595	262,250
26	9	24		Robbie Buhl	Dreyer & Reinbold Racing	G/O/F	99	Engine	4.00	112.00	2	230,655	27,845	258,500
27	23	75		Richie Hearn	Pagan Racing IRL Spcl.	D/O/F	97.00	Electrical	3.00	3.00	41.00	129,655	25,345	155,000
28	33	48	R	Andy Hillenburg	Sumar Special By Irwindale Speedway	D/O/F	91.00	Wheel Bearing	2.00	2.00	42.00	128,655	25,595	154,250
29	18	3	W	Al Unser Jr.	Galles ECR Racing Tickets.com Starz Encore Superpak	G/O/F	89.00	Over Heating	1.00	78.00	10.00	227,655	28,345	256,000
30	25	27		Jimmy Kite	Big Daddy's BBQ/Founders Bank/Blueprint Racing Spl.	G/O/F	74.00	Engine	1.00	19.00	30.00	137,655	26,345	164,000
31	19	15	R	Sarah Fisher	Walker Racing Cummins Special	D/O/F	71.00	Accident	1.00	31.00	25.00	126,655	39,095	165,750
32	32	90		Lyn St. James	Yellow Freight System	G/O/F	69.00	Accident	1.00	1.00	43.00	126,655	25,345	152,000
33	1	1		Greg Ray	Team Conseco/Quaker State/Moen/Menards	D/O/F	67.00	Accident	4.00	55.00	17.00	226,655	162,045	388,700
	NQ	81		Billy Boat	Team Pelfrey								1,000	1,000
					Speedway Engines								1,000	1,000
					Team Menard Engines								500	500
					Ed Pink Racing Engines								500	500
												TOTAL - $7,700,000	$1,776,505	$9,476,505

(Event Record)

Time of Race: 2:58:59.431 **Average Speed:** 167.607 mph **Margin of Victory:** 7.184 sec. **Fastest Lap:** #91 Buddy Lazier (Race lap 198, 218.494 mph, 41.191 sec.)
Fastest Leading Lap: #9 Juan Montoya (Race lap 199, 217.691 mph, 41.343 sec.) **PPG Pole Winner:** #1 Greg Ray (223.471 mph, 2:41.095) **MBNA "Fastest Bump Day Qualifier" Award:** #55 Raul Boesel (222.113 mph, 2:42.080)
Firestone "First at 100" Award: #9 Juan Montoya **"The Net Race Live Award" Lap Leader:** #9 Juan Montoya **RaceSearch.com "Top Finishing Rookie" Award:** #9 Juan Montoya **WorldCom Long Distance Award:** #41 Billy Boat
Coors Light Pit Stop Contest: #4 Scott Goodyear, Panther Racing **Legend:** R= Indianapolis 500-Mile Race Rookie, W= Former Indianapolis 500-Mile Race Winner **Chassis Legend:** D=Dallara (15); G=G Force (18)
Engine Legend: O=Oldsmobile (31); I=Nissan Infiniti (2) **Tire Legend:** F=Firestone (33)

Lap Leaders:

Laps	Car	Driver
1-26	#1	Greg Ray
27-29	#9	Juan Montoya
30	#10	Jimmy Vasser
31-32	#5	Robby McGehee
33-175	#9	Juan Montoya
176-179	#10	Jimmy Vasser
180-200	#9	Juan Montoya

Total: 6 lead changes among 4 drivers

Caution Flags:

Laps	Reason/Incident
66-70	#1 Ray, accident T2
74-84	#90 St. James, #15 Fisher, accident T1
99-102	Debris
127-130	Oil on track
144-150	#1 Ray, accident T2
158-161	#18 Hornish Jr., accident T2
174-177	Oil on track

Total: 7 caution flags, 39 laps

Lap Leader Summary:

Driver	Times	Total
Juan Montoya	3	167
Greg Ray	1	26
Jimmy Vasser	2	5
Robby McGehee	1	2

INDY RACING NORTHERN LIGHT SERIES
Texas Motor Speedway, Sunday, June 11, 2000

FP	SP		Car	Driver	Car Name	C/E/T	Laps Comp.	Running/ Reason Out	IRL Pts.	Total IRL Pts.	IRL Standings	IRL Awards	Designated Awards	Total Awards
1	12		8	Scott Sharp	Delphi Automotive Systems/MCI WorldCom	D/O/F	208	Running	50	122	6	$95,500	$28,800	$124,300
2	14		5	Robby McGehee	Mall.com	G/O/F	208	Running	40	103	9	79,200	2,250	81,450
3	9		3	Al Unser Jr.	Galles ECR Racing Tickets.com Starz Encore Superpak	G/O/F	208	Running	37	115	8	67,100	31,950	99,050
4	19		12	Buzz Calkins	Bradley Food Marts/Sav-O-Mat	D/O/F	208	Running	32	80	15	55,100	0	55,100
5	3		4	Scott Goodyear	Pennzoil Panther Dallara	D/O/F	208	Running	30	142	2	50,700	500	51,200
6	6		28	Mark Dismore	On Star/GM BuyPower	D/O/F	208	Running	28	122	6	45,300	0	45,300
7	1		91	Buddy Lazier	Delta Faucet/Coors Light/Tae-Bo/Hemelgarn Racing	D/O/F	207	Running	26	164	1	44,200	0	44,200
8	26	R	55	Shigeaki Hattori	EPSON	G/O/F	207	Running	24	24	31	21,100	10,000	31,100
9	5		51	Eddie Cheever Jr.	#51 Excite@Home Indy Race Car	D/I/F	207	Running	22	126	3	43,100	6,000	49,100
10	20	R	88	Airton Daré	TeamXtreme/USACredit.com/FreeInternet.com/G Force	G/O/F	207	Running	20	68	19	42,000	500	42,500
11	15		7	Stephan Gregoire	Mexmil/Tokheim/Viking Air Tools/Cigarette	G/O/F	205	Running	19	81	14	40,900	0	40,900
12	25	R	15	Sarah Fisher	Walker Racing Cummins Special	D/O/F	204	Running	18	49	22	17,800	0	17,800
13	16		20	Tyce Carlson	Hubbard-Immke Racing Dallara	D/O/F	204	Running	17	73	17	38,800	0	38,800
14	18		33	Jaques Lazier	Truscelli Team Racing	G/O/F	204	Running	16	60	20	37,600	0	37,600
15	17		1	Greg Ray	Conseco/Quaker State/Menards	D/O/F	202	Engine	15	70	18	36,600	0	36,600
16	23		27	Jimmy Kite	Big Daddy's BBQ/Founders Bank/Blueprint Racing Spl.	G/O/F	201	Running	14	33	25	13,500	0	13,500
17	4		11	Eliseo Salazar	Rio A.J. Foyt Racing	G/O/F	179	Engine	13	123	5	34,300	0	34,300
18	2		24	Robbie Buhl	Team Purex Dreyer & Reinbold Racing	G/I/F	179	Running	12	124	4	34,300	500	34,800
19	7		14	Jeff Ward	Harrah's A.J. Foyt Racing	G/O/F	168	Engine	11	97	11	33,300	0	33,300
20	13	R	18	Sam Hornish Jr.	Hornish Bros./Advantage Powder Coating/PDM Racing	D/O/F	131	Electrical	10	74	16	32,200	0	32,200
21	10	R	6	Jeret Schroeder	Kroger/Tristarmall.com	D/O/F	124	Gearbox	9	86	13	32,200	0	32,200
22	8		98	Donnie Beechler	Cahill Racing	D/O/F	115	Engine	8	93	12	32,200	0	32,200
23	11		81	Billy Boat	Team Pelfrey	D/O/F	107	Fuel Pump	7	98	10	32,200	0	32,200
24	22		16	Davey Hamilton	TeamXtreme/FreeInternet.com/G Force	G/O/F	84	Engine	6	42	23	10,200	0	10,200
25	27		19	Billy Roe	Logan Racing Special	D/O/F	60	Engine	5	5	42	10,200	0	10,200
26	21		30	Robby Unser	WorldBestBuy.com/Jonathan Bryd's Cafeteria	R/O/F	34	Mechanical	4	10	34	10,200	0	10,200
27	24	R	43	Doug Didero	Mid America Motorsports/Western Star Trucks	D/O/F	26	Handling	3	35	24	10,200	0	10,200
				Comptech Engines									600	600
				VDS Engines									400	400
											TOTAL -	$1,000,000	$81,500	$1,081,500

Time of Race: 1:47:19.835   **Average Speed:** 169.182 mph   **Margin of Victory:** 0.059 sec.

Fastest Lap: #51 Eddie Cheever Jr. (Race lap 61, 213.065, 24.584 sec.)   **Fastest Leading Lap:** #8 Scott Sharp (Race lap 179, 211.551 mph, 24.760 sec.)

MBNA Pole Winner: #28 Mark Dismore (208.502 mph, 25.899 sec.)

Firestone "First at 100" Award: #3 Al Unser Jr.   **Coors Light "Pit Performance" Award:** #3 Al Unser Jr.

"The Net Race Live Award" Lap Leader: #3 Al Unser Jr.   **WorldCom Long Distance Award:** #55 Shigeaki Hattori

Legend: R= Indy Racing Northern Light Series Rookie   **Chassis Legend:** D=Dallara (15); G=G Force (11); Riley & Scott (1)

Engine Legend: O=Oldsmobile (25); I=Nissan Infiniti (2)   **Tire Legend:** F=Firestone (27)

Lap Leaders:

Laps	Car#	Driver	Laps	Car#	Driver
1-2	#91	Buddy Lazier	82-86	#91	Buddy Lazier
3-4	#4	Scott Goodyear	87-87	#3	Al Unser Jr.
5-7	#91	Buddy Lazier	88-88	#91	Buddy Lazier
8-11	#4	Scott Goodyear	89-90	#3	Al Unser Jr.
12-16	#28	Mark Dismore	91-93	#91	Buddy Lazier
17-28	#91	Buddy Lazier	94-111	#3	Al Unser Jr.
29-29	#11	Eliseo Salazar	112-117	#51	Eddie Cheever Jr.
30-45	#91	Buddy Lazier	118-118	#5	Robby McGehee
46-54	#3	Al Unser Jr.	119-121	#28	Mark Dismore
55-55	#8	Scott Sharp	122-159	#3	Al Unser Jr.
56-62	#3	Al Unser Jr.	160-164	#91	Buddy Lazier
63-63	#91	Buddy Lazier	165-169	#28	Mark Dismore
64-65	#3	Al Unser Jr.	170-201	#8	Scott Sharp
66-78	#91	Buddy Lazier	202-203	#5	Robby McGehee
79-79	#3	Al Unser Jr.	204-208	#8	Scott Sharp
80-80	#91	Buddy Lazier			
81-81	#3	Al Unser Jr.	**Total: 31 Lead changes among 8 drivers**		

Lap Leader Summary:

Driver	Times	Total
Al Unser Jr.	9	79
Buddy Lazier	11	62
Scott Sharp	3	38
Mark Dismore	3	13
Scott Goodyear	2	6
Eddie Cheever Jr.	1	6
Robby McGehee	2	3
Eliseo Salazar	1	1

Caution Flags:

Laps	Reason/Incident
9-22	rain
62-67	#19 Roe, Engine smoking T4
171-176	#14 Ward, Engine T4
181-187	#14 Salazar, Engine T1

Total: 4 caution flags, 23 laps

INDY RACING NORTHERN LIGHT SERIES
Pikes Peak International Raceway, Sunday, June 18, 2000

FP	SP	Car	Driver	Car Name	C/E/T	Laps Comp.	Running/ Reason Out	IRL Pts.	Total IRL Pts.	IRL Standings	IRL Awards	Designated Awards	Total Awards
1	10	51	Eddie Cheever Jr.	#51 Excite@Home Indy Race Car	D/I/F	200	Running	50	176	1	$94,600	$29,800	$124,400
2	16	88 R	Airton Daré	Uproar.com/TeamXtreme/G Force	G/O/F	200	Running	40	108	14	79,000	13,950	92,950
3	4	8	Scott Sharp	Delphi Automotive Systems/MCI WorldCom	D/O/F	200	Running	37	159	3	67,200	21,250	88,450
4	3	28	Mark Dismore	On Star/GM BuyPower	D/O/F	199	Running	33	155	5	55,300	10,000	65,300
5	15	98	Donnie Beechler	Cahill Racing	D/O/F	198	Accident	30	123	9	51,000	500	51,500
6	6	11	Eliseo Salazar	Rio A.J. Foyt Racing	G/O/F	198	Running	28	151	6	45,700	0	45,700
7	5	6 R	Jeret Schroeder	Kroger/Tristarmall.com	D/O/F	198	Running	26	112	11	44,500	0	44,500
8	7	7	Stephan Gregoire	Mexmil/Tokheim/Viking Air Tools/Cigarette	G/O/F	198	Running	24	105	15	43,500	0	43,500
9	24	33	Jaques Lazier	Truscelli Team Racing	G/O/F	198	Running	22	82	20	43,500	5,000	48,500
10	18	3	Al Unser Jr.	Galles ECR Racing Tickets.com Starz Encore Superpak	G/O/F	197	Accident	20	135	7	42,500	0	42,500
11	20	20	Tyce Carlson	Hubbard Racing Dallara	D/O/F	197	Running	19	92	17	41,300	0	41,300
12	14	12	Buzz Calkins	Bradley Food Marts/Sav-O-Mat	D/O/F	197	Running	18	98	16	40,300	0	40,300
13	12	5	Robby McGehee	Mall.com	G/O/F	196	Running	17	120	10	39,200	0	39,200
14	8	16	Davey Hamilton	TeamXtreme/FreeInternet.com/G Force	G/O/F	195	Running	16	58	21	16,100	0	16,100
15	9	14	Jeff Ward	Harrah's A.J. Foyt Racing	G/O/F	195	Running	15	112	11	37,100	0	37,100
16	11	4	Scott Goodyear	Pennzoil Panther Dallara	D/O/F	194	Running	14	156	4	36,000	0	36,000
17	17	55 R	Shigeaki Hattori	EPSON	G/O/F	174	Running	13	37	26	12,900	0	12,900
18	21	81	Billy Boat	Team Pelfrey	D/O/F	158	Engine	12	110	13	34,900	0	34,900
19	19	18 R	Sam Hornish Jr.	PDM Racing/Uniden	G/O/F	108	Handling	11	85	18	33,800	0	33,800
20	1	1	Greg Ray	Conseco/Quaker State/Menards	D/O/F	95	Accident	13	83	19	32,800	12,500	45,300
21	26	30	Robby Unser	WorldBestBuy.com/Jonathan Byrd's Cafeteria	R/O/F	73	Handling	9	19	32	10,800	0	10,800
22	25	43 R	Doug Didero	Mid America Motorsports/Western Star Trucks	D/O/F	62	Engine	8	43	24	10,800	0	10,800
23	2	24	Robbie Buhl	Team Purex Dreyer & Reinbold Racing	G/I/F	61	Engine	9	133	8	32,800	0	32,800
24	23	27	Jimmy Kite	Big Daddy's BBQ/Founders Bank/Blueprint Racing Spl.	G/O/F	50	Fuel pressure	6	39	25	10,800	0	10,800
25	22	15 R	Sarah Fisher	Walker Racing Cummins Special	D/O/F	6	Accident	5	54	22	10,800	0	10,800
26	13	91	Buddy Lazier	Delta Faucet/Coors Light/Tae-Bo/Hemelgarn Racing	D/O/F	1	Engine	4	168	2	32,800	0	32,800
			Ed Pink Racing Engines									600	600
			Team Menard Engines									400	400
											TOTAL - $1,000,000	$94,000	$1,094,000

Time of Race: 1:28:44.257   **Average Speed:** 135.230 mph   **Margin of Victory:** under caution
Fastest Lap: #12 Buzz Calkins (Race lap 188, 167.131, 21.540 sec.)   **Fastest Leading Lap:** #8 Scott Sharp (Race lap 109, 167.108 mph, 21.543 sec.)
MBNA Pole Winner: #1 Greg Ray (179.874 mph, 20.014 sec., track record)
"The Net Race Live Award" Lap Leader: #8 Scott Sharp   WorldCom Long Distance Award: #33 Jaques Lazier
Firestone "First at 100" Award: #8 Scott Sharp   **Coors Light "Pit Performance" Award:** #28 Mark Dismore
Legend: R= Indy Racing Northern Light Series Rookie Chassis   **Legend:** D=Dallara (13); G=G Force (12); Riley & Scott (1)
Engine Legend: O=Oldsmobile (24); I=Nissan Infiniti (2)   Tire   **Legend:** F=Firestone (26)

Lap Leaders:

Laps	Car#	Driver	Laps	Car#	Driver
1-61	#24	Robbie Buhl	147-151	#8	Scott Sharp
62-133	#8	Scott Sharp	152-154	#28	Mark Dismore
134-143	#51	Eddie Cheever Jr.	155-171	#7	Stephan Gregoire
144-146	#98	Donnie Beechler	172-200	#51	Eddie Cheever Jr.

Total: 7 Lead changes among 6 drivers

Lap Leader Summary:

Driver	Times	Total
Scott Sharp	2	77
Robbie Buhl	1	61
Eddie Cheever Jr.	2	39
Stephan Gregoire	1	17
Mark Dismore	1	3
Donnie Beechler	1	3

Caution Flags:

Laps	Reason/Incident
7-15	#81 Boat spin T2, #15 Fisher, accident T2
62-66	#24 Buhl, engine
80-83	#55 Hattori, spin exiting T2
97-103	#1 Ray, accident T4
199-200	#3 A. Unser, #98 Beechler accident T1

Total: 5 caution flags, 27 laps

ROUND 7: MIDAS 500 CLASSIC

INDY RACING NORTHERN LIGHT SERIES
Atlanta Motor Speedway, Saturday July 15, 2000

FP	SP	Car	R	Driver	Car Name	C/E/T	Laps Comp.	Running/ Reason Out	IRL Pts.	Total IRL Pts.	IRL Standings	IRL Awards	Designated Awards	Total Awards
1	1	1		Greg Ray	Conseco/Quaker State/Menards	D/O/F	208	Running	55	138	11	$96,100	$47,300	$143,400
2	11	91		Buddy Lazier	Delta Faucet/Coors Light/Tae-Bo/Hemelgarn Racing	D/O/F	208	Running	40	208	1	80,100	18,450	98,550
3	24	3		Al Unser Jr.	Galles ECR Racing Tickets.com Starz Encore Superpak	G/O/F	208	Running	35	170	6	68,100	16,250	84,350
4	12	5		Robby McGehee	Treadway Racing	G/O/F	208	Running	32	152	10	56,000	0	56,000
5	3	98		Donnie Beechler	Cahill Racing	D/O/F	207	Running	31	154	9	51,500	500	52,000
6	8	24		Robbie Buhl	Team Purex Dreyer & Reinbold Racing	G/I/F	207	Running	28	161	8	46,100	5,500	51,600
7	20	7		Stephan Gregoire	Mexmil/Tokheim/Viking Air Tools/Cigarette	G/O/F	207	Running	26	131	13	45,000	0	45,000
8	19	81		Billy Boat	Team Pelfrey	D/O/F	207	Running	24	134	12	43,900	0	43,900
9	18	55	R	Shigeaki Hattori	EPSON	G/O/F	206	Running	22	59	23	28,200	5,000	33,200
10	2	11		Eliseo Salazar	Rio A.J. Foyt Racing	G/O/F	205	Running	22	173	4	42,900	0	42,900
11	16	4		Scott Goodyear	Pennzoil Panther Dallara	D/O/F	205	Running	19	175	3	41,700	0	41,700
12	25	27		Jimmy Kite	Big Daddy's BBQ/Blueprint Racing Special	G/O/F	199	Engine	18	57	24	24,900	0	24,900
13	15	20		Tyce Carlson	Hubbard Racing Dallara	D/O/F	196	Running	17	109	17	39,600	0	39,600
14	5	15	R	Sarah Fisher	Walker Racing Cummins Special	D/O/F	190	Accident	16	70	22	22,700	0	22,700
15	17	16		Davey Hamilton	freeinternet.com/TeamXtreme/G Force	G/O/F	184	Running	15	73	21	21,700	0	21,700
16	13	8		Scott Sharp	Delphi Automotive Systems/MCI WorldCom	D/O/F	179	Oil pressure	14	173	4	36,300	0	36,300
17	23	30		J.J. Yeley	WorldBestBuy.com/Jonathan Byrd's Cafeteria	G/O/F	177	Running	13	13	35	19,400	0	19,400
18	7	28		Mark Dismore	On Star/GM BuyPower	D/O/F	146	Engine	12	167	7	35,100	0	35,100
19	4	14		Jeff Ward	Harrah's A.J. Foyt Racing	G/O/F	123	Engine	11	123	14	34,100	0	34,100
20	21	43		Scott Harrington	Mid America Motorsports/Western Star Trucks	D/O/F	120	Engine	10	17	33	17,300	0	17,300
21	14	51		Eddie Cheever Jr.	#51 Excite@Home Indy Race Car	D/I/F	96	Engine	9	185	2	33,000	0	33,000
22	22	19	R	Stevie Reeves	Logan Racing Special	D/O/F	89	Engine	8	8	39	17,300	0	17,300
23	9	12		Buzz Calkins	Bradley Food Marts/Sav-O-Mat	D/O/F	68	Engine	7	105	18	33,000	0	33,000
24	6	6	R	Jeret Schroeder	Kroger/Tristarmall.com	D/O/F	37	Engine	6	118	15	33,000	0	33,000
25	10	88	R	Airton Daré	Uproar.com/TeamXtreme/G Force	G/O/F	13	Engine	5	113	16	33,000	0	33,000
				Team Menard Engines									600	600
				Speedway Engines									400	400
										TOTAL –		**$1,000,00**	**$94,000**	**$1,094,000**

Time of Race: 2:02:01.882   Average Speed: 153.403 mph   Margin of Victory: 3.054 sec.

Fastest Lap: #98 Donnie Beechler (Race lap 76, 214.626 mph, 25.160 sec.)   Fastest Leading Lap: #1 Greg Ray (Race lap 5, 214.209 mph, 25.209 sec.)"

MBNA Pole Winner: #1 Greg Ray (216.104 mph, 24.988 sec.)   Coors Light "Pit Performance" Award: #3 Al Unser Jr."

Firestone First at 100 Award: #1 Greg Ray   The Net Race Live Award Lap Leader: #1 Greg Ray"

WorldCom Long Distance Award: #3 Al Unser Jr.   RaceSearch.com Top Finishing Rookie: #55 Shigeaki Hattori

Legend: R= Indy Racing Northern Light Series Rookie   Chassis Legend: D=Dallara (14); G=G Force (11)

Engine Legend: O=Oldsmobile (23); I=Nissan Infiniti (2)   Tire Legend: F=Firestone (25)

Lap Leaders:

Laps	Car#	Driver	Laps	Car#	Driver
1-40	#1	Greg Ray	76-78	#28	Mark Dismore
41-44	#98	Donnie Beechler	79-122	#1	Greg Ray
45-52	#28	Mark Dismore	123-124	#28	Mark Dismore
53-69	#1	Greg Ray	125-156	#1	Greg Ray
70-71	#20	Tyce Carlson	157-158	#91	Buddy Lazier
72-74	#28	Mark Dismore	159	#5	Robby McGehee
75	#51	Eddie Cheever Jr.	160-208	#1	Greg Ray

Total: 13 Lead changes among 7 drivers

Lap Leader Summary:

Driver	Times	Total
Greg Ray	5	182
Mark Dismore	4	16
Donnie Beechler	1	4
Tyce Carlson	1	2
Buddy Lazier	1	2
Eddie Cheever Jr.	1	1
Robby McGehee	1	1

Caution Flags:

Laps	Reason/Incident
14-18	#88 Daré, spin front straightaway
40-43	#43 Harrington, stalled T1
69-73	#12 Calkins, stalled T1/T2
138-142	Debris on track
147-163	#28 Dismore, oil on track
194-198	#15 Fisher, accident T4

Total: 6 caution flags, 41 laps

ROUND 8: THE BELTERRA RESORT INDY 300

INDY RACING NORTHERN LIGHT SERIES
Kentucky Speedway, Sunday, Aug. 27, 2000

FP	SP	Car		Driver	Car Name	C/E/T	Laps Comp.	Running/ Reason Out	IRL Pts.	Total IRL Pts.	IRL Standings	IRL Awards	Designated Awards	Total Awards
1	7	91		Buddy Lazier	Delta Faucet/Coors Light/Tae-Bo/Hemelgarn Racing	D/O/F	200	Running	50	258	1	$95,500	$30,800	$126,300
2	1	4		Scott Goodyear	Pennzoil Panther Dallara	D/O/F	200	Running	45	220	2	79,200	34,550	113,750
3	4	15	R	Sarah Fisher	Walker Racing Cummins Special	D/O/F	200	Running	35	105	20	47,850	6,150	54,000
4	15	51		Eddie Cheever Jr.	#51 Excite@Home Indy Race Car	D/I/F	200	Running	32	217	3	55,100	6,000	61,100
5	21	7		Stephan Gregoire	Team Mexmil/Tokheim/Viking Air Tools/Cigarette	G/O/F	199	Running	30	161	12	50,700	5,500	56,200
6	5	14		Jeff Ward	Harrah's A.J. Foyt Racing	G/O/F	199	Running	28	151	13	45,300	0	45,300
7	3	1		Greg Ray	Conseco/Quaker State/Menards	D/O/F	199	Running	27	165	11	44,200	0	44,200
8	17	55	R	Shigeaki Hattori	EPSON	G/O/F	199	Running	24	83	23	43,100	0	43,100
9	20	18	R	Sam Hornish Jr.	Dubois Nordson USAF PDM Racing	D/O/F	199	Running	22	107	19	23,850	0	23,850
10	8	98		Donnie Beechler	Cahill Racing	D/O/F	198	Running	20	174	8	42,000	0	42,000
11	24	28		Mark Dismore	On Star/Bryant Heating & Cooling/GM BuyPower	D/O/F	198	Running	19	186	4	40,900	0	40,900
12	11	12		Buzz Calkins	Bradley Food Marts/Sav-O-Mat	D/O/F	197	Running	18	123	16	39,800	0	39,800
13	16	24		Robbie Buhl	Team Purex Dreyer & Reinbold Racing	G/I/F	196	Running	17	178	7	38,800	0	38,800
14	19	5		Robby McGehee	Meijer	G/O/F	196	Running	16	168	10	37,600	0	37,600
15	26	30		J.J. Yeley	WorldBestBuy.com/Jonathan Byrd's Cafeteria	G/E/T	189	Running	15	28	28	17,350	0	17,350
16	9	16		Davey Hamilton	Freeinternet.com/TeamXtreme	G/O/F	185	Running	14	87	22	16,250	0	16,250
17	12	27		Jimmy Kite	Aramis/Blueprint Racing Special	G/O/F	155	Engine	13	70	24	15,050	0	15,050
18	22	81		Billy Boat	Team Pelfrey	D/O/F	154	CV joint	12	146	14	34,300	0	34,300
19	23	88	R	Airton Daré	Uproar.com/TeamXtreme	G/O/F	133	Bell Housing	11	124	15	33,300	0	33,300
20	10	43		Jaques Lazier	Mid America Freight Systems/Western Star Trucks	D/O/F	121	Engine	10	92	21	12,950	10,000	22,950
21	27	19	R	Stevie Reeves	Logan Racing Special	D/O/F	97	CV joint	9	17	34	12,950	0	12,950
22	13	20		Tyce Carlson	Hubbard Racing Dallara	D/O/F	70	Gear box	8	117	18	32,200	0	32,200
23	25	40		Roberto Guerrero	Team Coulson Racing Zali	G/O/F	48	Engine	7	7	42	12,950	0	12,950
24	18	8		Scott Sharp	Delphi Automotive Systems/WorldCom	D/O/F	16	Engine	6	179	6	32,200	0	32,200
25	2	11		Eliseo Salazar	Rio A.J. Foyt Racing	G/O/F	2	Accident	7	180	5	32,200	0	32,200
26	6	6	R	Jeret Schroeder	Kroger/Tri Star Motorsports Inc.	D/O/F	2	Accident	4	122	17	32,200	0	32,200
27	14	3		Al Unser Jr.	Galles ECR Racing Tickets.com Starz Encore Superpak	G/O/F	2	Accident	3	173	9	32,200	0	32,200
				Speedway Engines								600	600
				Comptech Engines								400	400
											TOTAL -	$1,000,000	$94,000	$1,094,000

Time of Race: 1:49:21.309　Average Speed: 164.601 mph　Margin of Victory: 1.879 sec.
Fastest Lap: #91 Buddy Lazier (Race lap 154, 218.438, 24.721 sec.)　Fastest Leading Lap: #91 Buddy Lazier (Race lap 48, 217.742 mph, 24.800 sec.)
MBNA Pole Winner: #4 Scott Goodyear (219.191 mph, 24.636 sec.)　RaceSearch.com Top Finishing Rookie: #15 Sarah Fisher
Firestone "First at 100" Award: #43 Jaques Lazier　Coors Light "Pit Performance" Award: #4 Scott Goodyear
"The Net Race Live Award" Lap Leader: #4 Scott Goodyear　WorldCom Long Distance Award: #7 Stephan Gregoire
Legend: R= Indy Racing Northern Light Series Rookie　Chassis Legend: D=Dallara (15); G=G Force (12)
Engine Legend: O=Oldsmobile (25); I=Nissan Infiniti (2)　Tire Legend: F=Firestone (27)

Lap Leaders:

Laps	Car#	Driver	Laps	Car#	Driver
1-2	#11	Eliseo Salazar	98-103	#43	Jaques Lazier
3-31	#4	Scott Goodyear	104-106	#28	Mark Dismore
32-40	#18	Sam Hornish Jr.	107-138	#4	Scott Goodyear
41-55	#91	Buddy Lazier	139-154	#27	Jimmy Kite
56-66	#14	Jeff Ward	155-157	#91	Buddy Lazier
67-93	#18	Sam Hornish Jr.	158-161	#4	Scott Goodyear
94-95	#43	Jaques Lazier	162-170	#15	Sarah Fisher
96-97	#18	Sam Hornish Jr.	171-200	#91	Buddy Lazier

Total: 15 Lead changes among 9 drivers

Lap Leader Summary:

Driver	Times	Total
Scott Goodyear	3	65
Buddy Lazier	3	48
Sam Hornish Jr.	3	38
Jimmy Kite	1	16
Jeff Ward	1	11
Sarah Fisher	1	9
Jaques Lazier	2	8
Mark Dismore	1	3
Eliseo Salazar	1	2

Caution Flags:

Laps	Reason/Incident
3-16	#6 Schroeder, #11 Salazar, #3 Unser Jr.
	#8 Sharp T2 Accident
52-57	debris on track
102-106	#19 Reeves fire, wheel bearing
115-117	debris on track

Total: 4 caution flags, 28 laps

INDY RACING NORTHERN LIGHT SERIES
Texas Motor Speedway, Sunday, October 15, 2000

FP	SP	Car		Driver	Car Name	C/E/T	Laps Comp.	Running/ Reason Out	IRL Pts.	Total IRL Pts.	IRL Standings	IRL Awards	Designated Awards	Total Awards
1	2	4		Scott Goodyear	Pennzoil Panther Dallara	D/O/F	208	Running	52	272	2	$95,500	$28,200	$123,700
2	10	51		Eddie Cheever Jr.	#51 Excite@Home Indy Race Car	D/I/F	208	Running	40	257	3	79,200	7,650	86,850
3	22	81		Billy Boat	Team Pelfrey	D/O/F	208	Running	35	181	10	67,100	6,650	73,750
4	6	91		Buddy Lazier	Delta Faucet/Coors Light/Tae-Bo/Hemelgarn Racing	D/O/F	208	Running	32	290	1	55,100	1,000	56,100
5	21	11		Eliseo Salazar	Rio A.J. Foyt Racing	G/O/F	207	Running	30	210	4	50,700	0	50,700
6	16	98		Donnie Beechler	Cahill Racing	D/O/F	207	Running	28	202	6	45,300	0	45,300
7	15	55	R	Shigeaki Hattori	EPSON	G/O/F	207	Running	26	109	22	44,200	15,000	59,200
8	3	14		Jeff Ward	Harrah's A.J. Foyt Racing	G/O/F	207	Running	25	176	11	43,100	0	43,100
9	17	12		Buzz Calkins	Bradley Food Marts/Sav-O-Mat	D/O/T	207	Running	22	145	15	43,100	0	43,100
10	12	16		Jaques Lazier	Nabisco/TeamXtreme/G Force	G/O/F	207	Running	20	112	20	20,000	0	20,000
11	13	15	R	Sarah Fisher	Walker Racing Cummins Special	D/O/F	206	Running	19	124	18	18,900	0	18,900
12	19	88	R	Airton Daré	Uproar.com/TeamXtreme Racing	G/O/F	205	Running	18	142	16	39,800	0	39,800
13	24	8		Scott Sharp	Delphi Automotive Systems/WorldCom	D/O/F	200	Running	17	196	7	38,800	0	38,800
14	11	28		Mark Dismore	On Star/GM BuyPower/Bryant Heating & Cooling	D/O/F	189	Running	16	202	5	37,600	0	37,600
15	25	21	R	Zak Morioka	Revista Motors/Tri Star Motorsports	D/O/F	187	Accident	15	15	36	14,600	0	14,600
16	14	6	R	Jeret Schroeder	Kroger/Tristarmall.com	D/O/F	165	Running	14	136	17	35,500	0	35,500
17	4	3		Al Unser Jr.	Galles ECR Racing Tickets.com Starz Encore Superpak	G/O/F	155	Clutch	15	188	9	34,300	20,000	54,300
18	5	24		Robbie Buhl	Team Purex Dreyer & Reinbold Racing	G/I/F	148	Engine	12	190	8	34,300	0	34,300
19	7	43		Davey Hamilton	Western Star Trucks/PetroMoly Special	D/O/F	140	Wheel bearing	11	98	23	11,300	0	11,300
20	23	7		Stephan Gregoire	Team Mexmil/Tokheim/Viking Air Tools/Cigarette	G/O/F	116	Running	10	171	14	32,200	0	32,200
21	20	27		Jimmy Kite	National Sports Management/Blueprint Racing Special	G/O/F	89	Engine	9	79	24	10,200	0	10,200
22	26	19	R	Stevie Reeves	Logan Racing Special	D/O/F	80	Engine	8	25	33	10,200	0	10,200
23	9	20		Tyce Carlson	Hubbard Racing Dallara	D/O/F	67	Engine	7	124	19	32,200	0	32,200
24	8	5		Robby McGehee	Broadband Investment Group	G/O/F	62	Electrical	6	174	12	32,200	0	32,200
25	27	30		J.J. Yeley	WorldBestBuy.com/Jonathan Byrd's Cafeteria	G/O/F	27	Oil pressure	5	33	28	10,200	0	10,200
26	1	1		Greg Ray	Conseco/Quaker State/Menards	D/O/F	18	Electrical	7	172	13	32,200	12,500	44,700
27	18	18	R	Sam Hornish Jr.	Uniden Bearcat Scanners	D/O/F	8	Engine	3	110	21	32,200	0	32,200
					Ed Pink Engines								600	600
					Speedway Engines								400	400
											TOTAL -	$1,000,000	$92,000	$1,092,000

Time of Race: 1:43:35.926   **Average Speed:** 175.276 mph   **Margin of Victory:** 0.140 sec.
Fastest Lap: #16 Jaques Lazier (Race lap 206, 216.205, 24.227 sec.)   **Fastest Leading Lap:** #3 Al Unser Jr. (Race lap 65, 213.822 mph, 24.497 sec.)
MBNA Pole Winner: #1 Greg Ray (215.352 mph, 24.323 sec.) RaceSearch.com   **Top Finishing Rookie:** #55 Shigeaki Hattori
Firestone "First at 100" Award: #3 Al Unser Jr.   **Coors Light "Pit Performance" Award:** #55 Shigeaki Hattori
"The Net Race Live Award" Lap Leader: #3 Al Unser Jr.   **WorldCom Long Distance Award:** #81 Billy Boat
Legend: R= Indy Racing Northern Light Series Rookie   **Chassis Legend:** D=Dallara (16); G=G Force (11)
Engine Legend: O=Oldsmobile (25); I=Nissan Infiniti (2)   **Tire Legend:** F=Firestone (27)

Lap Leaders:

Laps	Car#	Driver		Laps	Car#	Driver
1-1	#4	Scott Goodyear		122-135	#51	Eddie Cheever Jr.
2-33	#3	Al Unser Jr.		136-143	#4	Scott Goodyear
34-48	#4	Scott Goodyear		144-145	#24	Robbie Buhl
49-49	#3	Al Unser Jr.		146-146	#81	Billy Boat
50-50	#16	Jaques Lazier		147-156	#4	Scott Goodyear
51-52	#8	Scott Sharp		157-194	#91	Buddy Lazier
53-100	#3	Al Unser Jr.		195-206	#51	Eddie Cheever Jr.
101-103	#4	Scott Goodyear		207-208	#4	Scott Goodyear
104-121	#3	Al Unser Jr.				

Total: 16 Lead changes among 8 drivers

Lap Leader Summary:

Driver	Times	Total
Al Unser Jr.	4	99
Scott Goodyear	6	39
Buddy Lazier	1	38
Eddie Cheever Jr.	2	26
Scott Sharp	1	2
Robbie Buhl	1	2
Jaques Lazier	1	1
Billy Boat	1	1

Caution Flags:

Laps	Reason/Incident
68-71	#20 Carlson, tow-in
86-94	#19 Reeves, oil on track
155-159	#6 Schroeder, tow-in
193-198	#21 Morioka, accident T2

Total: 4 caution flags, 24 laps

DON'T SET THE PACE.
DEMOLISH IT.

The speed, skill and tradition of the world's most time-honored auto racing series are yours to experience with INDY RACING® 2000. INDY RACING® 2000 is the only official Indy Racing® game available, capturing all the excitement and high-speed action of racing 225 mph toward victory.

INDY RACING 2000®

Race as 20 of Indy Racing's® biggest superstars on official Indy Racing® tracks!

Intense arcade racing action!

Go head to head with Multi-Player Split-Screen mode!

Dominate beyond Indy Racing®: 8 open wheel road courses with Midget, Sprint and Formula cars!

Track	Date	Winner (start)	Time of Race	Average Speed (mph)	Margin of Victory	Second	Third	Fourth	Fifth
WDWS	1/29/00	Robbie Buhl (22)	1:57:18.676	102.292 mph	3.165 sec.	B. Lazier	Cheever	Goodyear	Salazar
PIR	3/19/00	Buddy Lazier (26)	1:47:11:029	111.957 mph	4.191 sec.	Goodyear	Beechler	Salazar	Sharp
LVMS	4/22/00	Al Unser Jr. (21)	2:16:57.045	136.691 mph	12.531 sec.	Dismore	Hornish	Schroeder	Buhl
IMS	5/28/00	Juan Montoya (2)	2:58:59.431	167.607 mph	7.184 sec.	B. Lazier	Salazar	Ward	Cheever
TMS 1	6/11/00	Scott Sharp (12)	1:47:19.835	169.182 mph	.059 sec.	McGehee	A. Unser	Calkins	Goodyear
PPIR	6/18/00	Eddie Cheever Jr. (10)	1:28:44.257	135.230 mph	Under caution	Daré	Sharp	Dismore	Beechler
AMS	7/15/00	Greg Ray (1)	2:02:01.882	153.403 mph	3.054 sec.	B. Lazier	A. Unser	McGehee	Beechler
KS	8/27/00	Buddy Lazier (7)	1:49:21.309	164.601 mph	1.879 sec.	Goodyear	Fisher	Cheever	Gregoire
TMS 2	10/15/00	Scott Goodyear (2)	1:43:35.926	175.276 mph	.140 sec.	Cheever	Boat	Lazier	Salazar

Track	Pole (finish)	Average Speed	Starters	Running at Finish	Cars On Lead Lap	Race Leaders	Lead Changes	Caution Flags	Laps Under Caution
WDWS	Entrant Points*	—	26	19	10	8	11	8	65
PIR	Greg Ray (19)	176.566	26	16	9	8	9	7	56
LVMS	Mark Dismore (2)	208.502	28	13	2	7	11	7	47
IMS	Greg Ray (33)	223.471	33	22	6	4	6	7	39
TMS 1	Entrant Points**	—	27	17	6	8	31	4	23
PPIR	Greg Ray (20)	179.874	26	15	3	6	7	5	27
AMS	Greg Ray (1)	216.104	25	14	4	7	13	6	41
KS	Scott Goodyear (2)	219.191	27	16	4	9	15	4	28
TMS 2	Greg Ray (26)	215.352	27	16	4	8	16	4	24

*Greg Ray started the race from the number one position based on 1999 entrant points as qualifications were rained out.

**Buddy Lazier started the race from the number one position based on current entrant points as qualifications were rained out.

Key: WDWS-Walt Disney World Speedway; PIR-Phoenix International Raceway; LVMS-Las Vegas Motor Speedway; IMS-Indianapolis Motor Speedway; TMS-Texas Motor Speedway; PPIR-Pikes Peak International Raceway; AMS-Atlanta Motor Speedway; KS-Kentucky Speedway.

2000 INDIANAPOLIS 500 ENTRY LIST

Car	Driver	Car Name	C/E	Entrant
1	Greg Ray	Team Conseco/Quaker State/Moen/Menards	D/O	Team Menard, Inc.
1T	Greg Ray	Team Conseco/Quaker State/Moen/Menards	D/O	Team Menard, Inc.
3	Al Unser Jr.	Galles ECR Racing Tickets.com Starz Encore Superpak	G/O	Galles ECR Racing, LLC
3T	Al Unser Jr.	Galles ECR Racing Tickets.com Starz Encore Superpak	G/O	Galles ECR Racing, LLC
4	Scott Goodyear	Pennzoil Panther Dallara	D/O	Panther Racing, LLC
4T	Scott Goodyear	Pennzoil Panther Dallara	D/O	Panther Racing, LLC
5	Robby McGehee	Meijer/Energizer Advanced Formula/Mall.com	G/O	Treadway Racing
5T	Robby McGehee	Meijer/Energizer Advanced Formula/Mall.com	G/O	Treadway Racing
6	Jeret Schroeder	Armour Swift-Eckrich/Tristarmall.com	D/O	Tri Star Motorsports, Inc.
6T	Jeret Schroeder	Armour Swift-Eckrich/Tristarmall.com	D/O	Tri Star Motorsports, Inc.
7	Stephan Gregoire	Mexmil/Tokheim/Viking Air Tools/Dick Simon Racing	G/O	Dick Simon Racing
7T	Stephan Gregoire	Mexmil/Tokheim/Viking Air Tools/Dick Simon Racing	G/O	Dick Simon Racing
8	Scott Sharp	Delphi Automotive Systems/MCI WorldCom	D/O	Kelley Racing
8T	Scott Sharp	Delphi Automotive Systems/MCI WorldCom	D/O	Kelley Racing
9	Juan Montoya (R)	Target	G/O	Target/Chip Ganassi Racing
9T	Juan Montoya (R)	Target	G/O	Target/Chip Ganassi Racing
10	Jimmy Vasser	Target	G/O	Target/Chip Ganassi Racing
10T	Jimmy Vasser	Target	G/O	Target/Chip Ganassi Racing
11	Eliseo Salazar	Rio A.J. Foyt Racing	G/O	A.J. Foyt Enterprises
11T	Eliseo Salazar	Rio A.J. Foyt Racing	G/O	A.J. Foyt Enterprises
12	Buzz Calkins	Bradley Food Marts/Sav-O-Mat	D/O	Bradley Motorsports
12T	Buzz Calkins	Bradley Food Marts/Sav-O-Mat	D/O	Bradley Motorsports
14	Jeff Ward	Harrah's A.J. Foyt Racing	G/O	A.J. Foyt Enterprises
14T	Jeff Ward	Harrah's A.J. Foyt Racing	G/O	A.J. Foyt Enterprises
15	Sarah Fisher (R)	Walker Racing Cummins Special	R/O	Walker Racing, LLC
15T	Sarah Fisher (R)	Walker Racing Cummins Special	R/O	Walker Racing, LLC
16	Davey Hamilton	TeamXtreme/Lycos/G Force	G/O	TeamXtreme Racing, LLC
16T	Davey Hamilton	TeamXtreme/Lycos/G Force	G/O	TeamXtreme Racing, LLC
17	Scott Harrington	Nienhouse Motorsports Racing Special	D/O	Nienhouse Motorsports, Inc.
17T	Scott Harrington	Nienhouse Motorsports Racing Special	D/O	Nienhouse Motorsports, Inc.
18	Sam Hornish Jr. (R)	Hornish Bros. Trucking/Advantage Powder Coating	D/O	PDM Racing, Inc.
18T	Sam Hornish Jr. (R)	Hornish Bros. Trucking/Advantage Powder Coating	G/O	PDM Racing, Inc.
19	Andy Michner	Logan Racing Special	D/O	Logan Racing
20	Tyce Carlson	Hubbard Photographics/Immke Auto Group/Dallara	D/O	Hubbard-Immke Racing
20T	Tyce Carlson	Hubbard Photographics/Immke Auto Group/Dallara	D/O	Hubbard-Immke Racing
21	Jack Miller	Milk Chug/Opalescence/Century 21/Tristarmall.com	D/O	Tri Star Motorsports, Inc.
21T	Jack Miller	Milk Chug/Opalescence/Century 21/Tristarmall.com	D/E	Tri Star Motorsports, Inc.
22	Johnny Unser	Delco-Remy/Microdigicom/Homier Tools/G Force/Oldsmobile	G/O	Indy Regency Racing, LLC
22T	Johnny Unser	Delco-Remy/Microdigicom/Homier Tools/G Force/Oldsmobile	G/O	Indy Regency Racing, LLC
24	Robbie Buhl	Team Purex Dreyer & Reinbold Racing	G/O	Dreyer & Reinbold Racing
24T	Robbie Buhl	Team Purex Dreyer & Reinbold Racing	G/O	Dreyer & Reinbold Racing
25	TBA	Walker Racing Special	R/O	Walker Racing, LLC
25T	TBA	Walker Racing Special	R/O	Walker Racing, LLC
27	Jimmy Kite	Founders Bank Group/ZMAX/Blueprint Racing Special	G/O	Blueprint Racing Enterprises, LLC
27T	Jimmy Kite	Founders Bank Group/ZMAX/Blueprint Racing Special	G/O	Blueprint Racing Enterprises, LLC
28	Mark Dismore	On Star/GM BuyPower/Bryant Heating & Cooling	D/O	Kelley Racing
28T	Mark Dismore	On Star/GM BuyPower/Bryant Heating & Cooling	D/O	Kelley Racing
29	J.J. Yeley	Jonathan Byrd-McCormack Motorsports Jonathan Byrd's Cafeteria	G/O	Jonathan Byrd/McCormack Motorsports, LLC
29T	J.J. Yeley	Jonathan Byrd-McCormack Motorsports Jonathan Byrd's Cafeteria	G/O	Jonathan Byrd/McCormack Motorsports, LLC

2000 INDIANAPOLIS 500 ENTRY LIST

Car	Driver	Car Name	C/E	Entrant
30	Ronnie Johncox (R)	Jonathan Byrds/WorldBestBuy.com	R/O	Jonathan Byrd/McCormack Motorsports, LLC
30T	Ronnie Johncox (R)	Jonathan Byrds/WorldBestBuy.com	G/O	Jonathan Byrd/McCormack Motorsports, LLC
32	TBA	Team Conseco/Quaker State/Moen/Menards	D/O	Team Menard, Inc.
33	Jaques Lazier (R)	Miles of Hope/Truscelli Team Racing	D/O	Truscelli Team Racing
33T	Jaques Lazier (R)	Miles of Hope/Truscelli Team Racing	D/O	Truscelli Team Racing
37	TBA	Nienhouse Motorsports Racing Special	G/O	Nienhouse Motorsports, Inc.
40	TBA	Team Coulson G Force	G/O	Team Coulson Racing, Inc.
40T	TBA	Team Coulson G Force	G/O	Team Coulson Racing, Inc.
41	TBA	Foyt Brack Motorsports	G/O	A.J. Foyt/Kenny Brack Motorsports
41T	TBA	Foyt Brack Motorsports	G/O	A.J. Foyt/Kenny Brack Motorsports
43	Doug Didero (R)	Mid America Motorsports Inc./Western Star Trucks	D/O	Mid America Motorsports, Inc.
43T	Doug Didero (R)	Mid America Motorsports Inc./Western Star Trucks	D/O	Mid America Motorsports, Inc.
44	Guy Smith (R)	March Racing	D/O	Sinden Racing Service
44T	Guy Smith (R)	March Racing	D/O	Sinden Racing Service
48	Andy Hillenburg (R)	The Sumar Special	D/O	Fast Track Racing Enterprises, Inc.
48T	Andy Hillenburg (R)	The Sumar Special	D/O	Fast Track Racing Enterprises, Inc.
51	Eddie Cheever Jr.	#51 Excite@Home Indy Race Car	D/I	Team Cheever
51T	Eddie Cheever Jr.	#51 Excite@Home Indy Race Car	TBA/I	Team Cheever
52	TBA	Team Cheever/Infiniti/Firestone	TBA/I	Team Cheever
52T	TBA	Team Cheever/Infiniti/Firestone	TBA/I	Team Cheever
54	Hideshi Matsuda	Beck Motorsports	D/O	Beck Motorsports
54T	Hideshi Matsuda	Beck Motorsports	D/O	Beck Motorsports
55	TBA	EPSON	G/O	Treadway-Vertex Cunningham Racing
55T	TBA	EPSON	G/O	Treadway-Vertex Cunningham Racing
75	TBA	Pagan Racing	D/O	Pagan Racing
75T	TBA	Pagan Racing	D/O	Pagan Racing
77	Wim Eyckmans	Dick Simon Racing/EGP/Millennium Gate	G/O	Dick Simon Racing
77T	Wim Eyckmans	Dick Simon Racing/EGP/Millennium Gate	G/O	Dick Simon Racing
81	Billy Boat	Team Pelfrey	D/O	Team Pelfrey
81T	Billy Boat	Team Pelfrey	D/O	Team Pelfrey
82	Memo Gidley (R)	Team Pelfrey	D/O	Team Pelfrey
82T	Memo Gidley (R)	Team Pelfrey	D/O	Team Pelfrey
88	Airton Daré (R)	TeamXtreme/USACredit.com/G Force	G/O	TeamXtreme Racing, LLC
88T	Airton Daré (R)	TeamXtreme/USACredit.com/G Force	G/O	TeamXtreme Racing, LLC
90	TBA	Dick Simon Racing	G/O	Dick Simon Racing
90T	TBA	Dick Simon Racing	G/O	Dick Simon Racing
91	Buddy Lazier	Delta Faucet/Coors Light/Tae-Bo/Hemelgarn Racing	R/O	Hemelgarn Racing, Inc.
91T	Buddy Lazier	Delta Faucet/Coors Light/Tae-Bo/Hemelgarn Racing	R/O	Hemelgarn Racing, Inc.
92	TBA	March Indy International/Hemelgarn Racing	D/O	Hemelgarn Racing, Inc.
92T	TBA	March Indy International/Hemelgarn Racing	D/O	Hemelgarn Racing, Inc.
93	Dan Drinan (R)	Hemelgarn Racing	D/O	Hemelgarn Racing, Inc.
93T	Dan Drinan (R)	Hemelgarn Racing	D/O	Hemelgarn Racing, Inc.
98	Donnie Beechler	Cahill Racing	D/O	Cahill Auto Racing, Inc.
98T	Donnie Beechler	Cahill Racing	D/O	Cahill Auto Racing, Inc.

Legend: Chassis: D=Dallara, G=G Force, R=Riley & Scott
Engine: O=Oldsmobile, I=Nissan Infiniti
R=Indy 500 Rookie; TBA=To be announced

The Indianapolis Motor Speedway and participating sponsors in the 84th Indianapolis 500 are pleased to offer the following qualifying incentives.

PPG Industries returns to present the PPG Pole Award, worth $100,000 to the pole position winner, plus Oldsmobile will present the pole winner with a 2000 Oldsmobile Silhouette.

GTE awards each front row qualifier with $10,000, MBNA Motorsports pays $10,000 to the fastest driver to qualify on bump day. Ameritech presents the youngest starting driver with $7,500.

PPG Pole Award $100,000
PPG INDUSTRIES

Greg Ray

OLDSMOBILE POLE AWARD
2000 Oldsmobile Silhouette
Greg Ray

GTE "Front Runner" Award - $30,000
$10,000 awarded to each front row driver
GTE
Greg Ray, Juan Montoya, Eliseo Salazar

MBNA Motorsports "Fastest MBNA Bump Day Qualifier" Award - $10,000
MBNA MOTORSPORTS
Raul Boesel

Ameritech "Youngest Starting Driver" Award - $7,500
awarded to the youngest driver to qualify
AMERITECH/SBC
Sarah Fisher

American Dairy Association "Fastest Qualifying Rookie" Award - $5,000
AMERICAN DAIRY ASSOCIATION
Juan Montoya

Buckeye Machine/ Race Spec "Final Measure" Award - $5,000
awarded to last team to pass inspection and qualify for the race
BUCKEYE MACHINE/ RACE SPEC
Billy Boat

Ferguson Steel "Most Consistent Qualifier" Award - $5,000
awarded to the veteran who records the most consistent qualifying laps
FERGUSON STEEL COMPANY, INC.
Jeff Ward

Buildings To Go "Most Consistent Rookie Qualifier" Award - $5,000
awarded to the rookie who records the four most consistent qualifying laps
BUILDINGS TO GO
Sarah Fisher

Mi-Jack "Top Performance" Award - $5,000
awarded to the driver recording the fastest single qualifying lap
MI-JACK PRODUCTS
Eliseo Salazar

Snap-On/CAM "Top Wrench" Award - $5,000
recognizes mechanical excellence by a chief mechanic during practice and qualifying
SNAP-ON TOOLS/CAM
Glenn Scott, Kelley Racing

T.P. Donovan "Top Starting Rookie" Award - $5,000
T.P. DONOVAN INVESTMENTS
Juan Montoya

Toro - $8,000 value
a Toro 5xi tractor to the pole winner
TORO
Greg Ray

PPG Industries leads the way for all participating Contingency Awards sponsors of the 2000 Indianapolis 500 with their posting of $495,000 divided equally among each of the 33 starting drivers. PPG also presents each starting driver with a special PPG Starters' Ring.

Pennzoil follows PPG with a posting of $150,000. Other leading Accessory Award sponsors include the Robert Bosch Corporation offering $35,000 and Nissan, Oldsmobile and Raybestos each post $30,000. Premier Farnell Corporation offers $10,000 and Simpson Helmets offers $10,000.

PPG INDUSTRIES
$495,000

PENNZOIL
$150,000

  Oldsmobile

ROBERT BOSCH CORPORATION $35,000

NISSAN $30,000

OLDSMOBILE $30,000

RAYBESTOS/DANA BRAKE & CHASSIS $30,000

PREMIER FARNELL CORPORATION $10,000

SIMPSON HELMETS $10,000

BELL HELMETS $6,000

KLOTZ SPECIAL FORMULA PRODUCTS $6,000

EARL'S INDY $5,000

EMCO GEARS $5,000

HYPERCO $5,000

KECO COATINGS $5,000

THE MEXMIL COMPANY $5,000

POWER PERFORMANCE PRODUCTS $5,000

STANT MANUFACTURING, INC. $5,000

WORLDWIDE PETROMOLY CORPORATION $5,000

The 2000 Indianapolis 500 Mile Race purse exceeded $8 million dollars for the sixth time in Speedway history. While the Indianapolis Motor Speedway contributes over $6 million to this purse, over 50 participating sponsors have posted over $1 million in cash and prizes.

Borg-Warner Inc. leads the postings for Race Day awards with $130,000 in cash for the winner and a $100,000 bonus if a back-to-back win is recorded. Northern Light Technology Inc. offers $100,000 for each race in the Indy Racing Northern Light Series and awards the Northern Light Cup as well as $1,000,000 to the series champion. Coors Brewing Company has posted $80,000 for their Carburetion Day Coors Indy Pit Stop Challenge.

The 2000 race winner will also receive a 2001 Aurora from Oldsmobile.

BORG-WARNER INC. TROPHY AWARD
$130,000 plus trophy replica
$100,000 bonus if the 1999 winner repeats his victory
($20,000 added to the bonus each year until a back-to-back win is recorded)
Borg-Warner, Inc.
(race winner)
Juan Montoya

OLDSMOBILE OFFICIAL PACE CAR AWARD
2001 Oldsmobile Aurora
(race winner)
Juan Montoya

NORTHERN LIGHT "CIRCLE OF CHAMPIONS" AWARD
$100,000 - Northern Light Technology Inc.
(distributed among the twelve highest finishers)

$80,000 purse - Coors Brewing Company
(contest held May 25, 2000)
Panther Racing ($42,500)

TITAN MOTORCYCLE
$38,000 value - Titan Motorcycle Co. of America
(race winner)
Juan Montoya

BANK ONE "ROOKIE OF THE YEAR" AWARD
$25,000 - Bank One, Indianapolis
Juan Montoya

SCOTT BRAYTON DRIVERS TROPHY
$25,000
(awarded to the driver who most exemplifies the attitude, spirit and competitive drive of Scott Brayton)
Eddie Cheever, Jr.

FIRESTONE "FIRST AT 100" AWARD
$20,000 - Bridgestone/Firestone Inc.
(awarded to the highest running driver at lap 100 using Firestone tires)
Juan Montoya

MCI WorldCom "LONG DISTANCE" AWARD
$20,000 - MCI WorldCom
(awarded to the driver who most improves their position during the race)
Billy Boat

UNION PLANTERS BANK "LEADERS' CIRCLE" AWARD
$20,000 - Union Planters Bank
(awarded to the driver who leads the most laps)
Juan Montoya

MONARCH BEVERAGE "INSIDE TRACK" AWARD
$11,000 - Monarch Beverage
($1000 to each starter with an inside track starting position)

AMERICAN DAIRY AWARDS
$10,750 - American Dairy Association
(winner, fastest qualifying rookie, winning chief mechanic, each qualifying rookie)

C&R RACING "TRUE GRIT" AWARD
$10,000 - C&R Racing co-sponsored by Visteon Climate Control
(awarded to the mechanic that exemplifies outstanding achievement and excellence in preparation and management)
Craig Baranouski, AJ Foyt Racing

NATIONAL CITY BANK "CHECKERED FLAG" AWARD
$10,000 - National City Bank, Indiana
(race winner)
Juan Montoya

NET RACE LIVE/AniVision
$10,000 - Net Race Live/AniVision
(awarded to the driver who leads the most laps during the race)
Juan Montoya

RACE SEARCH.COM "Top Finishing Rookie" AWARD
$5,000
Juan Montoya

"TORO TRACTOR" AWARD
$8,000 value - Toro
(Toro 5xi tractor to the race winner)
Juan Montoya

CLINT BRAWNER "MECHANICAL EXCELLENCE" AWARD
$5,000 - Clint Brawner Mechanical Excellence Foundation
Paul Murphy, PDM Racing

INDIANA OXYGEN "PERSEVERANCE" AWARD
$5,000 - Indiana Oxygen
(presented to the team on race day that exemplifies the most exceptional sportsmanship in a non-winning effort)
PDM Racing

LINCOLN ELECTRIC "HARD CHARGER" AWARD
$5,000 - Lincoln Electric
Racing's #1 Choice in Welding
(awarded to the lowest qualifier to lead the race)
Robby McGehee

MOTORSPORTS SPARES INTERNATIONAL "PERSISTENCE PAYS" AWARD
$5,000 - Motorsports Spares International
(awarded to the highest finishing last day qualifier)
Jaques Lazier

PREMIER FARNELL "MECHANICAL ACHIEVEMENT" AWARD
$5,000 - Premier Farnell Corp.
Owen Snyder, Team Cheever

OFFICIAL SPONSORS OF THE 2000 INDIANAPOLIS 500

Blue Star	Official Battery
Canon	Official Camera
Chevrolet	Official Truck
Clarian Health	Official Healthcare Provider for the Indianapolis Motor Speedway
Coors Light	Official Beer
Emergency One	Official Fire Truck of the Indianapolis Motor Speedway
Featherlite Trailers	Official Trailer
Holmatro	Official Safety Equipment Supplier
Kidde	Official Fire Extinguisher
MBNA	Official Credit Card
MCI WorldCom	Official Long Distance, Calling Card, Pre-paid Calling Card & Local Service Provider
Net Race Live	Official Online Entertainment Network
Northern Light	Official Search Engine
Oldsmobile	Official Pace Car
Pennzoil	Official Motor Oil
Pepsi	Official Soft Drink
Perkin Elmer	Official Instrumental Supplier & Fuel Certification
St. Clair Apparel	Official Clothier
Vulcan	Official Race Recovery Vehicle of the Indianapolis Motor Speedway

PROMOTIOMAL PARTNERS

	WDWS SP	WDWS FP	PIR SP	PIR FP	LVMS SP	LVMS FP	IMS SP	IMS FP	TMS 1 SP	TMS 1 FP	PPIR SP	PPIR FP	AMS SP	AMS FP	KS SP	KS FP	TMS 2 SP	TMS 2 FP
Donnie Beechler	15	6	11	3	13	26	15	12	8	22	15	5	3	5	8	10	16	6
Billy Boat	9	9	16	6	5	7	31	15	11	23	21	18	19	8	22	18	22	3
Raul Boesel							24	16										
Robbie Buhl	22	1	9	7	23	5	9	26	2	18	2	23	8	6	16	13	5	18
Buzz Calkins	11	8	15	23	19	25	22	18	19	4	14	12	9	23	11	12	17	9
Tyce Carlson	23	13	6	15	27	8			16	13	20	11	15	13	13	22	9	23
Eddie Cheever Jr.	6	3	8	10	7	11	10	5	5	9	10	1	14	21	15	4	10	2
Airton Daré	25	11	24	22	11	14	21	25	20	10	16	2	10	25	23	19	19	12
Doug Didero	20	14	22	25	26	19			24	27	25	22						
Mark Dismore	3	16	2	16	1	2	11	11	6	6	3	4	7	18	24	11	11	14
Sarah Fisher			21	13	12	17	19	31	25	12	22	25	5	14	4	3	13	11
Scott Goodyear	8	4	7	2	10	12	13	9	3	5	11	16	16	11	1	2	2	1
Robby Gordon							4	6										
Stephan Gregoire	13	18	12	8	15	28	20	8	15	11	7	8	20	7	21	5	23	20
Roberto Guerrero															25	23		
Davey Hamilton	17	26	10	18	28	20	28	20	22	24	8	14	17	15	9	16	7	19
Scott Harrington					14	23							21	20				
Shigeaki Hattori									26	8	17	17	18	9	17	8	15	7
Richie Hearn							23	27										
Jon Herb	26	22																
Andy Hillenburg							33	28										
John Hollansworth Jr.	14	21																
Sam Hornish Jr.	19	20	19	17	18	3	14	24	13	20	19	19			20	9	18	27
Ronnie Johncox			18	14	24	13												
Niclas Jonsson	21	12	25	21														
Jimmy Kite			14	26	17	16	25	30	23	16	23	24	25	12	12	17	20	21
Steve Knapp							27	19										
Buddy Lazier	5	2	26	1	20	22	16	2	1	7	13	26	11	2	7	1	6	4
Jaques Lazier	12	23			22	10	26	13	18	14	24	9			10	20	12	10
Jason Leffler					9	15	17	17										
Robby McGehee	4	10	4	24	16	6	12	21	14	2	12	13	12	4	19	14	8	24
Dr. Jack Miller					25	24												
Juan Montoya							2	1										
Zak Morioka																	25	15
Greg Ray	1	17	1	19	2	9	1	33	17	15	1	20	1	1	3	7	1	26
Stevie Reeves													22	22	27	21	26	22
Bobby Regester			23	20														
Billy Roe									27	25								
Eliseo Salazar	10	5	17	4	4	18	3	3	4	17	6	6	2	10	2	25	21	5
Jeret Schroeder	16	19	5	12	8	4	29	14	10	21	5	7	6	24	6	26	14	16
Scott Sharp	7	15	3	5	3	27	5	10	12	1	4	3	13	16	18	24	24	13
Lyn St. James							32	32										
Al Unser Jr.	24	25	20	9	21	1	18	29	9	3	18	10	24	3	14	27	4	17
Johnny Unser							30	22										
Robby Unser	18	24							21	26	26	21						
Jimmy Vasser							7	7										
Jeff Ward	2	7	13	11	6	21	6	4	7	19	9	15	4	19	5	6	3	8
Stan Wattles							8	23										
J.J. Yeley													23	17	26	15	27	25

Rank	Car	Entrant	WDWS	PIR	LVMS	IMS	TMS 1	PPIR	AMS	KS	TMS 2	Total	Leader	Previous
1	91	Hemelgarn Racing	40	50	8	40	26	4	40	50	32	290		
2	4	Panther Racing	32	40	18	22	30	14	19	45	52	272	-18	-18
3	51	Team Cheever	35	20	19	30	22	50	9	32	40	257	-33	-15
4	11	A.J. Foyt Enterprises	30	32	12	36	13	28	22	7	30	210	-80	-47
5	28	Kelley Racing	14	16	45	19	28	33	12	19	16	202	-88	-8
6	98	Cahill Racing	28	35	4	18	8	30	31	20	28	202	-88	0
7	8	Kelley Racing	15	33	4	20	50	37	14	6	17	196	-94	-6
8	24	Dreyer & Reinbold Racing	52	26	30	4	12	9	28	17	12	190	-100	-6
9	3	Galles ECR Racing	5	22	50	1	37	20	35	3	15	188	-102	-2
10	14	A.J. Foyt Enterprises	26	19	9	32	11	15	11	28	25	176	-114	-12
11	5	Treadway Racing	20	6	28	9	40	17	32	16	6	174	-116	-2
12	1	Team Menard	13	14	24	4	15	13	55	27	7	172	-118	-2
13	7	Dick Simon Racing	12	24	2	24	19	24	26	30	10	171	-119	-1
14	81	Team Pelfrey	22	28	26		7	12	24	12	35	166	-124	-5
15	12	Bradley Motorsports	24	7	5	12	32	18	7	18	22	145	-145	-21
16	88	TeamXtreme Racing	19	8	16	5	20	40	5	11	18	142	-148	-3
17	55	Treadway Racing			15	14	24	13	22	24	26	138	-152	-4
18	6	Tri Star Motorsports	11	18	32	16	9	26	6	4	14	136	-154	-2
19	15	Walker Racing		17	13	1	18	5	16	35	19	124	-166	-12
20	20	Hubbard Racing	17	15	24		17	19	17	8	7	124	-166	-12
21	16	TeamXtreme Racing	9	12	10	10	6	16	15	14	20	112	-178	-12
22	18	PDM Racing	10	13	35	6	10	11	22	3		110	-180	-2
23	27	Blueprint Racing Enterprises	18	4	14	1	14	6	18	13	9	97	-193	-13
24	33	Truscelli Team Racing	7	10	20	17	16	22				92	-198	-5
25	30	Jonathan Byrd-McCormack Mspts.	8	16	17		4	9	13	15	5	87	-203	-5
26	43	Mid America Motorsports	16	5	11		3	8	10	10	11	74	-216	-13
27	9	Target/Chip Ganassi Racing				54						54	-236	-20
28	19	Logan Racing					5		8	9	8	30	-260	-24
29	32	Team Menard				28						28	-262	-2
30	21	Tri Star Motorsports	6		6						15	27	-263	-1
31	10	Target/Chip Ganassi Racing				26						26	-264	-1
32	17	Nienhouse Motorsports		9	7							16	-274	-10
33	41	A.J. Foyt Enterprises				15						15	-275	-1
34	50	Treadway Racing				13						13	-277	-2
35	23	Dreyer & Reinbold Racing				11						11	-279	-2
36	22	Indy Regency Racing				8						8	-282	-3
37	92	Hemelgarn Racing				7						7	-283	-1
38	40	Team Coulson								7		7	-283	0
39	44	Sinden Racing Service	4									4	-286	-3
40	75	Pagan Racing				3						3	-287	-1
41	48	Fast Track Racing Enterprises				2						2	-288	-1
42	90	Dick Simon Racing				1						1	-289	-1

Key: WDWS-Walt Disney World Speedway; PIR-Phoenix International Raceway; LVMS-Las Vegas Motor Speedway; IMS-Indianapolis Motor Speedway; TMS-Texas Motor Speedway; PPIR-Pikes Peak International Raceway; AMS-Atlanta Motor Speedway; KS-Kentucky Speedway

Indianapolis 500 Winners

AAA SANCTIONING

Year	St. Pos.	Car #	Driver	Car Name & Sponsor Chassis/Engine	Qualify Speed	Race Time	Race Speed
1911	28	32	Ray Harroun	Nordyke & Marmon / Marmon / Marmon		6:42:08.000	74.602
1912	7	8	Joe Dawson	National Motor Vehicle / National / National	86.130	6:21:06.000	78.719
1913	7	16	Jules Goux	Peugeot / Peugeot / Peugeot	86.030	6:35:05.000	75.933
1914	15	16	Rene Thomas	L. Delage / Delage / Delage	94.540	6:03:45.000	82.474
1915	2	2	Ralph DePalma	Mercedes/E.C. Patterson / Mercedes / Mercedes	98.580	5:33:55.510	89.840
1916	4	17	Dario Resta	Peugeot Auto Racing / Peugeot / Peugeot	94.400	3:34:17.000	84.001 a
1919	2	3	Howdy Wilcox	Peugeot/Indpls Sptway Team / Peugeot / Peugeot	100.010	5:40:42.870	88.050
1920	6	4	Gaston Chevrolet	Monroe/William Small / Frontenac / Frontenac	91.550	5:38:32.000	88.618
1921	20	2	Tommy Milton	Frontenac/Louis Chevrolet / Frontenac / Frontenac	93.050	5:34:44.650	89.621
1922	1	35	Jimmy Murphy	Jimmy Murphy / Duesenberg / Miller	100.500	5:17:30.790	94.484
1923	1	1	Tommy Milton	H.C.S. Motor / Miller / Miller	108.170	5:29:50.170	90.954
1924	21	15	L.L. Corum-J. Boyer	Duesenberg / Duesenberg / Duesenberg	93.330	5:05:23.510	98.234
1925	2	12	Peter DePaolo	Duesenberg / Duesenberg / Duesenberg	113.080	4:56:39.460	101.127
1926	20	15	Frank Lockhart	Miller/Peter Kreis / Miller / Miller	95.780	4:10:14.950	95.904 b
1927	22	32	George Souders	Duesenberg/William White / Duesenberg / Duesenberg	111.550	5:07:33.080	97.545
1928	13	14	Louie Meyer	Miller/Alden Sampson, II / Miller / Miller	111.350	5:01:33.750	99.482
1929	6	2	Ray Keech	Simple Piston Ring/Yagle / Miller / Miller	114.900	5:07:25.420	97.585
1930	1	4	Billy Arnold	Miller-Hartz / Summers / Miller	113.260	4:58:39.720	100.448
1931	13	23	Louis Schneider	Bowes Seal Fast/Schneider / Stevens / Miller	107.210	5:10:27.930	96.629
1932	27	34	Fred Frame	Miller-Harry Hartz / Wetteroth / Miller	113.850	4:48:03.790	104.144
1933	6	36	Louie Meyer	Tydol/Louie Meyer / Miller / Miller	116.970	4:48:00.750	104.162
1934	10	7	Bill Cummings	Boyle Products/Henning / Miller / Miller	116.110	4:46:05.200	104.863
1935	22	5	Kelly Petillo	Gilmore Speedway/Petillo / Wetteroth / Offy	115.090	4:42:22.710	106.240
1936	28	8	Louie Meyer	Ring Free/Lou Meyer / Stevens / Miller	114.170	4:35:03.390	109.069
1937	2	6	Wilbur Shaw	Shaw-Gilmore / Shaw / Offy	122.790	4:24:07.800	113.580
1938	1	23	Floyd Roberts	Burd Piston Ring/Lou Moore / Wetteroth / Miller	125.680	4:15:58.400	117.200
1939	3	2	Wilbur Shaw	Boyle Racing Headquarters / Maserati / Maserati	128.970	4:20:47.390	115.035
1940	2	1	Wilbur Shaw	Boyle Racing Headquarters / Maserati / Maserati	127.060	4:22:31.170	114.277
1941	17	16	F. Davis-M. Rose	Noc-Out Hose Clamp/Moore / Wetteroth / Offy	121.100	4:20:36.240	115.117
1946	15	16	George Robson	Thorne Engineering / Adams / Sparks	125.540	4:21:16.700	114.820
1947	3	27	Mauri Rose	Blue Crown Spark Plug/Moore / Deidt / Offy	120.040	4:17:52.170	116.338
1948	3	3	Mauri Rose	Blue Crown Spark Plug/Moore / Deidt / Offy	129.120	4:10:23.330	119.814
1949	4	7	Bill Holland	Blue Crown Spark Plug/Moore / Deidt / Offy	128.670	4:07:15.970	121.327
1950	5	1	Johnnie Parsons	Wynn's Friction/Kurtis-Kraft / Kurtis / Offy	132.040	2:46:55.970	124.002 c
1951	2	99	Lee Wallard	Murrell Belanger / Kurtis / Offy	135.030	3:57:38.050	126.244
1952	7	98	Troy Ruttman	J.C. Agajanian / Kuzma / Offy	135.360	3:52:41.880	128.922
1953	1	14	Bill Vukovich	Fuel Injection/Howard Keck / KK500A / Offy	138.390	3:53:01.690	128.740
1954	19	14	Bill Vukovich	Fuel Injection/Howard Keck / KK500A / Offy	138.470	3:49:17.270	130.840
1955	14	6	Bob Sweikert	John Zink / KK500C / Offy	139.990	3:53:59.130	128.213

Indianapolis 500 Winners

USAC SANCTIONING

Year	St. Pos.	Car #	Driver	Car Name & Sponsor / Chassis/Engine	Qualify Speed	Race Time	Race Speed
1956	1	8	Pat Flaherty	John Zink / Watson / Offy	145.590	3:53:28.840	128.490
1957	13	9	Sam Hanks	Belond Exhaust/George Salih / Salih / Offy	142.810	3:41:14.250	135.601
1958	7	1	Jimmy Bryan	Belond AP/George Salih / Salih / Offy	144.180	3:44:13.800	133.791
1959	6	5	Rodger Ward	Leader Card 500 Roadster / Watson / Offy	144.030	3:40:49.200	135.857
1960	2	4	Jim Rathmann	Ken-Paul / Watson / Offy	146.370	3:36:11.360	138.767
1961	7	1	A.J. Foyt, Jr.	Bowes Seal Fast/Bignotti / Trevis / Offy	145.900	3:35:37.490	139.130
1962	2	3	Rodger Ward	Leader Card 500 Roadster / Watson / Offy	149.370	3:33:50.330	140.293
1963	1	98	Parnelli Jones	J.C. Agajanian/Willard Battery / Watson / Offy	151.150	3:29:35.400	143.137
1964	5	1	A.J. Foyt, Jr.	Sheraton-Thompson/Ansted / Watson / Offy	154.670	3:23:35.830	147.350
1965	2	82	Jim Clark	Lotus powered by Ford / Lotus / Ford	160.720	3:19:05.340	150.686
1966	15	24	Graham Hill	American Red Ball/Mecom / Lola / Ford	159.240	3:27:52.530	144.317
1967	4	14	A.J. Foyt, Jr.	Sheraton-Thompson/Ansted / Coyote / Ford	166.280	3:18:24.220	151.207
1968	3	3	Bobby Unser	Rislone/Leader Cards / Eagle / Offy	169.500	3:16:13.760	152.882
1969	2	2	Mario Andretti	STP Oil Treatment / Hawk / Ford	169.850	3:11:14.710	156.867
1970	1	2	Al Unser	Johnny Lightning/Parnelli Jones / P.J. Colt / Ford	170.220	3:12:37.040	155.749
1971	5	1	Al Unser	Johnny Lightning/Parnelli Jones / P.J. Colt / Ford	174.520	3:10:11.560	157.735
1972	3	66	Mark Donohue	Sunoco McLaren/Penske / McLaren / Offy	191.400	3:04:05.540	162.962
1973	11	20	Gordon Johncock	STP Double Oil Filter/Patrick / Eagle / Offy	192.550	2:05:26.590	159.036 d
1974	25	3	Johnny Rutherford	McLaren Cars / McLaren / Offy	190.440	3:09:10.060	158.589
1975	3	48	Bobby Unser	Jorgensen/All American Racers / Eagle / Offy	191.070	2:54:55.080	149.213 e
1976	1	2	Johnny Rutherford	Hy-Gain/McLaren / McLaren / Offy	188.950	1:42:52.000	148.725 f
1977	4	14	A.J. Foyt, Jr.	Gilmore Racing/A.J. Foyt / Coyote / Foyt	194.560	3:05:57.160	161.331
1978	5	2	Al Unser	First National City/Chaparral / Lola / Cosworth	196.470	3:05:54.990	161.363
1979	1	9	Rick Mears	The Gould Charge/Penske / Penske / Cosworth	193.730	3:08:47.970	158.899
1980	1	4	Johnny Rutherford	Pennzoil/Chaparral Racing / Chaparral / Cosworth	192.520	3:29:59.560	142.862
1981	1	3	Bobby Unser	The Norton Spirit/Penske / Penske/ Cosworth	200.540	3:35:41.780	139.084
1982	5	20	Gordon Johncock	STP Oil Treatment/Patrick / Wildcat / Cosworth	201.880	3:05:09.140	162.029
1983	4	5	Tom Sneva	Texaco Star/Bignotti-Cotter / March / Cosworth	203.680	3:05:03.066	162.117
1984	3	6	Rick Mears	Pennzoil Z7/Penske / March / Cosworth	207.840	3:03:21.660	163.612
1985	8	5	Danny Sullivan	Miller American/Penske / March / Cosworth	210.290	3:16:06.069	152.982
1986	4	3	Bobby Rahal	Budweiser/Truesports / March / Cosworth	213.550	2:55:43.480	170.722
1987	20	25	Al Unser	Cummins-Holset/Penske / March / Cosworth	207.420	3:04:59.147	162.175
1988	1	5	Rick Mears	Pennzoil Z7/Penske / Penske / Chevy Indy V8	219.190	3:27:10.204	144.809
1989	3	20	Emerson Fittipaldi	Marlboro/Patrick Racing / Penske / Chevy Indy V8	222.320	2:59:01.490	167.581
1990	3	30	Arie Luyendyk	Domino's Pizza/Shierson / Lola / Chevy Indy V8	223.300	2:41:18.404	185.981
1991	1	3	Rick Mears	Marlboro Penske Chevy 91 / Penske / Chevy Indy V8	224.113	2:50:00.791	176.457
1992	12	3	Al Unser, Jr.	Valvoline Galmer '92 / Galmer/Chevy Indy V8A	222.989	3:43:05.148	134.477
1993	9	4	Emerson Fittipaldi	Marlboro Penske Chevy '93 / Penske/Chevy Indy V8C	220.150	3:10:49.860	157.207
1994	1	31	Al Unser, Jr.	Marlboro Penske Mercedes / Penske/Mercedes Benz	228.011	3:06:29.006	160.872
1995	5	27	Jacques Villeneuve	Player's LTD/Team Green / Reynard/Ford Cosworth XB	228.397	3:15:17.561	153.616
1996	5	91	Buddy Lazier	Delta Faucet/Montana/Hemelgarn / 95 Reynard/Ford Cosworth XB	231.468	3:22:45.753	147.956
1997	1	5	Arie Luyendyk	Wavephore/Sprint PCS/Miller Lite/Provini / G Force/Aurora	218.263	3:25:43.388	145.827
1998	17	51	Eddie Cheever, Jr.	Rachel's Potato Chips / Dallara/Aurora	217.334	3:26:40.524	145.155
1999	8	14	Kenny Brack	AJ Foyt Power Team / Dallara/Aurora	222.659	3:15:51.182	153.176
2000	2	1	Juan Montoya	Target / G Force/Aurora	232.372	2:58:59.431	167.607

a 1916 - 300 Miles (Scheduled)   b 1926 - 400 Miles (Rain)   c 1950 - 345 Miles (Rain)
d 1973 - 332.5 Miles (Rain)   e 1975 - 435 Miles (Rain)   f 1976 - 255 Miles (Rain)

INDY 2001 RACING

SUN.	March 18	Phoenix International Raceway (1 mile)	ABC	4pm
SUN.	April 8	Homestead - Miami Speedway (1.5 miles)	ABC	2pm
SAT.	April 28 ·	Atlanta Motor Speedway (1.54 miles)	ESPN 2	7pm
SUN.	May 27	Indianapolis Motor Speedway (2.5 miles)	ABC	11am
SAT.	June 9 ·	Texas Motor Speedway (1.5 miles)	ESPN	8pm
SUN.	June 17	Pikes Peak International Raceway (1 mile)	ABC	4pm
SAT.	June 30 ·	Richmond International Raceway (.75 mile)	ESPN	8pm
SUN.	July 8	Kansas Speedway (1.5 miles)	ESPN	1pm
SAT.	July 21 ·	Nashville Superspeedway (1.33 miles)	ESPN	8pm
SUN.	Aug. 12	Kentucky Speedway (1.5 miles)	ABC	3:30pm
SUN.	Aug. 26	Gateway International Raceway (1.25 miles)	ESPN	3pm
SUN.	Sept. 2	Chicagoland Speedway (1.5 miles)	ABC	4pm
SUN.	Sept. 16	Texas Motor Speedway (1.5 miles)	ESPN	4:30

· **Night Race**   AIR TIMES SUBJECT TO CHANGE   ALL TIMES EASTERN